Mahlon M Yeakle

The city of Saint Louis of to-day

Its progress and prospects...

Mahlon M Yeakle

The city of Saint Louis of to-day
Its progress and prospects...

ISBN/EAN: 9783337336264

Printed in Europe, USA, Canada, Australia, Japan

Cover: Foto ©ninafisch / pixelio.de

More available books at **www.hansebooks.com**

THE

CITY OF

SAINT LOUIS

OF TO-DAY:

ITS

PROGRESS AND PROSPECTS.

**TRUTH IN HOMELY WORDS,
AND FACTS IN FAITHFUL FIGURES.**

BY M. M. YEAKLE. SEN'R.

ILLUSTRATED.

SAINT LOUIS:
J. OSMUN YEAKLE & CO..
1889.

ACTION OF THE

BOARD OF DIRECTORS

OF THE

SAINT LOUIS REAL ESTATE EXCHANGE

IN RELATION TO THIS TREATISE.

WHEREAS. The City of Saint Louis, having attained a position so commanding amongst all its Peers of every State: a just feeling of pride arises in the breast of its citizens, and prompts the wish to have their city better known to other communities: And,

WHEREAS. To accomplish such natural desire, we consider paper and type, in a Treatise, which shall set forth facts and figures—fairly and faithfully—delivered through the medium of the mail, the best and most facile means and method for increasing our population from abroad and of reaching capitalists, investors and manufacturers of distant localities: And,

WHEREAS. Having become acquainted with the able Treatise of Mr. M. M. Yeakle. Senior, entitled "THE CITY OF SAINT LOUIS OF TO-DAY: ITS PROGRESS AND PROSPECTS." And, having taken said Work under careful consideration: we find it most judicious in its themes, and admirably suited—through its large supply of fresh and reliable information—to the representation of our city abroad, and to cause it to be more favorably known where such information would be cheerfully received, and the result be beneficial to St. Louis: Wherefore, Be it

RESOLVED. That this Board approves said Work, and urges upon the Author its early publication: And, Be it further

RESOLVED. That this Board earnestly recommends the Members of this Exchange to obtain the said Work, and circulate it widely, wherever their judgment shall determine.

LEON L. HULL. *President.*

This is to certify, that at a meeting held this day at the Saint Louis Real Estate Exchange, the Board having been addressed by Mr. M. M. Yeakle. Sen'r, the author of a Work entitled, "THE CITY OF SAINT LOUIS OF TO-DAY: ITS PROGRESS AND PROSPECTS." And, having previously read and carefully considered the said Work, the foregoing PREAMBLE and RESOLUTIONS were unanimously adopted.

Attest: THOS. F. FARRELLY. *Secretary.*

St. Louis, September 6. 1888.

THE LINDELL HOTEL.

TO THE READER.

At the inception of this work it was expected it would be a *pamphlet* of ordinary length. But the author early found that no reasonable justice could be done to his subject without enlarging the original limits. Again he fixed a bound—still too short—but sufficient to give a fair measure of satisfaction to himself.

The work is the outgrowth of the opinion—entertained in thoughtful circles—that the city of Saint Louis is too little understood or appreciated abroad, especially in the Eastern and Middle States, and that were thorough information of its rare and abounding advantages suitably set forth in manner and form, that more enlarged views and juster opinions might be entertained, and the result be beneficial to the general interests of this city.

All advertisements have been excluded from this work, in order to utilize its pages for the presentation of Saint Louis as a single and all absorbing subject. Further, it has not been written in the interest or for the benefit of any particular class of citizens, nor of any person or association of persons, but with the sole design of conveying to strangers such knowledge of this city as was presumed they do not possess, but would cheerfully receive.

In conclusion, should these pages be read by any who would ask the question: "What might I do toward improving my fortune by investing my money, time or skill, at the so-called Metropolis of the Mississippi Valley?" he could be answered: Come and see, investigate, compare and contrast. Then, you will probably reach the conclusion that it is the most inviting field between the Atlantic and Pacific.

Respectfully,

THE AUTHOR.

St. Louis, February 28, 1889.

SECOND BAPTIST CHURCH, ST. LOUIS, MO.

PREFACE.

The succeeding pages go from the author's workshop without any pretention as to the quality of the Work. But, he is confident that value may be found in his fidelity to fact, the reliability of his statements, and the authenticity of his figures. Nevertheless, he may be proud of the approval of intelligent gentlemen to whom he submitted his manuscript.

The views presented in these pages relative to the quickened growth and large development of the City of St. Louis are only such as the most casual observer meets at every hand. The recent results have proceeded from the fresh life blood bounding in the manhood of the leaders of the people, who have created a NEW CITY out of the OLD, within a period of less than fifteen years. Citizens are apt to consider the present a New Era in their city's history, and that its able and active men are not behind, but fully abreast-of-the-times! The Modern City was not "built *wiser* than its people knew," but *wisely* as they knew. The frail brick buildings upon slender foundations of the earlier days, have given place to huge structures whose base of granite is broad, deep and enduring. The successful attainments in the past few years have had the effect of encouraging the inception and undertaking of other works, some of great value and necessity, such as the Merchants' Bridge, which might have slept. If the awakening is as profound as it seems to be, the forward movement cannot be stayed, but will be hastened.

The views which the author has presented of the wide field of action open to the capitalist and investor, the manufacturer and merchant, and the advantages of St. Louis for home-life are such as a stranger of intelligence could scarcely dissent from after careful examination of the ground, and, he might early find the "potentiality of great riches" clinging to the gates of St. Louis. No attempt was made to draw a line between the Present and Past, but rather to direct attention to improvements which forcibly mark the contrast.

In sending his work to the press the Author trusts, that a generous appreciation will follow his humble effort. The critic surely will discover faults, but he is expected to make no exception to the style of composition, since he well knows that each individual man and writer, who is not an imitator or copyist, is more or less *sui generis*.

Finally, to those friends who have kindly favored the Author with their advice and encouragement, he begs to tender his sincere thanks.

THE AUTHOR.

St. Louis, February 28, 1889.

EDEN COLLEGE, ST. LOUIS.
OF THE GERMAN EVANGELICAL SYNOD OF NORTH AMERICA.

THE CITY OF ST. LOUIS OF TO-DAY:

ITS PROGRESS AND PROSPECTS.

IN SEVEN PARTS.

TABLE OF CONTENTS.

11

THE FAGIN BUILDING.

PART SECOND.

PART FOURTH.

PART FIFTH.

*A Description of the New Buildings of the St. Louis University and Mercantile Library will be found in Part V, pages 163 and 183.

PART SIXTH.

PART SEVENTH.

APPENDIX.

TABLE OF ILLUSTRATIONS: A FEW OF THE BUILDINGS RECENTLY ERECTED AND OTHER PROMINENT STRUCTURES — CLASSIFIED.

ERRATA.

The *paging* after page 20, and up to page 60, is *eight pages behind the proper number:* Page 13 should be page 21, and each succeeding page up to page 60 should be advanced eight pages.

The cut at foot of page 180 should be named " Building of the National Government."

These variations, together with a few typographical errors, will be corrected in the next edition.—AUTHOR.

New Building at S. W. Cor. Eleventh and St. Charles Sts., for DREY & KAHN.
A. F. Rosenheim, Architect.

The City of St. Louis of To-Day.

PART FIRST.

CHAPTER I.

A SKETCH OF ITS FOUNDING, RISE AND PROGRESS.

LACLEDE, THE PIONEER!

PIERRE LACLEDE LIGUEST, a Frenchman by birth, possessed of education, enterprise and intelligence, founded St. Louis on February 15th, 1764, as a fur-trading post. But within a few years it became the recognized centre of the government, as it was of trade, of the territory of Upper Louisiana. Together with Louisiana *at large*, it was successively dominated over by the French and Spanish government, until, by the treaty of Paris, April 30, 1803, it was ceded to the United States, for the sum of fifteen million dollars. The town had then a population of 925 souls, all French, with the exception of a few Spaniards and Americans. At that period, the trade was exclusively in furs and peltries, and amounted annually to about a quarter of a million dollars.

In 1809, the territorial government erected St. Louis, which then had a population of 1,100 souls, into a town, to be governed by a Board of Trustees. After Missouri became a State, in 1822, St. Louis was incorporated as a city, and in 1823, the first Mayor and Aldermen were chosen. At this period the population numbered about 5,000 souls, of whom two-thirds were French, and one-third American.

In 1831, the population was 5,960 souls, and the scale of nationality began to take larger weight on the side of Americans. In 1841, the area of the corporate limits of the city was enlarged to 2,865 acres; and, during the succeeding five years, building and development were proportionately greater than for any previous term of equal length.

In 1850, the National Census of population was 56,803 souls. At this period occurred the Asiatic Cholera, from which seven thousand inhabitants died; and the Great Fire, which destroyed three millions value in houses, steamboats and merchandise.

In 1860, the Census was 160,773 souls. The following year the civil war began, and its disastrous effects upon the trade and commerce of St. Louis, and all its material interests, was equal to a check of an entire decade of growth and development. But the city—with abundant latent strength, and present energy—leaped onward after the close of the war. It experienced another " let-up " after the general financial crisis of 1873, but in 1880, the federal census of the city was 350,561 souls.

Since then its growth in population and business has been beyond previous precedent. To reach a satisfactory estimate of the population at the close of the year 1888, the calculation is materially helped by the reply, in September last, to an inquiry made of the chief of the Bureau of the Census at the federal capital (by the Mayor of this city), who inquired "what estimate was made of the increase in population of the State of Missouri, in 1880?" The reply was, "forty per cent. increase." It is well understood, that the State *per se* has not increased as rapidly, or as much, as the City of St. Louis by at least ten per cent., or if the State has increased 40 per cent, then the city has increased 50 per cent., and by such data the present population of this city is 525,000 souls, which number many of the most astute of the active business 'men claim.

It is not within the scope assigned to this work to go into lengthy details upon any single subject bearing upon the material, social and other interests of St. Louis, especially into comparisons of growth in trade, commerce and manufactures, which is left to publications dealing in statistics. Nevertheless, it is aimed in this work to present certain facts and figures, in a concise and summary manner, relative to those valuable interests, which, whilst they go little into details, still show very large current gains, and suggest very great possibilities of increase in the future.

Now, that the theatre of business life is trodden by a larger number of more energetic actors, in men of business, than ever before in this city, it is looked for, that every advantage will be taken of each passing opportunity to raise this city to a greater and greater height in every interest relating to her welfare, wealth and grandeur.

CHAPTER II.

ST. LOUIS HAS TAKEN RANK AMONGST ALL ITS PEERS—THE MOST MODERN AND MOST PROGRESSIVE.

—

"This city now doth, like a garment, wear
The beauty of the morning."—*Wordsworth.*

From the date of the inauguration of that great work of the magnificent bridge — uniting the west and east sides of the "Father of Waters"—at St. Louis, in 1867, and more especially from its *completion*, (together with its terminal facilities by tunneling the most populous part of the city), and the union of numerous great railway lines at a common point of ingress and egress — affording the largest facilities for the incoming and outgoing traffic in freight and passengers, until at length the volume of inter-communication and commerce has grown — in less than fifteen years—so enormously as to choke the bridge and its connections, with a plethora of transit business, and to make manifest the very great need of another such structure— spanning the "Inland Sea."

From the advent of the "Eads" Bridge till its readiness for occupation, the public mind was in anxious expectation of very large benefits to follow immediately upon its construction. It was not possible that other than the most beneficial results should ensue, yet the highest expectations of the most sanguine have been greatly exceeded by the great growth of the trade and commerce of this city, in which the Bridge has been an indispensable factor and adjunct.

The Bridge, a titanic structure, has aided both in making and maintaining the fortunes of the business men and owners of real estate of St. Louis; and, from the auspicious era of its opening and successful use in 1874, there dawned a new day of golden effulgence! Then, modern St. Louis was born! That day developed a fresh, red blood flowing in the arteries of citizens representing all ranks and avocations. The elder men were filled with new life, and the younger inspired—all resolved on what Demosthenes termed eloquence: action! ACTION! ACTION! Since then, the elder and younger men have seen with clearer preceptions the grand present and grander future of their city, resolved with intenser earnestness, and performed with greater vigor. They have not waited but watched, and promptly taken advantage of opportunities to develop their personal resources in active measures to increase the commerce, manufactures and real estate values of their city, by wise and legitimate agencies, and to employ the vast resources of the great territory around it.

Such efforts, prompted by commendable pride and ambition, led them earnestly onward to accomplish still something greater each year—seeking new schemes of enterprise which involved the public good with their personal advantage—and it is not unfiting compliment to those citizens to say that they had the public good at heart, whilst aiding and leading in public and private works and enterprises, such as the encouragement of the municipality in purchasing the land for the Great Park, and in adorning all the public parks, the granite paving of their thoroughfares, and in numerous other ways. But, of themselves, they reared the great Exposition Building, and other magnificent buildings, such as the Fair Grounds and Jockey Club attractions, etc., all the outcome of private stock subscriptions. They clearly saw the large personal pecuniary benefits which they should realize, if not directly, then indirectly, from such investments. The annual illuminations, parades and street shows—some ludicrous, yet in the

main chaste and artistic—have continued to add new features to the city's attractions, and draw several hundred
thousand visitors from the surrounding states.

Turning to the improved styles, greatly enlarged
dimensions, and increased cost and number of new office,
bank, mercantile, manufacturing and other business buildings and blocks; church, college and school edifices; the
large number of magnificent private palaces, and the
immense number of new residence houses, in every variety
of style and size, and of all degrees of cost, (adapted to the
rich, the well-to-do, and the humbler citizen of smaller
means) for their own occupation, sale, lease or rent.
These results, of late, are most pleasing, being an index of
the immense strides made within the last few, especially
the last three years: whilst the buildings, finished and
finishing, of this year, are the grandest, costliest and most
splendid that have ever been built in this city, and are
rivals and peers of the superb structures of any city of the
United States.

The changes and improvements which have been made
in this city in the public thoroughfares, the cable railroads,
street lighting, the thorough system of drainage and
sewerage, large additional supply of wholesome water,
able fire extinguishing and salvage systems, public and
private attention to sanitation of houses and premises, have
all been means and agencies to make a *new* city out of *old*
Saint Louis, in fine, this city has been transformed, and the
aspect on all sides is most cheerful and encouraging, being
full of promise of still greater improvement and development in each succeeding year.

CHAPTER III.

THE CENTRAL SITE OF ST. LOUIS—ASSURING ITS PRE-EMI-NENCE IN THE "GREAT VALLEY" FOREVER!

" Who shall place a limit
To the giant's unchained strength,
Or curb his swiftness in the forward race? "—*Bryant.*

Nature herself has provided the site of every great and permanent City; and even in its crude, and at its, prestine period, there is no difficulty in *finding* it! Laclede Liguest—the founder of St. Louis—was a man of observation and experience. He had seen cities of the Old World (as Paris, the metropolis of his native country), and paused to consider their situation and surroundings. When he saw the spot which he chose—the site of the present great city, for the first time—he was so forcibly impressed with its rare advantages of situation, at the confluence of the mighty Missouri, and upon the bank of the "Father of Waters"—that, he gave utterance to his surprise and delight! and as Chouteau—his companion—relates, the same day on meeting the French officer in command of Fort de Chartres (and the only other person of note within more than a thousand miles), he told him in rapturous words of admiration and joy that, "he had *that day* found a site for his home and business, that it was all he could desire, and he would make a beginning on that spot, which might some day become one of the *finest cities of America*, and that he did not hesitate in the choice he had made!" *

*NOTE.—Auguste Chouteau accompanied Laclede in his search for a site for his trading post and left a Dairy, of which only a fragment remains, and is preserved in the Mercantile Library of St. Louis.—*Author.*

The opinion of an able and observing man—noted for high intelligence and sound judgment, upon any subject, is always received with respect, even should his views not be taken: but, when *several agree* upon the same subject—their conclusion is usually final. More than half a century has passed since the last of the two opinions—we shall now quote—was uttered, but now there are countless proofs patent to every intelligent mind—of the Grand Present, and still *Grander Future* of St. Louis!

Judge H. M. Brackenridge of Pittsburgh, a very able man and discriminating traveler—who visited St. Louis in 1811, after seeing large portions of the Great Valley, says, in his very entertaining Journal: "The chief cause of its great prospective growth (St. Louis), is her unrivaled position as a distributing centre: that there *must be a place of distribution* somewhere between the mouth of the Ohio and the Missouri: that a trade would be opened with New Spain:* and that *direct* communication with the East Indies—[via the Isthmus] was only a question of time: and *that* accomplished, St. Louis would become the commercial emporium of the "American Nile!" At that time no steamboat had yet been launched on any western water, and Oliver Evans' "*steam wagon*," had not even been planned, except in his brain.

The other quotation presents the views of another eminent man and citizen, the first mayor of Saint Louis, William Carr Lane (distinguished alike for his great abilities and virtues during a prolonged, useful and honorable life ended years since). In 1823, at his instalation, addressing himself to the aldermen, he said:

"The fortunes of the inhabitants may fluctuate, you and I may sink into oblivion, and even our families become extinct, but the progressive rise of our city is morally certain. The causes of its prosperity are inscribed on the

*NOTE.—As old Mexico was then called.—*Author.*

very face of the earth, and are as permanent as the foundations of the soil and sources of the Mississippi! These matters are not brought to your recollection for the mere purpose of eulogy, but that a suitable system of improvements may always be kept in view, that the rearing of the infant city may correspond with the expectations of such a mighty futurity!"

Let a stranger visit Saint Louis, view its site, and have knowledge of its surroundings—including its great tributary territory of permanent resources, of ever increasing volume, pouring its wealth incessantly into the lap of this city, and he cannot fail to imbibe an opinion in respect to St. Louis, similar to that of another noted man—whose talents and genius are acknowledged in the two hemispheres,*—in regard to London, when witnessing in wrapt attention the sale of the plant and effects of Thrale's brewery. Being asked what he could find in such a scene to *interest him*, he replied, "I see in and around me, sir, the potentiality of great riches!" This opinion (at a period when London was not much larger than St. Louis of to-day) and justly spoken of a *single* manufacturing plant, and its possibilities,—applies with apt and argumentative force to this city in *its entirety*. All the earlier and seemingly extravagant predictions, (when they were uttered) have been more than fulfilled within the observation and experience of living men, who need none to tell them—for they *see around them the potentiality of great riches*, both in the present and future of the solid growth of this city in wealth and grandeur.

*NOTE.—Doctor Samuel Johnson, author and lexicographer, who, more than a hundred years ago, discerned the future of the vast growth in the wealth of London through *one* only of its established industries. Of the *same sort* of industry, Saint Louis has to-day the greatest on the globe! (paying an annual direct tax to the government of a half million dollars); but this city possesses many other and very diversified industries,—in manufactures, producing annually a coin value *many times* more than all those of London of that period.—*Author.*

ELOQUENT EULOGIUM UPON THE FUTURE GREATNESS OF ST.
LOUIS. DELIVERED IN 1851.*

"Life is not a time of dreaming,
Standing still, or asking when—
Mere resolves, or worldly seeming—
Duty calls for earnest men."

The Author considers that he is doing a service to
Saint Louis, whilst rendering a just tribute, (in which all
citizens would unite), to the high character and ability of
a former eminent citizen, now deceased, by reproducing,
at least a part of an eloquent essay, of thirty-eight years
ago. The indications of the future destiny of the city
of St. Louis were there so strong that the utterance
of sentiments such as his was appreciated by large numbers of the leading and observing citizens of that day: but
it is no disparagement of their intelligence and foresight to
say, that their highest views, and grandest expectations
have been so far transcended in the growth and greatness
of this city (witnessed now after the lapse of nearly forty
years), that "the dreamy flight of a visionary," as a few
viewed his opinions, was not nearly equal to the realizations
of to-day!

"Earnestness is the watchword of the men of St. Louis.
At the present day especially, they will prove themselves
worthy to be citizens of this goodly city—whose future is
rich in promise. / A bright, enviable destiny awaits it—as the
time is not distant when from one hundred to two hundred
millions of our race will find their homes, in this most
fertile valley that a Beneficent Being has bestowed upon
the human race. And when these valleys and plains shall

*NOTE.—Extract from the fifth annual report of the Mercantile Library Association,
of St. Louis, January 14, 1851, by Hudson E. Bridge, President.—*Author.*

resound with the hum of the ceaseless industry of teeming millions, what then will be the bounds of our city? May she not become an Island City? with the mighty, restless Missouri for its northern, the magnificent Mississippi, as now, its eastern, and the pure, limpid, beautiful Meramec its southern border. Situated as St. Louis is, in the very heart of the valley, and, comparatively speaking in the centre of this continent, may not the time come when the pulsations of her commerce shall be felt from Baffin's Bay to the Mexican Gulf, and vibrate, with equal intensity along the shores of the placid Pacific, and from Panama to Prince Williams' Sound?/

The ruins of the ancient cities of the valley of the Nile excite our wonder and admiration. Yet we are laying the foundations of a city, on the banks of the Mississippi, that shall excel them in extent, wealth and refinement, as the Mississippi exceeds in volume that of the Nile, or the Anglo-Saxon or Celtic races excel in energy and intellectual greatness the ancient Copts. Those hopes and expectations may be pronounced wild and visionary.''

REMINISCENCES OF LACLEDE BY AUGUSTE CHOUTEAU, HIS COMPANION WHEN CHOSING THE SITE OF ST. LOUIS. GLOWING TRIBUTE TO LACLEDE BY A DISTINGUISHED CITIZEN.

" He planted wiser than he knew."

Auguste Chouteau, who was chosen by Liguest to accompany him in his search of a location, which should at once be his residence and a central trading post, (but shortly became the capital of "Upper Louisiana," as well) kept a journal of early events, which was destroyed by an accident, except a fragment only. He relates: "That in the month of December, 1763, Laclede set out (by batteaux from the landing nearest Fort Chartres), to look for a suitable site for the establishment of his settlement, taking with him Auguste Chouteau, who possessed his confidence, and (commencing at a point nearly opposite the Fort) he examined all the ground to the Missouri river: then returned, and decided upon the spot where St. Louis now stands. He was delighted to see the situation (to find a location so eligible), and did not hesitate to fix upon it as his home, and to begin a settlement. Besides the beauty of the spot, he found all the advantages which he could desire for a settlement, and one that might in time become considerable. After examining the place and surroundings, he fixed upon the exact locality where he wished to settle and build, marked some trees with his own hands, and, turning to Chouteau, said: "You will come here in the spring—on the opening of the river—and cause this spot to be cleared of the trees in order to begin our settlement after the plan I shall give you." Chouteau continues, "we returned immediately to Fort de Chartres, and Mons. Laclede, addressing himself to Captain De Noyon, the commander—in the presence of his officers—said with enthusiasm: That he had found a location where he should begin a settlement, and which might *hereafter become one of the finest cities in America*, that there were so many advantages embraced in the sight and locality for the forming of other settlements around it."

No attempt shall be made to comment on this fragmentary leaf of Chouteau's Journal; but instead, to reproduce an extract from an address made to a St. Louis audience, eighteen years ago by a distinguished citizen still living, in language, than which it would be difficult to choose words more befitting the theme, and in which every citizen may

sympathize and feel a becoming pride and grateful satisfaction that his lot has been cast at so highly favored a
spot.

He said: "Laclede seems to have had a prophetic
vision of the coming greatness of the city which he was lo-
cating—it at least dawned upon his mind. Could the hand
of Omnipotence have drawn aside the veil, so he could have
had a glimpse of it, with its busy population, its crowded
streets teeming with life, its miles of storehouses, its palatial residences, its foundries and furnaces, its machine
shops and manufactories, its churches and school houses
and colleges, its waters no longer traversed by barges of a
few tons burden, propelled by sinews and muscles of strong
men—occupying many months in making a voyage from
New Orleans to Saint Louis; but by great vessels propelled
by steam, carrying vast burdens, and moving almost with
the speed of the wind; the land traversed by numerous railroads with their long trains freighted with human
beings and the rich products of every clime, arriving and
departing each hour, contributing to the wealth and growth
of the little trading post established by him, and which he
said 'might become one of the finest cities of America,'
this seemed no less probable to Mons. De Noyon and his
officers at Fort de Chartres, than do the predictions of
those now in our midst—who tell us that St. Louis is not
to be *one* of the greatest, but *the* greatest city on this continent, and the capital of an empire."*

---

* Extract from the address of James E. Yeatman, at the 25th anniversary of
the founding of the St. Louis Mercantile Library Association, Jan. 13, 1871.—*Author.*

CHAPTER IV.

SAINT LOUIS, A GREAT AND GROWING CENTRE OF PRODUC-
TION, CONVERSION AND EXCHANGE.

"To you, ye Gods, belongs the Merchant! o'er
　The waves, his sails the wide world's wealth explore:
　And, all the while, wherever waft the gales,
　The wide world's wealth sails with him as he sails."
　　　　　　　　　　　　　　　　—*Schiller.*

Saint Louis is planted in the centre of a very great area of rich and populous country—greater than that of any other city in America—of either continent. The agricultural resources are the products of the Valley of the Great "Longitudinal" River, which covers more than 30 degrees of longitude and 25 of latitude, down to the semi-tropics. Scarcely a fourth of this vast territory has yet been tamed or developed from the primeval forest, and native prairie: the immensity of the volume of production of the future, in whatsoever ministers to the comforts or delights of man, when it shall all be utilized, from the sources of the Mississippi, thence to the Mexican Gulf, and from the western slope of the Alleghenies to the mountains at the west, cannot be estimated, but the yearly increase is simply incalculable.*

St. Louis, as by magnetic attraction, draws into her lap a very large and increasing proportion of the productions and trade of that magnificent territory, and is acquiring more and more each recurring season: until, in time, the swelling flood shall roll in, not to harm or destroy, but to

*NOTE—Within the geographical limits of the valley of the Mississippi—includ-ing its branches—it is estimated that a population of three hundred million human beings could subsist and yet not exceed to the square mile a larger number than many countries in Europe.—*Author.*

enrich its people, and build up each vacant lot of ground with the dwellings of a mighty population, and with warehouses, groaning under a surfeit of stores; then—having already verified Laclede's prediction—"of becoming in time one of the finest cities of America"—it may be the greatest./

To assume the ultimate consummation of such future for this city, there must be a foundation for the claim, and the possession, within itself, of all the elements necessary to receive, and the ability to utilize the incoming flood of commerce and population. The solid basis of this claim will not be questioned, any more than the mighty future of the surrounding territory. Then, the accretions from the remotest circumference, shall be so considerable as to make of St. Louis a World's Depot; and, its people rivals in opulence and influence of the greatest cities of the globe!

THE BUSINESS "PLANT" OF ST. LOUIS IS REPLETE IN NEARLY EVERY ELEMENT AND DEPARTMENT.

Moreover, it is suggested, that, to be a great Commercial and Manufacturing Centre—such as St. Louis is—requires the possession, in active daily business routine, of all that, which, in the language of the counting-room, is called Exchange, Conversion and Production.

By *Production*, we understand that which is derived from "field, forest and mine." *Conversion* implies the consumption of food products and fuel, use in manufactures—changing the crude or rough material into different, and more valuable forms and conditions, but, including all the uses and dispositions made of nature's productions. *Exchange*, is manifestly Commerce and Banking, the

purchase and sale of all productions received from abroad,
or manufactured at home, and their distribution at large.
Transportation is a necessary adjunct, and an essential
factor, but must be easy, direct and cheap.

A PARALLEL BETWEEN ST. LOUIS AND OTHER WESTERN CITIES.

In drawing a parallel between other western cities and
St. Louis, we naturally take Chicago, Pittsburgh, Cincinnati and Louisville, whose geographical position and
business relations toward this city are well understood.

These cities are all centres of commerce and manufactures, but, in the case of the two last named, their
surrounding, available territory is hedged, as compared
with that of this city, and its area cannot be enlarged,
except on the south, the northwest being held by Chicago,
and the west by St. Louis.

Chicago, at the divide between the great water-shed of
the Mississippi valley, is a great commercial site and city,
but is vastly inferior to St. Louis as a manufacturing site,
and whose greater advantages will continue to grow with
the years. This city being possessed of cheap fuel, that
which "made" Pittsburgh, and gave her the prime element
of advantage over less favored spots, is at no disadvantage
in comparison with the most favored manufacturing sites
in respect to an abundance of fuel, in raw coal and fuel-
gas.

Pittsburgh, planted at the junction of two important
rivers, the sources of the Ohio, which begins the valley of
the Mississippi at the northeast, was a grand manufacturing
site and centre before the discovery and use of natural gas.

which, in recent years gave that city a great advantage in manufacturing over some other places, but at the present time, by the very successful production from our coal of a fine quality of fuel-gas. St. Louis is placed upon an equality of advantage—in the cheapness of its manufactured products with any natural gas locality.

Saint Louis possesses all the advantages of the cities mentioned, but in a degree which surpasses them all. (without any of their disadvantages), and is at once a great *central mart* of commerce—in Exchange, Conversion and Production—the focus towards which the trade of the Mississippi valley, and a vast territory beyond, is constantly tending: and shall become, before many years have elapsed, the zone of the population of North America.

ST. LOUIS GREAT NOW, BUT OUT OF COMPARISON WITH ITS FUTURE IN POPULATION AND OPULENCE.

The site and surroundings, conditions of trade and commerce of this city are all most favorable—located on the great "Inland Sea," at its centre, and near the confluence of the other greatest river of North America, (the Missouri); between the mouths of the Ohio and Illinois; and closely connected with, and joined to the Great Railroad Systems of the United States, Canada and Mexico—it is pre-eminently situated for attracting, acquiring, and holding a very great trade in ever increasing proportions and value. Besides, other systems of railroads are annually being built and will continue to be constructed toward St. Louis—as to both a necessary and profitable connection.

The producers and agents in the agricultural and grazing, the mineral and timber districts on all sides, from great

2

distances seek this city as their point of conversion and
exchange to many the most accessible, direct and profitable market; and, in return, they take the wares, merchandise and manufactures found here in variety in every department; the extent of the accessible and tributary territory dealing with this city from the four points of the
compass, their populations and productions amazing in
extent and variety—increasing at a rate unexampled in any
other country or age—can a limit be fixed to their growth?
The prospects are such as are not surpassed, or scarcely
equalled by any other site! Such is the happy experience, and such the grand prospects of St. Louis whose
natural and acquired advantages are supplimented and utilized by the enterprise and intelligence of her active men
of business.

The tens of thousands of miles of railroads, leading
from and centering at this city, as the initial and focal
point, and the fifteen thousand miles of navigable rivers—
forming the ''Inland Sea''—and connecting it with all the
globe beyond—conveying the productions of the Great
Valley, and of the hills, mountains and plains—in gold,
silver, fruit, wine and wool; rice, sugar, cotton and tobacco; wheat, maize, butter, cheese and meats; timber,
lumber, lead, iron and coal—all delivered at the depots
and wharves of St. Louis.   Think of the amazing annual
increase of all productions and facilities; then inquire,
where shall the limit be? and the echo answers where?
This tide of commerce and trade can no more be stemmed,
or turned away from this city than the floods of men,
money and merchandise which irresistably and incessantly
pour their tides into the cities of New York and London.

Other towns and cities, within the circumference of
the vast territory which surrounds St. Louis, will continue
to grow and flourish, and others still shall spring up—in
valley and plain, on mountain and shore, but, this city

shall keep, cannot lose, its preeminence—as the Central
Mart of a Great Continental District—any less surely than
that the City of New York should ever fail of her supremacy over all other cities of the United States!

ST. LOUIS—A FACTORY OF PRODUCTION AND MARKET OF DIS-
TRIBUTION.

Through the enterprise of the active business men and
capital of St. Louis, the city of to-day presents most of the
able aids to modern progress, supplemented to great natural advantages of site and surroundings. As a railway
centre connected with all parts of the continent, central,
accessable, and in direct communication with all other business centres, it is available on the most economical
terms of freightage to the manufacture, handling and distribution of the products of the soil, mine and forest, and
of the workshop and factory. Whilst the limits pre-
scribed for this work do not permit of extended tables of
statistics, there will be found elsewhere, in a condensed
form, the results of the last years business of this city
obtained from standard authority, and most reliable and
direct sources. Our space permits of only the summary
sales in leading lines of merchandise—of wholesale and
jobbing merchants—but the reader will find ample reference to all the leading industries of this city.

Producers and dealers from part of the states east of
the Mississippi, and from the greater part west of the
Great River, market productions and purchase supplies to
a greater or lesser extent at St. Louis. In the Northwest
and State of Illinois, this city competes with Chicago: and
in Indiana with Cincinnati and Indianapolis: whilst with

the Southern Valley States, the great trade of ante-bellum days is enjoyed in excess of all previous times.

St. Louis is second in the production of flour, first in manufactured tobacco, and all products of fire-clays; and in sales of hardware, drugs, chemicals and groceries, is a rival both of Chicago and New York; whilst in malt liquors it exceeds in value any other spot on the globe.

Through the efforts of the able men conducting the Merchants' Exchange, a valiant contest has been waged against railroad freight and bridge toll discriminations, which have been the greatest obstacles to all intelligent plans and earnest endeavors to enlarge the commerce of this city, and put it in the forward rank. The operation of the Inter-State Commerce Law has not met the general expectations of benefit which it promised; but, the construction of the New Merchants' Bridge across the Mississippi, at a most favorable point, with its terminal railway facilities, will abate excessive tolls to a minimum of the cost; the assurance that this most needful structure will be built and completed within thirty months, raises to blood-heat the zeal of merchants and manufacturers to lend their aid in hastening the day of disenthrallment from an odious monopoly, in the present bridge, which has so greatly hampered commerce.

The owners of real estate at the east end of the new bridge, in Illinois, all in north St. Louis, especially along the east front wharves, will be enriched by the rise in the active value of their property, which, by the time the Bridge and Terminal are completed, will be raised to triple the present values; but property values will be largely increased throughout the entire city.

CHAPTER V.

Bituminous and Cannel Coal are both found throughout the larger portion of the State of Missouri, in limitless quantity, and of fine quality; but, in the immediate vicinity of St. Louis—"across the river in Illinois"—great mines of bituminous coal supply the city of St. Louis with an excellent quality; upwards of one hundred coal companies of that State offer their coal on the markets. The State Geologist, Professor Swallow, thirty years since, estimated the quantity of good available bituminous coal in the State of Missouri at 134 million tons, but later discoveries and estimates make the figures very much larger.

The recent "finds" of great beds of fine quality of cannel coal, in different counties of Missouri, swell the total of fuel deposits still larger.

The late discovery of improved processes for the making of fuel-gas from coal of varieties furnished for consumption at St. Louis—adds still more to the fuel supply of this city; and, as it has been found, that the supply of natural gas is unreliable, and growing more expensive by reason of the failure of wells, and the great expense of boring others; the cost of fuel-gas is no greater in the long run, which places this city, certainly on an equality of advantage in fuel with any other manufacturing site.

MOUNTAINS OF IRON.

The "Iron Mountain" is a mountain of iron, and is situated in Saint Francois county, Missouri, distant eighty-

one miles from St. Louis, and is composed almost exclusively of iron ore in the purest form, denominated "specular" ore.

The other immense deposits of iron ores are found in
Iron county, which adjoins St. Francois, and are Pilot
Knob, Shepherd, Arcadia and Bogy Mountains; these
wonderful formations probably possess more iron ores of
purer qualities than any other of equal area on the globe,
and Iron county is in truth the *iron county* of the United
States.

Originally the Iron Mountain was 228 feet in height,
its base covered an area of 500 acres, and it was estimated
to contain 1,655,280,000 cubic feet, or 230,187,375 tons
of ore.

Pilot Knob is 581 feet in height, and 1118 feet above
the bed of the Mississippi river at St. Louis, it covers an
area of 360 acres, the ore yields sixty-five per centum, and
the quantity was ascertained to be fourteen million tons.

Shepherd Mountain is 660 feet in height, nearly two
miles in length by one mile in width, and covers an area of
800 acres. Its ores are mainly a mixture of magnetic and
specular oxides: the polarity of the former frequently
caused it to be called loadstone.

The Iron Mountain is located forty-one miles from the
Mississippi river at Ste. Genevieve. It was first mined
extensively in 1845, and the ore hauled over the hill road
to the river by wagons in thousands of tons. In 1852, the
quantity delivered at Ste. Genevieve was largely increased
after the completion of a plank road; but since 1857, upon
the construction of the Iron Mountain Railroad, the ore has
been hauled to St. Louis by rail in vast quantities.

The earliest iron mine in this group was opened in 1840;
but, the mountains of ore were known to Missourians long
previously. A little more than fifty years ago, geologists
at the East knew of these vast piles of iron ore and even

that they were very pure, but the general public scorned the possibility of the existence of "a mountain of iron," and considered the story a myth, or boast of western people accustomed, as they said, to "spin yarns." Even the President of the United States did not receive the information of the existence of such huge masses of ore as a veritable fact.*

In later years the enormous masses of iron, of marvelous value, which the hand of nature has so lavishly bestowed upon the State of Missouri, have excited the wonder and admiration of the world.

The vast yearly consumption of iron products in numberless and indispensable forms, has made it a commercial barometer, indicating the rising and falling of the tide of the general public prosperity. It has become an axiom, that when the market for iron is dull, or the demand light, it is significant of a drop in trade, or decline in industrial activity; but, when the demand is active or large, it is indicative of the reverse condition, namely, that the general

*NOTE.—An entertaining story is recalled to memory—related directly to the author thirty years since—by the widow of the former United States Senator Lewis F. Linn, so highly esteemed in his day, and colleague of Thomas H. Benton. Mrs. Linn—a most estimable and accomplished woman and true daughter of Missouri—told in a charming manner the following incident, which occurred at the White House, about the year 1838. It was during the administration of President Van Buren, and at a dinner party to which they (Senator and Mrs. Linn) were invited guests; sitting near the President at the banquet, she spoke of that great natural wonder—not very distant from her home at Ste. Genevieve—a mountain of iron! and of such wonderful purity, as to be utilized directly at the forge of the workman! Mr. Van Buren listened attentively, but looked incredulous, and remarked: "Oh, Mrs. Linn, you western people are too poetical." The lady quickly rejoined, "very well, Mr. President, I shall be enabled to show you on our return from Missouri next winter, that if poetical, we are practical, as well." Mrs. Linn stated, that she had often visited the iron mountains, and had knowledge of a competent workman accustomed to utilize the ore; and of an old pioneer, who had seen buffalo in south-east Missouri, and preserved several horns of the bison. Upon returning to Ste. Genevieve, Mrs. L. went horseback over the rough hills, and obtained sufficient of the ore with her own hands and carried it to the workman, who, under her direction, forged a large knife, and polished it; and, out of the bison's horn, she had a handle made for it, then a scabbard of morocco. Being thus furnished with a specimen-proof of her true story of the mountain and its peculiar ore, Mrs. Linn waited upon the President the following winter, in womanly triumph, and presented the knife to the ungallant host, who made ample apology.—*Author.*

lines of industries are prosperous, and trade at par, wherefore, Iron is King!

We might, like Sparta, do without gold or silver, but
would become barbarians without iron. Iron—unknown
to the Britons until the Roman domination—has been the
main lever in raising England to her pinnacle of wealth:
the same with Pennsylvania—it has become her ablest factor in opulence: to the State of Missouri, and the City of
Saint Louis, in particular, manufactured iron products will
continue to be a source of greatest wealth.

The ores of this metal are found in great variety for all
purposes in the manufacture of iron in three-fourths of
all the counties of the State of Missouri; but in all those
of the southeastern part with only one or two exceptions,
and always in great abundance.

RAW COAL VERSUS FUEL-GAS FOR GENERATING STEAM POWER. NATURAL GAS AND FUEL-GAS COMPARED.

As is well known, fuel-gas is not a *new* steam-generating
fuel, but the improved processes of its manufacture, within
the last two or three years, have greatly increased its useful value, for instance over the Siemens' process—and
patented by Mr. Westinghouse, of Pittsburgh.* His discovery consists in making a fuel-gas which can be stored,
or conveyed directly in wrought-iron pipes to factories—
where steam is required—or to stores and dwellings, for
heating or cooking; and further, he has succeeded in
eliminating from this flowing and portable fuel-gas the

*Note. That gentleman stated to a committee of St. Louis Capitalists, who visited
his plant to investigate and experiment with our coal, that he had expended a quarter million of dollars in experiments before meeting with success in making a superior fuel-gas.—*Author.*

tar, which, under old processes adhered to, and choked the pipes and gasometer. In this success consists the special advantage in greater part over the Siemens', or old process.

A few of the St. Louis iron and glass manufacturers have adopted the use of fuel-gas, which they make at their works, and use *hot* from the generator; their process of making it is not yet perfected, and for the present they will continue to consume it in the hot state, otherwise, they would be speedily troubled with a tar coating of conveying pipes; but, they are engaged in experiments to expel the tar, and use the fuel-gas *cold*.

Nevertheless, the late improvements in the manufacture of fuel-gas are so great as to give the assurance, that it is *the coming fuel* for generating steam; indeed, enthusiastic manufacturers declare that the value of fuel-gas over raw coal is like a tallow-dip candle, a half century ago, in comparison with electric lighting at the present day.

The experience of the St. Louis establishments in the use of fuel-gas shows that it has an enormous advantage over the raw coal as used; first, in economy, and secondly, in obtaining a better quality of product. As a result, other large manufacturers of this city are about to build gas plants at their works, and adopt this wonderful fuel. As compared with natural gas, it is more reliable, and as cheap! At one of the very large iron works of this city, the use of fuel-gas—made on the premises—has realized an enormous saving in cost of fuel. So completely has the new fuel come to be valued, that a member of this firm has declared, that even if natural gas had been found in immense volume near Webster in St. Louis County—where a company expended a large sum of money in sinking wells without success—he would not take it, as he is now getting better results and cheaper fuel by the use of fuel-gas.

In iron and glass works, and other manufactories where a large quantity of fuel is consumed, independent

gas generators will be employed, but other consumers of
fuel—manufacturers, business establishments, and dwellings—will shortly have offered them the benefit of fuel-gas.

It can be said, that a company composed of some of
the ablest men of this city, is now being organized to
make and supply this fuel to consumers, delivered from
wrought iron pipes. The company will be enabled to furnish fuel-gas at no higher cost than the present price of
natural gas at the City of Pittsburgh. At that city it has
become necessary of late, owing to the exhaustion of wells,
to advance the price of gas, which caused a remonstrance
on the part of consumers, who decline to pay a higher rate.
The company which furnished the gas, threatened to cut
off the supply; but, the courts being appealed to, granted
a temporary injunction. The furnishing of natural gas is
followed, after establishing a very costly plant required
in its distribution, by the enormous expense of sinking
new wells to replace exhausted ones; and, even in the best
fields, its price is more expensive than the fuel-gas made
and used by St. Louis manufacturers.

Less than two years ago, all the great iron and glass
works of Wheeling, West Virginia, were using natural gas;
but, only recently the last one of these works gave it up,
and, are again using either raw coal, or fuel-gas of their
own making.

Some manufacturers of St. Louis, two or three years
ago, had fears least they might not be able to compete in
prices with similar works at Pittsburgh; but, now they
realize their full ability to manufacture as cheap as that, or
any other locality using natural gas; and, that they have
nothing to fear from competition; having now in the
fuel-gas a permanent fuel, just at their doors—cheaper in
the long run than natural gas—and giving them such advantages as are equalled by few spots, and not surpassed
by any manufacturing site.

AMOUNT OF BITUMINOUS AND ANTHRACITE COAL AND COKE
RECEIVED IN ST. LOUIS THE LAST THREE YEARS.

	1887.	1886.	1885.
	Bushels.	Bushels.	Bushels.
Bituminous Coal	66,524,925	61,258,525	53,387,664
Coke	9,584,350	5,463,950	3,500,000
	Tons.	Tons.	Tons.
Anthracite Coal	65,000	70,000	80,000

THE IRON INDUSTRIES OF ST. LOUIS.

No statistics of the iron industries are available (there
being no special record of their multiform productions) and
it is only by observation and deduction, that an estimate
of their extent and money value may be formed. But, in the
production of the blast furnaces, we have some reliable
statistics, and they alone turned out, in 1887, 187,000
tons of pig iron and iron for manufacturing steel, the
market value of which, at an average price of $18.00 per
ton, amounted to $3,386,000. Besides, there were 151,500
tons of net product of the rolling mill and steel works last
year, the value of which, in varying degrees of work and
finish, could not be estimated, nor can the output of the
other lines of manufactures in iron be stated with any
accuracy. But, when, to seven blast furnaces, five rolling
mills and steel works, are to be added the many foundries
and forges—all working in the rough material—and the
numerous manufactures in iron, of varying degrees of
moderate and high cost, of every description, including an
enormous output in barbed and other wires, an idea, at
least, may be formed of the great value of the annual trade.

It is but reasonable, that the iron industries should have
great prosperity at St. Louis from their accessibility to ores,
fuel and every adjunct necessary to the business, and
should occupy a very chief position in the manufacture of
iron and steel products, in comparison with other localities.

PILGRIM CONGREGATIONAL CHURCH.

CHAPTER VI.

ST. LOUIS AN AMERICAN CITY.

"Nature's vast ever-acting energy
In will, in deed, impulse All to All."

—*S. T. Coleridge*.

There is an outside impression prevalent, that, as St. Louis was at one period altogether French, there must yet remain, if not a large element of that nationality, at least well defined proofs in society and business walks of its former existence. Neither opinion, however, is correct. At the period of the "Cession," or transfer of the country to the United States' authorities, in 1804—under the Treaty of Purchase of the Territory of Louisiana,— the entire population numbered only 925 souls, of which number all were French, save a few Spaniards, Americans and slaves of African descent. But, within the succeeding twenty years, the American emigrants out-numbered the original population: and in 1823, (when the first City Government was established), the population amounted to nearly five thousand souls. A few French immigrants continued to arrive after the "cession," during the wars of the first Napoleon, and succeeding the Revolution in France, which dethroned King Charles X, in 1830. There were men of large wealth, and many of culture and refinement, of both sexes, amongst the French resident population, who, for many years, continued to be amongst the leaders in society, business and public affairs: they were always foremost in the Fur-trade; took a leading part with Americans in merchandising and banking; and in mining and manufacturing, as well. The oldest of

the original French inhabitants passed away forty years
ago:* but numerous descendants remain, and are prominent in society, business and professional life. By intermarriage outside, their nationality was lost, and now there
are very few citizens of purely French blood remaining,
whilst in business or society circles, the French language is
rarely ever spoken. The French ladies were distinguished
for elegance in dress and refinement of manners.

Of foreign immigrants, the Germans were the most numerous, and the Irish next, the latter speedily blending with
Americans. There were not a few English and Scotch,
and some Italians, but even the latter show few characteristics of their race, with the exception of recent immigrants.

In the years 1849-50 and 51, thirty-four thousand Germans immigrated to St. Louis, one-third of whom settled
outside of this city. The impulse began with the Revolution in that country, in the year 1848. Many brought
small fortunes in money and means, and were generally an
excellent class: some were persons of note and distinction
in their native country, a part of whom acquired celebrity in a few years in our country, as soldiers, statesmen,
etc., amongst whom were Siegel, Osterhaus, Hecker,
Flad, Shurz and others.

The immigration of Germans to St. Louis continued
freely up to 1856, and has lasted to the present time, but
in comparatively small numbers. Still this city has not
been "Germanized," † as some have supposed at the East.
The German population has ever been orderly and law-

*NOTE—Pierre Chouteau, Sen., who died in 1849, aged 91 years.

† NOTE.—Not that it is presumed there is any thing worse in Germans than is
found in other people, but that Americans dislike *all* foreign peculiarities, whether
of German, English, or other peoples, and prefer the American type of men, accompanied with its "Yankee" enterprise and push. It would not hurt, but help the
Germans of St. Louis were they to follow American ideas and methods more
than they do. But, as regards national prejudices and preferences, where can
be found greater admirers of German Soldiers, Scholars, Scientists, Philoso-

abiding; in general they are moral, and the religious element is considerable; their churches are usually large, after European models, and have great bells and organs, most have their parochial schools. The German element has instituted many social, benevolent, musical and artistic societies. In music they rank high; a number of prima donnas, and performers on instruments, have gone forth from these societies, and taken rank amongst the first singers and musicians of America and Europe; and besides, there are some artists of ability in painting and sculpture.

A large percentage of the Germans, and German-Americans, are of the best people in intelligence, refinement and morality; they are found in every avocation, including merchants, manufacturers and bankers, and other departments of useful and professional life. A marked degree of intelligence and culture is evidenced among the German population not only by a number of daily, weekly and other publications in their language, but in their social and family relations. They always readily adapted themselves to American ideas in dress and otherwise, and eagerly sought to learn the English language, and to acquire a knowledge of our laws.

The president of the public schools in his last annual report (issued Nov., 1888), referring to the elimination of the German language from the district schools of this city, in January 1888, says: "The unselfish devotion of our fellow citizens of German ancestry to our public school system was signally illustrated in that the schools suffered no perceptible loss of attendance in any part of the city, and the most urgent demands for new school accommodations continued from what were known as distinctively German districts."

phers, Artists, and composers of the Divine Art of Music, than among cultured Americans? and do not Americans heartily unite with the people of every land, in admiration of that noble specimen of ripe manhood presented in the character of the late Emperor Frederick?—*Author.*

It can justly be said, that the Germans and German-Americans are not surpassed by any, nor equaled by but few other people in those social ministrations by which life is humanized and softened.*

The blending of Germans into the one predominating nationality, by intermarriage, is of constant occurrence. In fine, St. Louis is as distinctly American as most of the large cities of the United States, and, in the nativity of its people, more so than either Chicago or Cincinnati.

*NOTE.—The author on his paternal side, derives his lineage and name from a German, born and reared in the Upper Rhine Country, Germany and immigrated to the Carolinas via Charleston, (within ten years succeeding the arrival of that distinguished man, Henry Melchior Muhlenberg, the earliest missionary to the German Lutheran colonists in America, about 1740 ; and on his maternal side from English "Quakers," who came part of Penn's colony to Philadelphia, in 1680, and, although an American of Americans he speaks in praise of the Germans and German-Americans of St. Louis because they deserve to be commended, and the German race in general, as well.—Author.

VIEW AT FOURTH AND PINE STREETS.

CHAPTER VII.

SAINT LOUIS' ABLE AND ACTIVE MEN.

"Be strong therefore, and
Show thyself a man."—*Sacred Writ.*

Men of marked ability were always found in all professions and pursuits at St. Louis; they were drawn hither as
to a fitting field of action, and once upon it, remained.
In business pursuits, men of rare judgment and energy,
largely endowed with brain and will power, have never
been wanting, nor ever so numerous as now; they would
be so considered in any community. Since examples of
the *abler* always go downward to the *weaker*, it is obvious
that the influence of these men of push and power is
widely felt in the community.

The stale accusation that St. Louis men have ever
been slow and timid to enter upon plans of development
and improvement, which would benefit themselves and
their city, and that they discouraged and balked enterprise,
deserves review to find its truth or inaccuracy. The
history of this city disproves that assertion, if frequency
of splendid action, followed by great benefits to themselves
and fellow-citizens be proof of pluck, public spirit and
enterprise.

Beginning with the fur-traders (earliest at the town of
St. Louis), there were men of more than mediocre ability
possessed of fair education, large intrepidity and courage.
They encountered the dangers of the wilderness, whose
only inhabitants were wild animals and wilder men. To
reach the Pacific coast they traversed the pathless plains,

3

scaled the hills, crossed the Rocky Mountains, planted two trading posts on Columbia river, as early as 1808, and preceded Astor in the establishment of the fur-trade on that coast!

When the Spanish-French domination ended, the business men of St. Louis became voluntary and able aids of the National government in controlling the Indian tribes, with whom these pioneers held constant business relations. At this period, talented Americans joined the French in prosecuting the valuable and lucrative trade in furs, and in opening the way to the settlement and civilization of the interior country.

St. Louis men surveyed the " Santa Fe trail " amidst the hunting grounds of the savage Kiowa and Comanche; and were the earliest to send an annual expedition to New Mexico from the eastward for the purpose of trade.

St. Louis men promoted the settlement of all the territory contiguous to the Missouri and Mississippi rivers; they filled those streams with steamboats, and established regular lines to the Yellowstone, and from St. Paul to New Orleans!

A St. Louis man* in Congress, was the father of the Pre-emption Land Act, which enabled the poor emigrant to select his home and hold it, previous to the survey of the public lands. That law brought untold benefits to millions of the pioneers and their families, and settled the West in one-half the time!

St. Louis men were not behind in city improvements; water-works were early constructed, and enlarged as required, until thirty million gallons are now used daily; and works are under construction for an additional water supply, equal to the demand of the next half-century, the cost of which is provided for, without contracting any additional loan or any debt therefor!

*NOTE.—Thomas H. Benton, U. S. Senator.—*Author*.

Within a few months after the earliest flash of the electric telegraph, in 1844, a telegraph line was demanded and built to St. Louis!

In 1849 and 1850, Saint Louis endured two plagues at one time. Asiatic cholera, which alone destroyed seven thousand lives, and the "Great Fire," which consumed three or four millions of property; the city survived these calamities, and recovered without aid from abroad!

Immediately after these two great disasters, St. Louis men commenced to build the *first* great railroad to the Pacific, and another to the Atlantic. Then it was that Senator Benton made his great speech on behalf of these pioneer railroads; and, as if it were only necessary to *remind* St. Louis men of the great works to be undertaken and completed, he said—pointing towards the East, and then to the West—"hither is the Orient, and thither is the Occident!"

St. Louis built furnaces, mills, foundries, factories, and great store houses; her commerce filled the rivers, and their tributaries; and her customers came from every stream and valley!

St. Louis endured the shock of the Civil War upon her commercial and manufacturing foundations, and stood the loss of her southern trade—involving a hundred millions annually of reciprocal trade—with the additional loss of millions of credit debts never paid, and yet survived, and flourished!

St. Louis men planned, engineered and built the titanic Bridge and Tunnel, the former the world's wonder, less than a score years ago, and they are about to build, and complete within thirty months, another similar Great Bridge, spanning the Mississippi—having terminal facilities of the highest utility—all which, (by the enterprise of St. Louis men) its great and growing commerce demands for profitable use even to-day.

A St. Louis man constructed the "Jetty" system at the
mouth of the Great River, and deepened the channel from
eight feet to thirty feet to the Sea, forever!

Thirty years ago St. Louis established street railways;
built great grain elevators as required; founded some of
the largest manufacturing establishments in the United
States, and carried trade and commerce into more than
two-thirds of all the States and territories, and to numerous
foreign countries, as well!

Now, when the increased railroad traffic, and enlarged
business of the city require it, St. Louis men vigorously
undertake the work of another Great Steel Bridge—spanning the Mississippi!

St. Louis men have established the most successful
Agricultural and Mechanical Annual Fair of any country,
and an annual Exposition of the Fine Arts, and grand
entertainments in Music, all which have cost several million of dollars, and are visited annually by a half million
people from the surrounding and distant States and territories!

St. Louis men have reared, and built on a solid foundation one of the first and most promising cities of America—done from increased value of their holdings, and the
fruit of their enterprise and business, and not with bor-
rowed capital!

The merchants, manufacturers, bankers, and business
men at large of St. Louis, have always been pre-eminent
in "tact, push and principle;" and are now employing
push in excess of their predecessors, whilst carrying forward all the great interests of this city with such energy
and ability as is not overmatched elsewhere!

Not only in material matters, but in education, and all
the liberal and refined arts, St. Louis men have been active
and munificent in the past, as at the present; in evidence
one instance only need be named: The magnificent endow-

ment, a generation since, of Washington University, one
man alone giving a quarter million dollars in money, besides
valuable real estate; but, there have been numerous other
endowments of educational, art, benevolent, charitable and
religious institutions. Names are inappropriate here, but
the sentiment and action have ever been broad in the community, since sordidness is not a characteristic of Saint
Louis men!

Yet, it is not to be considered that all the able and
active men of St. Louis have departed (few ever emigrate,
and depart only with end of life), but it possesses to-day a
host of men the equals of their predecessors, and who,
whilst emulating the noble examples left them, are impelled
by the vital energy of the present day—seen on every side
—and are living to excel, both in action and skill, the
great men who preceeded them. But, the aforegoing are
given as specimens only of the works of the able and active
men of Saint Louis.

In fine, it should no longer be said that Saint Louis men
are deficient in enterprise and activity, since their will and
ability to do is as large as their great field of action.

THE NOBLE WOMEN OF ST. LOUIS.

"O fairest of creation, last and best
Of all God's works, creature in whom excelled
Whatever came to sight, or thought be formed,
Holy, divine, good, amiable, or sweet."—*Milton.*

Having written upon the men of St. Louis, its noble
women may not be passed in silence. It would be invidi-
ous to mention names in a work of this description, but it
will suffice to say, that not a few women born and reared at

this city, and others from abroad who have made it their home—gifted for womanly worth—have gained a graceful distinction. Some possessed of wealth have founded benevolent and charitable institutions; whilst others, having the riches of "faith, hope and charity," have given of these in abundant works; others still, endowed with talent and genius, have attested their gifts in literature, music and art; in all which some have acquired well merited celebrity. In authorship alone, in almost every department of thought and sphere of observation, this city has brought out in half a century, more than five hundred writers, a large number of whom were and are women.

From the begining of the establishment of the national ownership of the territory of "Upper Louisiana," (of which Missouri formed a part), and especially from the date of the founding of Jefferson Barracks, near this city, and its occupation by a *corps de reserve* of the United States Army, the city of St. Louis has given, from the ranks of her fair and accomplished women, her daughters in marriage to officers stationed at the Post, amongst whom were some of the ablest and most distinguished soldiers of the Mexican and civil wars.

In fine, it may be said, that in all that makes woman the peer of man in activity and usefulness, and his superior in purity and worth, in beauty and refinement, the women of St. Louis have not been, nor are they excelled by their sisters of other places.

The City of St. Louis of To-Day.

PART SECOND.

CHAPTER I.

THE MUNICIPALITY: ITS GOVERNMENT.

"Oh! it is excellent
To have a giant's strength."— *Shakespeare.*

THE "Scheme and Charter," setting forth the organic rights and privileges of the city government, its legislative construction and powers, and limiting its power of taxation, was prepared by thirteen freeholders who were elected by the people for that purpose under an act of the State Legislature. The City is governed by two legislative bodies chosen by the people one of them is known as the "Council," and the other as the "House of Delegates." The latter is called the Lower House, one member being chosen from each city ward; and the former body, the Upper House, and is comprised of thirteen members, chosen from the city at large on a general ticket.

The Executive Department of the City Government consists of the Mayor, Officers and Board, who are elected for a term of four years. The department consists of the Mayor, Comptroller, Treasurer, Auditor, Register, Collector, Marshal, President of the Board of Assessors, Coroner, Sheriff, Recorder of Deeds, President of the Board of Public Improvements, President of the Council (who is Acting Mayor, in the absence of the Mayor), and Inspector of Weights and Measures, all of whom are elected by the people. In addition to these officials there are the *appointive* officers and boards having charge of the streets, water supply, wharves and harbors, public parks, public buildings, inspection of boilers, law department, etc. The Health Department is presided over by a Commissioner and Board. The heads of the Fire Department are appointed by the Mayor, by and with the advice and consent of the Council. The Police Board is appointed by the Governor of the State, and the Mayor is ex-officio President.

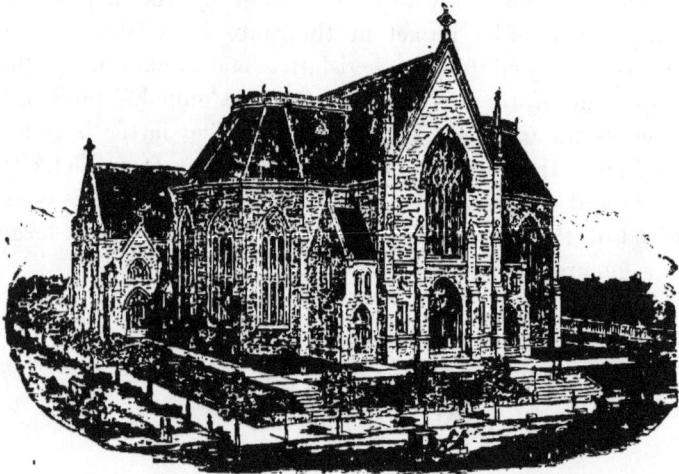

GRAND AVENUE PRESBYTERIAN CHURCH.

ELECTIVE OFFICERS

CITY OF ST. LOUIS.

FROM APRIL 1885, TO APRIL 1889.

Mayor,	DAVID R. FRANCIS,
Comptroller,	ROBERT A. CAMPBELL,
Treasurer,	FRED. F. ESPENSCHIED,
Auditor,	A. J. SMITH,
Register,	DANIEL O'C. TRACY,
Collector,	H. CLAY SEXTON,
Marshall,	MARTIN NEISER,
Supt. Weights and Measures,	ANDREW HALEY,
Pres. Board of Assessors,	JOHN J. O'BRIEN,
Pres. Board Pub. Improvements,	HENRY FLAD,
Pres. of the Council,	GEO. W. ALLEN,
Coroner,	SAMU'L K. FRAZER.

CHAPTER II.

THE BONDED DEBT, AND FINANCIAL STATEMENT FOR THE YEAR ENDING APRIL 9, 1888.

THE BONDED DEBT OF THE CITY OF ST. LOUIS. THE DEBT IS CONTROLLED WITHIN LIMITS FIXED BY THE CHARTER.

A statement of the bonded indebtedness and general financial condition of the City, is made up at the close of each fiscal year, the 9th of April. On the 9th of April, 1887, the city's bonded debt was $22,105,000. A reduction of the debt was made during that year of $821,000 by payment and cancellation of maturing bonds.

On the 9th of April, 1888, the Bonded Indebtedness of the city was $22,045,000, having been reduced $60,000 by the Sinking Fund during the fiscal year. The debt bears interest, as follows:

```
$   600,000.....................at 7  per cent. per annum.
   14,064,000.....................at 6   "    "      "       "
    1,049,000...        .......at 5   "    "      "       "
    3,481,900.....................at 4   "    "      "       "
    2,850,100.....................at 3.65 "   "      "       "
```

During the fiscal year just ended, the Mayor and Comptroller were authorized to provide for the redemption of maturing bonds to the amount of $4,529,000 by the sale of renewal bonds, at a rate of interest not to exceed four per cent. per annum: of that sum all bore interest at the rate of six per cent. except $122,000, which was at 7 and 8 per cent., the whole requiring an appropriation of $273,210 for annual interest thereon. The renewal bonds were readily sold, and bear interest as follows, viz: 2,850,100, bearing interest at 3.65 per cent. at par;

$1,559,000, bearing interest at 4 per cent., and at a premium of $17.80 for each bond of $1,000; $60,000, bearing 4 per cent. interest, (to sinking fund), at par; $59,900 not sold, but $27,750.20 of that sum was absorbed by the premium gained in the sale of the 4 per cent. bonds mentioned.

VIEW IN BENTON PARK.

The sum required to pay annual interest on these renewed bonds of $170,073.33, is a yearly saving to the city of $103,136.67, or for the twenty year term of the bonds, the large sum of two million sixty-two thousand, seven hundred and thirty-three and $\frac{40}{100}$ dollars.

The bonded debt of the city *cannot be increased over the limit* provided for in the City's Charter. The credit of St. Louis is second to none in the United States. If securities were exempt from taxation at this city, as similar securities are in some other cities, where issued, it

is presumed that the renewal bonds mentioned could have
been placed at 3 per cent. interest per annum.

There will mature during the fiscal year, ending April,
1889, the sum of $2,038,000 of the city's bonded indebt-
edness, which the Mayor and Comptroller are authorized to
renew, for a term of years, whose length is left to their
discretion; but it is under consideration to place the limit
at thirty years, instead of twenty, as in the case of last
year's renewals, in order to *spread* the period of the
maturiety of renewed bonds.

The city has no "floating" indebtedness, nor can it
make any debt which cannot be paid during any fiscal
twelve months. The Mayor, Comptroller and Treasurer of
the city, in 1887, so placed the current municipal deposits
as to be allowed interest thereon on the daily surplus at
the rate of $3\frac{91}{100}$ per cent. per annum, which is greater
than has heretofore been obtained,

THE FINANCES.

The finances of the city are in a highly satisfactory
condition. The total revenue collected during the past
year, and the sources whence it was derived, was as
follows;

Interest and public debt revenue	$1,491,271 91
Municipal revenue	3,769,367 19
Water Works revenue	1,531,636 12
Harbor fund	98,190 52
Total	$6,890,465 74

The following amounts, belonging to their respective
funds, were the unappropriated balance in the treasury
at the beginning of the fiscal year.

Interest and public debt revenue	$254,066 92
Municipal revenue	165,777 13
Water Works revenue	766,091 83
Harbor fund	26,714 38
Total	$1,212,650 26

This sum exceeded the unappropriated balances in the treasury at the beginning of the fiscal year, 1886–87, by $338,760.23, and that was far greater than that of the previous year. The estimated revenue from all sources for the fiscal year of 1888–89 is $6,970,501.47, or about $80,000 greater than that of 1887–88. The assessment of the revenue for 1888, is $224,740,470 against $216,917,720 for 1887, and $214,427,670 for 1886, showing a very satisfactory increase each year. This increase, together with the reduction of the rate of interest on the bonded debt, enabled the city *to reduce the rate of taxation* for 1888, from $2.50 to $2.30 on the $100.00, which includes State tax of four mills.

AUDITOR.

The Receipts and Expenditures of the city government during the fiscal year are stated in detail in the Auditor's report. The cash balance in the Treasury on April 12, 1887 was $1,422,037.64. The receipts into the treasury during the year were $9,873,648.39. The expenditures during the year (including unpaid warrants from fiscal years 1886–87 and 1887–88) were $10,514,143.44, leaving the Cash Balance in the treasury on April 9, 1888, $781,542.59.

TREASURER.

The above figures are also contained in the Treasurer's report. The Treasurer asks that the force employed in his office be increased to meet the increased business appertaining thereto.

COLLECTOR.

The total collections for State, City and Schools were $6,911,003.27, of which, after deducting expenses of collection, there was paid into the State Treasury the sum of $1,066,884.39; into the Public School Treasury, $853,-386.79; and into the City Treasury, $4,898,650.98.

CHAPTER III.

BOARD OF PUBLIC IMPROVEMENTS.

The Expenses of the Board of Public Improvements were $23,823.65. The number of special tax bills issued was 3,874, covering work the cost of which was $366,247.-01. The contracts awarded to public work involved an estimated expenditure of $1,687,938.27.

STREET PAVING.*

Up to April 1, 1888, the number of miles of Paved Streets were as follows, viz:

	Miles.
Of Macadam-stone paving	276.77
" Limestone Blocks "	1.07
" Granite " "	33.25
" Asphaltum " "	0.09
" Asphaltum Pavement (Monolithic, or Concrete base)	3.86
" Telford Pavement	9.49
" Wood-Nicholson (old system)	0.39
" Wooden Blocks on concrete base	2.72
Length of Streets. Total Miles†	327.64

OF ALLEYS.

Paved with Limestone Blocks chiefly, and some Granite Blocks. Length of Alleys. Total Miles 73.14

The Street Commissioner states that for the year end-

*Note.—The municipal law requires the owner of real estate to pay an assessment of not over twenty-five per cent on the tax levy for the current year (on a specified lot) of the cost of construction in paving a new street, or the reconstruction of an old one; the remainder is paid out of the city treasury from the special fund appropriated annually for streets.—*Author.*

†Note.—The improvement of streets during the year ending April, 1888, was less than the preceding year in consequence of the omission to make timely appropriation for that purpose the previous year; but, that did not happen again, and the report of the year ending April, 1889, will show a large increase both in construction and reconstruction. Up to December 10, 1888, the increase in street paving and repairing was as follows: In Granite Block, 6 10-100 miles, in Wooden Block, 2 55-100 miles, and in other descriptions, 39 65-100 miles, making a total increase in eight months, from end of city's year, April, 1888, of forty-eight and one-half miles. The entire cost of *grading* all new streets is paid out of the City Treasury.—*Author.*

ing April 9, 1888, the city expended in the construction
of new streets and the reconstruction of old ones, exceeding one million one hundred thousand ($1,100,000) dol-
lars.

COMPARISONS—SHOWING THE GROWTH OF THE CITY.

In 1861 the aggregate length of the Public and District
Sewers was 31 52-100 Miles; in 1871, 117 16-100 Miles;
in 1881, 202 66-100 Miles; in 1888, 270 68-100 Miles.

The Cost of the Sewers up to 1861 was almost $800,000;
in 1871 slightly over three million; in 1881 five and a half
million; and in 1888 nearly seven million dollars.

PUBLIC AND DISTRICT SEWERS

completed April 1, 1888, were two hundred and seventy
68-100 miles in length; and built at an aggregated cost
since the city began to build sewers of six million, six
hundred and sixty-five dollars. *The Mill-Creek Sewer is
the largest sewer in the world.** Its dimensions are 15x20
feet for 16,389 feet of its length, and 15x18 feet for
3,199 feet length, and has a total length of nearly four
miles. It was constructed at a cost of $1,387,030.73, or
plus $70.00 per lineal foot, equal to three hundred and
seventy thousand dollars per mile! The Mill-Creek Sewer
receives the sewerage and storm-water, of an area comprising twelve thousand three hundred acres. The materials of this mammoth sewer are stone and brick. It dis-
charges into the Mississippi at foot of La Salle Street.

* NOTE.—The Commissioner of Public Improvements so informed the Author.

CHAPTER IV.

WATER SUPPLY.

The City's Water Supply although ample is being largely increased, and the work under progress of construction includes a Conduit of Seven Miles in length and a diameter of *nine feet*. It is expected to be completed in 1893, and will furnish an adequate supply of water for one million population. The cost of this large work will be met by annual appropriations from the city's revenues as the work progresses, and when finished *no debt* will have been incurred for the work, which had not been provided for in advance.

There was an unappropriated balance in Water Works Revenues at the beginning of the present fiscal year (April, 1888), of $766,091.83, enabling the pushing of the work during the present year, and the annual surplus from (water rents) revenue will be ample for steady continuance. The increased supply of water will come from the Mississippi river at the "Chain of Rocks," ten miles north of Market street. Forty acres of ground at that point, and the right of way (the seven miles) has been purchased: excepting a small part now under condemnation and assessment of its valuation.

The average *daily consumption of water* for the last regular year was nearly *thirty and one-half million gallons*, or nearly five hundred thousand gallons more than the daily use during the preceding year. The Receipts of the Department for the last fiscal year were $919,975.18 in water rents.

In 1871, the daily water supply was twelve and a half million gallons, which in seventeen years has increased to two and one-half times that amount.

The Water Bonds of this city are in amount $5,200,-000, bearing interest at six per cent. per annum.

In 1901, the Revenue on Water Rates will enable a reduction on the principal of the Bonds, and, by gradual payment during the succeeding twelve years, it is expected that all will be liquidated; and in that year, 1913, it is estimated that there will be a surplus after full payment. This result will be accomplished out of the annual water-rate revenue, but includes the current annual interest on the bonds, and all expenditures for new pipes and distributing mains, besides the annual sums required in operating the Water System.

The New Works are to have a capacity of fifty mil-

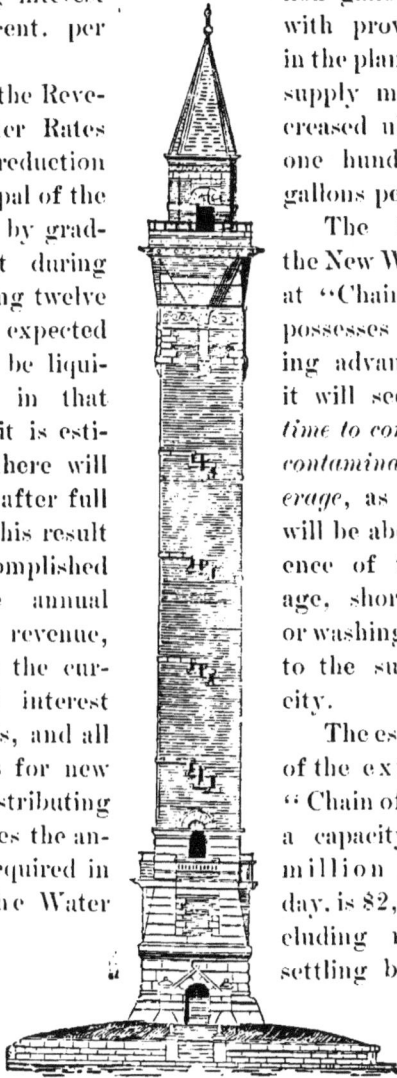

THE NEW WATER TOWER.

lion gallons per day, with provision made in the plant so that the supply may be increased ultimately to one hundred million gallons per day.

The location of the New Water Works at "Chain of Rocks" possesses the following advantages: that it will secure for *all time to come water not contaminated by sewerage*, as the in-take will be above all influence of town drainage, shore nuisances or washings incidental to the suburbs of a city.

The estimated cost of the extension to "Chain of Rocks" of a capacity of fifty million gallons per day, is $2,836,520, including river work, settling basins, filter beds, the 7 miles conduit and land

4

damages. The aforegoing is condensed from the annual
report of the Commissioner of Public Improvements to
April 9, 1888.

MILES OF WATER PIPE.

The number of miles of water pipe laid and in service
in the city is as follows, viz:

```
Laid previous to October 6th, 1877..............177 miles.
Laid since and up to April 1, 1888..............144  "

      Total April, 1888 ........................321  "
Pipes in service April 1, 1888 ..................314  "
```

THE FIRE DEPARTMENT

Is in the highest state of order and efficiency. There
are thirty steam fire-engines—(an increase of five over the
previous year), five chemical engines, twenty-seven hose
carriages, eight hook-and-ladder apparatuses, fourteen
wagons, 185 horses, and 30,000 feet of hose. The force
numbers 339 men and officers.[*]

ASSESSMENT OF THE REVENUE.

The Total Valuation of taxable property for the year
1888 (in old and new limits), was $222,679,760, being an
increase of $7,480,670 over the preceding year.

BUILDING FOR TWO YEARS, ENDING APRIL 1, 1889.

The sum expended for Building for the year ending
April, 1888, was about eight million dollars, or one million
in excess of the previous year. The year ending in April,
1889, is expected to show a still larger increase; but it has
been found that the sums reported are largely less than
the actual investments.

* NOTE.—On December 15, 1888, two additional Steam Fire Engines, and their
adjuncts, were added to the fire extinguishing department.—*Author.*

The building permits issued from the 9th of April to
the 12th of December, 1888, amounted to $6,793,208.

BANK OF COMMERCE BUILDING.

CHAPTER V.

SAINT LOUIS: THE LATITUDE, TEMPERATURE, RAIN-FALL,
TOPOGRAPHY, HEALTH.

"Yes, nature here draws close to man,
   With lenient eyes,
Dissolves with tender touch the ban
   Of griefs and sighs."

The Latitude is 38 degrees 23 minutes North, Longitude 89 degrees 36 minutes West, the Mean Temperature 57 degrees: the Annual *Rain-fall* is an average of forty-one inches; the average number of clear days during the year is found to be 142; of partly cloudy weather 174, and of entirely cloudy days 49. The Topography shows a varying rise above the City "Directrix," (the level at top of the Levee of the Mississippi at the East front), of from thirty-five to two hundred feet, or more, at the west side of the city, distant seven miles. Numerous hills, elevated plateaux, and benches afford grand building sites. The environs of the city, and suburban country for more than ten miles west, north and south of the city, is a continuous succession of fine elevations unsurpassed for their beauty of natural scenery and grand building sites without number, reached by rapid transit of several railway lines of numerous daily trains.

Very great extremes of cold or heat in Summer and Winter are not experienced at Saint Louis. The mean temperature for 1887 was 57.50, Fahrenheit, and the normal, 55.3 degrees. Number of days minimum below zero 5; maximum above 90 degrees 45 days. Total precipitation, 35.30 inches, greatest rain-fall in any 24 hours 2.32 inches.

The *mortality-rate* is less than some other large cities, as will be found by comparison. The annual mortality rate for the city of St. Louis for the last ten years is taken from the reports of the Health Commissioner, and is as follows:

1878, 1879, 1880, 1881, 1882, 1883, 1884, 1885, 1886, and 1887.

18.2 18.1 18.9 22.07 19.06 20.4 19.9 18.7 20.6   20.67

The progress in "sanitation" at St. Louis is steadily marked each succeeding year; and it will shortly become one of the cleanliest, as now among the healthiest cities of any country; and for salubrity of situation on the west bank of the Mississippi is not surpassed, by any city of the United States.

MISCELLANEOUS.

AREAS OF CITY LIMITS AT DIFFERENT PERIODS.

(Excluding the River.)

			Acres.	Sq. Miles.
Territory within Limits of 1839			477.25	0.75
"	"	"	1841.... 2,865.10	4.48
"	"	"	1855.... 8,923.25	13.94
"	"	"	1870....11,504.75	17.98
"	"	"	1876....39,276.25	61.37
"	"	"	1888.... same	same

DISTANCES.

(Air Line.)

			Miles.
1.	Length of River Front		19.15
2.	"	Western City Limits	21.27
3.	"	City from extreme North to South	17.00
4.	"	" " " East to West	6.02

ELEVATIONS.

The City Directrix upon which all elevations are based, is the top of *a square flat stone*, set level with the curb on the west side of the Wharf, between Walnut street and

Market street—0.00 (being the high water mark of the
year 1826).

(Above the City Directrix.)

Height of City Directrix above mean tide of the Gulf of Mexico, as
determined by the Mississippi River Commission......412.71 feet

Highest Stage of River—Jan. 27, 1844........... 7.58 "
Stage of River—June 10, 1851.................. 2.80 "
"   " — " 15th, 1858................ 3.30 "
"   " — " 26th, 1883............... 0.99 "

(Below the City Directrix.)

Lowest Stage of River December 21st, 1863..... 33.81 "
Stage of River- December 27th, 1860.......... 33.21 "
Difference bet. highest and lowest stage of river. 41.39 "

VIEW IN TOWER GROVE PARK.

CHAPTER VI.

THE STREET RAILROADS.

The number of Chartered Companies is seventeen, operating twenty-one lines, and covering the city in all directions with more than one hundred and sixty miles of street railways, counting single tracks only, but nearly all are double tracked. Four of these companies operate the Cable System, and several others are experimenting with electric power. Again, the project of Elevated City Railways has been broached, and a strong effort is being made to obtain municipal privileges which have hitherto been denied, partly in consequence of the opposition of property owners on the proposed routes.

More Street Railways, Electric or Cable, are demanded for the public convenience, and will be constructed at an early date.

In December last, 1888, a company, composed chiefly of Chicago capitalists, purchased the property and franchises of three important street railway lines in this city. The three roads were consolidated under a single proprietorship, or syndicate. The prices paid were favorable to the St. Louis companies, the late owners; and, the new owners assumed all liabilities. Two were horse-car lines, and one cable power. The officials of the new company announced their intention, not only to extend the roads into new territory, but to apply cable or electric power upon all early in the ensuing spring season, of 1889.

These purchases are signs of a rapidly growing conviction amongst watchful capitalists of other cities—both eastern and western—that St. Louis is a place of prime, but early to become of greater importance. At the present writing, (February, 1889), capitalists of Philadelphia and Pittsburgh are standing in readiness to place large sums of money in *elevated* street railways, charters for which energetic projectors of this city are pushing in the councils of the municipal legislature.

The Passenger Traffic on the Street Railroads, in 1887, as reported by the different companies to the City Register, was as follows: Number of trips made 3,922,009; and the number of passengers carried was 52,054,242. The passenger traffic for the year, ending December 31, 1888, was as follows: The number of single trips made was 4,204,929; and the number of passengers conveyed, 55,043,930; showing an increase of about 283,000 trips, and nearly 3,000,000 passengers; or a gain of 5¾ per cent over the year 1887.

It is expected, that 10 miles will be added to the length of the street railroads during 1889, and horse power be dispensed with on all the principal lines.

STREET NUMBERING.

Market Street and Laclede Avenue—running east and west—form the dividing line of all streets crossing them. North of this line are North Main, North Second, etc. South of this line is South Main, South Second, etc. The numbering of all houses fronting on the public streets is arranged as follows: the *odd numbers* apply to the north and west sides of the streets, and the *even numbers* to the east and south sides.

The general rule is that 100 numbers shall represent each block going westwardly from the river front, and a like number for each block north or south from Market street and Laclede avenue.

THE BUILDING MATERIAL OF ST. LOUIS—FOUND AT ITS DOORS.

The City of St. Louis is built on limestone rock, upon the upper stratum of which is found a superior quality of red-brick clay of which all the brick used in building is made. The red shade of color is clear and brilliant. The St. Louis smooth pressed red brick are so much admired abroad that many places using them, notably the cities of St. Paul and Minneapolis, have constructed the fronts of their fine houses of brick imported from this city.

The same clay is used in making brick of various forms for the embellishment of fronts of buildings and used with the brick of even shade of color. The combination of forms and figures with the plain brick makes a most attractive frontage, as shown in the New Mercantile Library Building, corner Sixth and Locust streets, the fronts of which present a very handsome effect.

Building Sand is obtained for the cost of hauling. Lime is very cheap. Limestone Rock of fine quality is abundant and convenient at a low price per perch. Superior quality of building material in Sand-stones, red and gray Granite; and Marbles in white, black and variagated, are to be obtained at no great distance from the city, in Missouri, in quantity without limit.

Fire Clay.—The deposits of this Clay are inexhaustible within and without the city limits, and are equal to the best clays of Europe, numerous factories are engaged in the manufacure of fire-brick, drain-pipe, retorts, house-chimneys, etc. Of drain pipe, the largest made by any works in the country is that of the Laclede Works of this city, being six and a half feet in diameter!

The Missouri Granite is susceptible of a polish equal to fine steel; and is much used in house fronts, both rock faced and polished.

In side-walk paving, the "Granitoid" description, composed of fine chip-granite and cement, is considerably used and makes a smooth and durable walk.

In Lumber and Timber for building and manufacturing purposes the supply is most ample—in white and yellow Pine, in Oak, Maple, Walnut, Sycamore, Poplar, and other varieties, at prices low as elsewhere with the exceptions of hard woods, yellow pine, and poplar, which are lower than at other large western points, and are obtained from the almost inexhaustable forests of Missouri, Arkansas and Tennessee.

CHAPTER VII.

SOME OF THE BUILDINGS OF THE MUNICIPALITY OF ST. LOUIS.

THE COURT HOUSE.

This imposing structure covers an entire block of ground, bounded by Fourth, Fifth, Chestnut and Market streets, and fronting on all; it was completed in 1862, at a

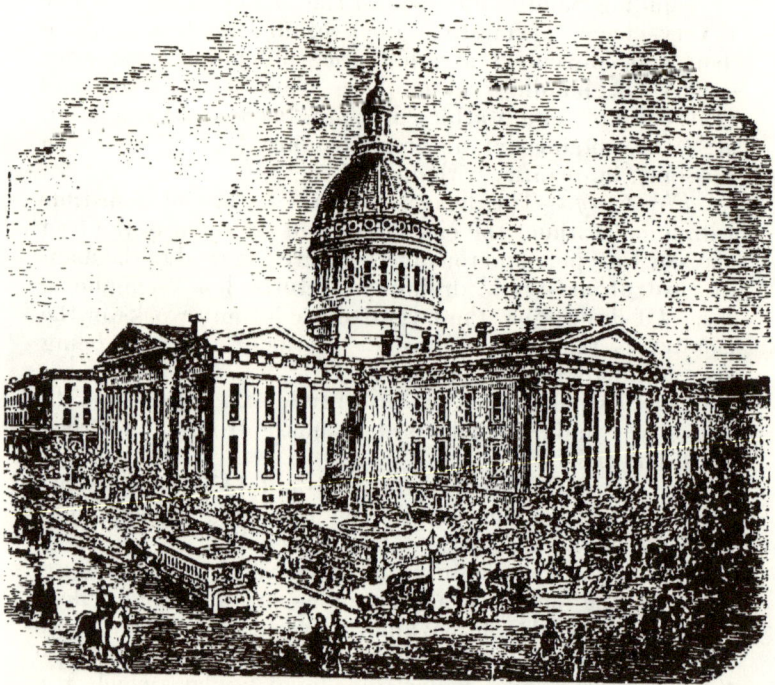

total cost of *seven million* dollars, not including the value of the plot. The Plan of the Building is in the form of a

cross, the material used in the construction is Missouri
gray granite, and it is fire-proof. The Central part is modeled after the Capital at Washington—a lofty Rotunda
and Dome—having elaborate paintings in fresco of leading historical events in American history, by a distinguished Italian artist. An iron stairway leads to the
Dome, from which a magnificent view of the City, River
and Aboriginal Mounds in Illinois may be obtained.

This building accommodates, besides the City Civil
Courts, the Recorder, Assessor, Collector, Sheriff, etc.

THE CITY HALL

Occupies very ample space, and fronts on Eleventh, Chestnut and Market streets. It is three lofty stories in height,
and accommodates the Mayor, Comptroller, Treasurer, Auditor, etc.; also the Street, Water, Fire and Health Departments, and besides the legislative halls of the Council and
House of Delegates.

The City Hall, finished and first occupied fifteen years
since, is no longer suited to the enlarged needs of the
Municipality. The authorities have at the present time
(February, 1889), in earnest consideration, and are taking
active steps in the direction of the construction of a New
City Hall. Excepting a frontage on Twelfth street, between Market and Chestnut streets, of 201 feet by 100
feet depth, the city owns the valuable block of ground
from Eleventh to Twelfth streets, and fronting on Chestnut and Market streets. Should the Municipality purchase
the lot mentioned, and add it to the ground it now owns—
in view of building a new Hall upon it—the block would
have a frontage of 201 feet on Twelfth, and 221½ feet on
Eleventh, by 415 feet on both Chestnut and Market streets.
The unusual width of the street on the west front, (Twelfth
street, of 150 feet), and the proximity of Washington
Square, add appreciably to the eligibility of the site for a

City Hall. A new structure would be erected on the west end of the block; and, in due time, the site of the present City Hall would be utilized for the extension of the new building, all to be adapted to the requirements of this rapidly growing city for the next quarter or half of a century.

With the sum of two hundred thousand dollars heretofore appropriated for a new City Hall, and lying in the treasury, together with suitable ground already paid for, it is quite probable, that the authorities will act soon in the direction of building a new fire-proof City Hall after the latest modern plans, and of suitable magnificence. *

THE FOUR COURTS AND JAIL BUILDINGS

Occupy the entire block of ground bounded by Eleventh Twelfth and Spruce streets, and Clark avenue. Facing the last is the elegant structure known as the Four Courts, built of cream colored stone, and modeled after the Palace of the Louvre at Paris, France. It has a frontage of 130 feet on Clark avenue by a depth of 75 feet. The site is commanding; in construction it is admirably suited to its uses—namely the Criminal and Police Courts, etc.; and was erected, in 1871, at a cost of nearly one million dollars.

---

* NOTE.—But, Washington Square is, in several valuable particulars, a much more eligible site for a City Hall, or building which should concentrate within its walls all the offices of the Municipality—one structure, grand for size, utility and beauty—whose usefulness and magnificence would be, at once the joy and pride of the people!

Practical reasons for preferring Washington Square, are plentiful: it is paid for, the area is very ample, and affords a rare central site, convenient to all street-car lines; the building ground is spacious enough for a wide margin on the four sides—of a rightangled parallelogram—for unobstructed light and air, away from dust and noise; besides, to form a fringe, which is essential for architectural effect in a great structure.

Finally, the value of the city's property mentioned in connection with the site of the present City Hall, the money awaiting use, and a reasonable additional sum, would pay for a new City Hall.

Lastly, and better still, *sell the Court House*, add its large proceeds. Then, erect an edifice designed for all the offices of the Municipality—administrative, executive and legislative—the whole—for convenience, centrality, economy and good sense.
                                                                AUTHOR.

The Jail is situated upon the southern portion of the same Block, and is suitably adapted to its purposes, including light, ventilation and sanitation. The "Morgue" fronts on Spruce street.

THE OTHER BUILDINGS BELONGING TO, AND MAINTAINED BY THE MUNICIPALITY

Are numerous, as the Blind and Insane Asylums, Women's Hospital, Alms and Work Houses, House of Refuge, etc., they are chiefly in the South Western portion of the city, and four miles from the Court House.

THE UNITED STATES' BUILDINGS.

First: The Magnificent Block of Buildings, covering the entire square between Eighth and Ninth streets, and fronting on Olive, with its rear on Locust street—is occupied by the Post office, Sub-Treasury, Internal Revenue, Courts, etc. The dimensions are 236 by 181 feet: there are four lofty stories above the basement, and all surmounted by a graceful dome. The materials are granite, marble and iron—completely fire proof; the granite is of Missouri red, and Maine gray varieties,—in about equal proportions. The cost approached the sum of six million dollars, including the block of ground.

Second: The fine Granite—fire proof structure— (finished and occupied in 1859), S. E. corner of Olive and Third streets, was constructed by the United States Government, at a cost of upward of a million dollars, and used for all the Federal Offices and purposes of the National Government, until inadequate longer to accommodate the increased and increasing needs for additional buildings.

At the present time, still more space is required for the transaction of Government Official Business, and for which this building is now being enlarged and rebuilt from ample congressional appropriations.

THE CITY OF ST. LOUIS OF TO-DAY.

PART THIRD.

CHAPTER I.

THE POPULATION OF ST. LOUIS: ACTIVE AGENCIES OF ITS GROWTH.

' Ye were but little at the first, but mighty at the last."—Charles Mackay.

NO enumeration of the population of the city of Saint Louis has been made since the national census of June, 1880, when the population was 350,561 souls. Its growth in the present decade exceeds the previous experience, but an estimate of the present population is to be found only in knowledge and observation. These afford satisfactory data in estimating the number at the close of the year 1888, or eight and a half years from the period of the last census, and point to the conclusion that it is a half million souls. The grounds for this estimate are ample, patent to all observing and thinking citizens, and may be stated concisely, as follows: During the last decade, this city has witnessed extraordinary development of its rare resources of site and surroundings. All the ready and latent energy of citizens, both of older and younger blood, have been aroused to intenser life and energy. Its industries have been enlarged through the constant increment of capital and commerce. Its wholesale and jobbing trades have realized greater expansion in solid growth. The suburban development has been very large, both in population and real estate improvements, while the urban has been most extensive and varied in buildings of every description. Residences, large and small, stores and warehouses, colleges and churches, halls, machine shops and factories, the extension of the old, and opening of new streets, the construction of more and lengthened sewers, the largely increased consumption of water and gas, the building of new school houses required by the need of increased school service, the greatly increased number of workmen employed in private and municipal improvements, especially in the making of many miles of new street pavements, and the reconstruction of old ones; and lastly, but not least, the increased throngs of men, women and children observed at every turn on the sidewalks, and crowding the street railways, to which many miles of new track have been added, while demands are constantly made for increase in the facilities of rapid transit.

The new manufacturing plants, and the extension of the old ones — a process constantly going on — add yearly a large population to St. Louis from abroad, through the demand for skilled workmen, and in providing employment for an army of the youth of both sexes. A mild climate, exemption from epidemic diseases, cheap living, great advantages of primary, academic and collegiate education, the numerous schools in science, art, technical instruction, complete curriculum of education in all professions and pursuits, the public libraries, and numerous other attractions, are constantly filling this city with a population of the refined and cultured. Those ambitious of an education, the artisan and laborer seeking work and employment, and a countless class of new-comers, constantly make additions to the number of the inhabitants in a swelling tide each season.

The volume of the present population of St. Louis has reached that point of fullness, when, as has been observed in the growth of other cities, (remarkable for which were the cities of London, New York and Brooklyn), it will begin to take increase in a *ratio disproportioned to its previous experience;* and, it is apparent, that such an era of quickened growth has reached this city, whose increase in population in succeeding decades will be in accordance with the experience of those other very large communities.

WHERE THE CENTRE OF POWER IS NOW FOUND IN THE UNITED STATES.

But, we whom a gracious Providence hath brought
To this bright, central spot of earth—
To live and labor, to plant our seed—than ought
More fruitful, or replete with worth.

That distinguished statesman, William H. Seward, averred in a speech made before a Western audience nearly twenty years ago, that: "Power would not much longer linger on the narrow strip between the Atlantic and the slopes of the Alleghenies, but that the commanding field would be in the Upper Mississippi Valley, where men and institutions would speak and communicate their will to the Nation and the world!"

The year 1889 witnesses the fulfilment of that prediction. Just one hundred years ago, the commonwealth of Virginia ratified her gift, by deed of conveyance to the United States, of the "Northwest Territory," which then did not contain one hundred white persons, if we except the French settlements in the "Illinois country," opposite St. Louis. And five hundred French inhabitants of that town constituted the whole remainder of the Caucasian race west of Pittsburgh.

Of the 401 electoral votes cast for the chief magistrate of the nation in 1888, only 164 belong to the original thirteen colonial states; and to the 237 votes which remain, will shortly be added those of new states applying for admission into the Federal Union.

VIEW IN FOREST PARK.

5

CHAPTER II.

THE SAINT LOUIS REAL ESTATE EXCHANGE ASSOCIATION.

> The solid, steadfast ground,
> Our mother earth—so fair!
> Brings forth her golden sheaves,
> Her certain task, nor leaves
> It long, but surely there
> She sheds her gifts around.

OFFICERS FOR YEAR 1888–89.

President, Leon L. Hull; *Vice-President*, Charles F. Vogel; *Board of Directors:* Charles C. Crone, John T. Percy, Charles H. Turner, James S. Farrar; * *Secretary and Treasurer*, Thomas F. Farrelly.

The real estate business of this city is mainly in the hands of the members of the Real Estate Exchange, an organization which has grown from a small beginning, in 1877, to be most important and useful. In its membership may be found the most prominent and influential real estate, loan and rental agents of Saint Louis.

The advantages of the Association are numerous, both to the public and to the agents themselves. It provides a large exchange hall, where the agents may meet and discuss matters relative to their business; and for the holding of auction sales of property. It is expected that ere long the (legal or) "judicial" sales of real estate will be authorized by law to be held at the Exchange, instead of at the Court House doorsteps. The change would be most advantageous by increasing the number of competitive bidders. The Exchange keeps for public inspection, lists of stores, houses, rooms, flats, and other property for rent, lease or sale. The renter, buyer, and public generally are con-

---

* NOTE.—Judge James S. Farrar, died Sep. 1888.

stantly furnished with current information in matters of
city real estate through the medium of *The Real Estate
Bulletin,* a well conducted weekly paper.

The high standing in community of the members of
the Exchange, is a sufficient guarantee for fidelity to their

RESIDENCE OF W. B. MANNY.

trusts. The Board of Directors is composed of members
chosen for their special activity. The advantages of the
Exchange are large and increasing.

ABSTRACTS OF TITLE TO THE REAL ESTATE OF ST. LOUIS. *

The first and most important consideration when dealing in real estate is to secure a clear and unimpeachable title, in which respect investors in St. Louis realty are especially safe. The "Concessions," or grants of land and lots of ground, made during the French and Spanish ownerships, were duly made, and were executed in the presence, and under the seal of the Governor of "Upper Louisiana," and recorded in the "Livres Terriens." These were afterwards transferred, together with all the "Papers" and "Documents" of the "Archives," to the custody of the United States, in 1804, *and are preserved*, together with duplicates—at the City Record Office, (Saint Louis)—having been transcribed into other books of record.

A description is given in the fifth chapter of this book of the "Livres Terriens," or Books of Record; and, the "Archives."

---

* NOTE—The real estate investigator is referred to Chapters V and VI upon the "Commons," and other French and Spanish "Concessions."—*Author.*

COOK AVENUE M. E. CHURCH.

CHAPTER III.

REVIEW OF THE PROPERTY INTERESTS OF ST. LOUIS IN RE-
CENT YEARS. TABLES OF VALUATIONS: OF REAL AND
PERSONAL PROPERTY FOR TWENTY-FIVE YEARS, AND
IN THE OLD AND NEW CITY LIMITS FOR NINE
YEARS. VALUE OF BUILDING PERMITS FOR TEN
YEARS. GROWTH IN VALUE OF REAL ESTATE.
THE RECENT ADDITIONS IN PARKS,
PLACES, BOULEVARDS, ETC.

Unlike some of the cities and towns in the West, Saint
Louis has not been given to wild speculation in real estate.
Prices have been measured according to the value when
changing hands; and it has, as a general rule, ever been
safe to buy the real estate of this city, whether improved
or unimproved. After the financial panic of 1873, St. Louis
experienced a depression in the market value of its real
estate—in common with the whole land—but the property
being held largely by strong owners, the decline was less
than in any other large city. Few other cities of the
United States present equal prospects, or are able to offer
as ample assurances of substantial returns on capital
invested in real estate. Besides, St. Louis for loans on
property is one of the very best localities.

This city is chiefly owned by its citizens, and in this
respect differs from many other large cities. Out of a
population of half a million souls there are over 55,000
tax payers, which is indicative of the comfortable position
of the inhabitants at large.*

It is of interest in this connection to note the following
table, showing the assessed value of property for the last

*NOTE—Careful inquiry at the Tax Office elicited the information that for the
year ending June 30, 1888, there were 55,563 tax bills paid, some of which were for
several owners' property paid through agents.—*Author.*

twenty-five years, beginning one year prior to the close of the civil war.

It is necessary to state, that in Saint Louis it has never been the custom in the assessment of real estate—to make valuations *for outside effect*, but to lean to the side of the tax payers, and make each valuation considerably less than the property would bear.

ASSESSED AMOUNT OF REAL ESTATE AND PERSONAL PROPERTY.*

YEAR.	CITY OF ST. LOUIS.		RATE OF TAXATION.	
	REAL ESTATE.	REAL & PERSONAL.	Old Limits.	New Limits.
1864	$ 53,205,820	$ 63,059,078	2.60	....
1865	73,960,700	87,625,534	2.76¾	....
1866	81,961,610	105,245,210	3.00	....
1867	88,625,600	112,907,660	2.95	....
1868	94,362,370	116,582,140	2.85	....
1869	113,626,410	138,523,480	2.85	....
1870	119,080,800	147,969,660	....	....
1871	123,833,950	158,272,430	2.80	....
1872	129,235,180	162,689,570	2.78	....
1873	149,144,400	180,278,950	2.76	....
1874	141,041,486	172,109,270	2.88½	....
1875	131,141,020	166,999,660	3.48½	....
1876	132,785,450	166,441,110	3.42½	....
1877	148,012,750	181,345,560	2.80	....
1878	140,976,540	172,829,980	2.60	1.35
1879	136,071,670	163,813,920	2.60	1.35
1880	135,824,980	160,493,000	2.60	1.35
1881	139,897,470	167,364,230	2.60	1.35
1882	161,679,250	191,948,450	2.58	1.35
1883	163,479,060	192,563,640	2.55	1.30
1884	178,596,650	210,124,370	2.55	1.30
1885	177,857,240	207,910,350	2.55	1.30
1886	187,291,540	218,271,260	2.55	130 and 180
1887	184,815,560	217,142,320	2.50	130 and 205
1888	195,578,249	227,169,979	2.30	170 and 220

* NOTE.—See Appendix: Article "A."—*Author.*

VIEW IN LAFAYETTE PARK.

THE VALUATIONS WITHIN THE OLD AND NEW CITY LIMITS,
FOR NINE YEARS, WERE AS FOLLOWS:*

YEAR.	SAINT LOUIS.	OLD LIMITS.	NEW LIMITS.
1880	Real Estate.	$122,752,140	13,072,540
	Real and Personal.	146,162,060	14,330,940
1881	Real Estate.	126,205,320	13,692,150
	Real and Personal.	152,165,210	15,199,020
1882	Real Estate.	146,536,400	15,142,850
	Personal	28,809,580	1,459,620
1883	Real Estate.	146,482,410	15,085,390
	Personal	15,139,180	1,420,820
1884	Real Estate.	159,773,580	. . .
	Personal	28,684,600	1,539,010
1885	Real Estate.	159,527,340	18,561,370
	Personal	27,292,990	1,887,010
1886	Real Estate.	162,793,920	22,330,990
	Personal	29,059,560	1,920,160
1887	Real Estate.	162,611,250	22,204,310
	Personal	30,082,110	2,244,650
1888	Real Estate.	167,535,870	26,162,240
	Personal	28,885,540	2,306,190

A steady increase in real estate valuations continued
up to the year 1874, when a decline set in occasioned by
the financial depression of that year throughout the nation,
and which lasted several years from the same cause. Also
in 1878, when a general decline in real estate values was
experienced throughout the country as the result of
preparation for the resumption of coin payment, Jan. 1,
1879, property at St. Louis fell under a temporary depression in price. But, since then, there has been a steady
increase in value. Each year has witnessed a growing
demand both for desirable unimproved ground and
improved property. New districts have been platted into
lots, streets opened and extended, followed by sewerage

* NOTE.—The reader is referred to the note at foot of page 81.—*Author.*

and general improvements. Of late, the demand has been
large for desirable residence plots, and single lots. West
of Grand Avenue, ground which seven years ago was sold
for at from ten to twenty dollars per front foot, now brings
from seventy to one hundred and ten dollars per front foot.
Within the business centres, and beyond, as well, prices
have largely increased, and legitimately too; notably on
special streets. Most of the purchases, made within the
few past years in business localities, were for investment,
and the holders are not desirous to give up property that
has a still greater future.

It will be noticed from the foregoing table of the
annual assessment of the real and personal property, that
there has been a growth of sixty million dollars within

FOUR COURTS.

the ten years, from 1878 to 1888. A much greater proportionate increase may very reasonably be expected within
the next decade.

The late extensions of established streets and avenues,
including additions of fine plots of ground, are in process of
construction and improvement. Several grand public boulevards and private "places," recently finished, are
occupied and in use at the close of 1888. Among them

is a public boulevard, of one mile in length, the road-
way 100 feet, and sidewalks each 25 feet in width. The
latter is granitoid and the former Telford pavement
with a top layer of Maremec red gravel level as a lawn.
Another boulevard of equal length and similar construction, is being made a few blocks distant, and both
end at Forest Park. These magnificent avenues and drives,
beside others not specially referred to, are unsurpassed by
any others in the land.

BUILDING PERMITS FOR TEN YEARS.*

Most of all of the purchases of lots, in recent years,
have been for early or immediate improvement, and
building permits have kept pace with the transfers of
ownership. The permits of the last ten years have been
as follows:

1878	$2,432,568.00
1879	3,851,673.00
1880	3,783,832.00
1881	4,980,885.00
1882	6,163,545.00
1883	7,123,878.00
1884	7,316,685.00
1885	7,376,519.00
1886	7,030,819.00
1887	8,162,914.00

1888, Beginning with the municipal fiscal year, April 9th, to
December 12th, a period of eight months and three days, the permits
were for $6,793,208.00.

These figures do not represent the actual sum expended,
since few buildings are ever completed for the estimated
cost, and for this reason, the total sum should be at least one-
fifth more. This is known to be the case in the estimates
of the outlay on several large structures finished, and yet
building, in the year 1888. The buildings completed in

*NOTE—The building permit office keeps its account for the *calendar* year, whilst
the Mayor follows the *fiscal* year, ending April 9th. The table here given is that of
the permit office.—*Author.*

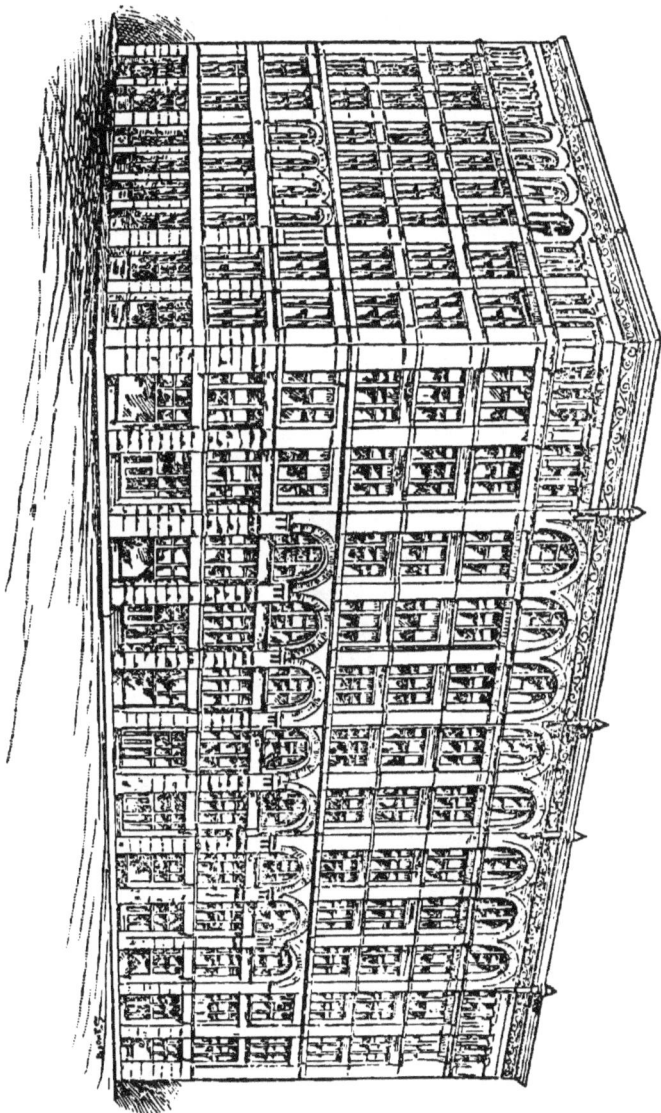

THE LIGGETT & MYERS BLOCK.

that year, namely, those for banks, offices, stores, churches, palatial dwellings, etc., excel in architectural splendor and size, with few exceptions, any that have ever been constructed in this city.

Within the city limits during the year 1888, several eligible and desirable tracts and plots of ground have changed hands, each costing with the surface improvements from a quarter to three-fourths of a million dollars. They have been platted, graded and sewered, and are on sale by the agents of the proprietors. Among the finest of all the splendid drives is Lindell Boulevard, which with others, vie with those of any city of the land.

ST. GEORGE'S EPISCOPAL CHURCH.

CHAPTER IV.

ST. LOUIS' REAL ESTATE. ITS DESIRABLENESS FOR INVEST-
MENT AND EARLY APPRECIATION IN VALUE.

St. Louis has only recently begun to draw the careful
and marked attention of capitalists and investors of other
localities; it has almost suddenly become apparent to them
that here is as promising a spot for investments as Chicago
ever was; and that in the future race for pre-eminence
in population, and its accompaniments, of commerce
and manufactures, it is a rival, whose grand future
may not be disparaged in comparison with the Lake City.
Now, at the threshold of the twentieth century, the time
is marked with such improvement, culture and refinement—
advancing steadily with the growth of population—that this
city will bear comparison with any other metropolis.

The present is a favorable period in the growth and
development of St. Louis, for the investment of capital in
unoccupied grounds, which may be chosen as promisingly,
with slight exceptions, in any portion of the city. Through
all parts new streets have been made and others extended. Sewerage advances apace with the improvement
and development of new localities. No wild inflation nor
"booming"—as that word is commonly understood—is in-
dulged in at St. Louis, but the instrinsic and rapidly ap-
preciating value of its real estate—both urban and suburban
—is manifest to all intelligent observers, and especially to
those who take the pains to make examination.

There is ample room for the profitable employment
of more capital in banking, in the establishment of
more manufacturing industries, and in trade and com-

merce in general; to meet the wants of the great valley, and
populous territory beyond, which seek Saint Louis as the
most convenient and direct market of supply and demand.

THE ADVANTAGES OF ST. LOUIS FOR HOME LIFE.

Few large cities of our country have as many solid
attractions for the residence of a family, composed of

J Blee. Arbt   Residence of Mrs. Mary E. Brownell Eng St   St Louis Mo

parents and children, as this city. To state the facts
briefly, a house may be purchased, or rented, at a reason-
ble—even low—price. Schools, churches and modern improvements are found in every quarter. Stores and markets
are convenient. An abundant supply of good water, gas and

thorough sewerage is found in every developed district. Rapid transit on upwards of 160 miles of street railways, is available, every five minutes and under, at a five cent fare for any distance. Institutions and societies for intellectual and physical improvement, and for rational delight are numerous. Libraries are open to the public at a merely nomial cost. The necessaries and luxuries of life are abundant and cheap. Saloons are closed 24 hours on Sundays. Gambling is forbidden by State and Municipal laws, which are rigidly enforced. And the policing of the city being rigid and active, there are few temptations or allurements which youth may not avoid, provided, the training be proper at home, and *that* made attractive as it can be. Finally, the climate is mild, and in healthfulness St. Louis is equal to the most favored cities of the United States. And, in many other respects, this city is a delightful place of residence.

Residence of L.L.Culver Esq.

CHAPTER V.

TITLES TO REAL ESTATE OF THE ORIGINAL "COMMONS," AND OTHER FRENCH AND SPANISH "CONCESSIONS."

The titles to the original "Common Fields" of the early Town of St. Louis were derived: *First*, from the French and Spanish governments, whose titles were afterwards maintained by special Acts of the Congress of the United States at the instance of the municipality of St. Louis, in all to 3837 acres. *Secondly*, from the City of St. Louis. These lands were sold by the city, and the title conveyed is both undisputed and indisputable. Reference is made to chapter six on the "Common Fields" for a detailed account of these lands.

OTHER "CONCESSIONS" OR GRANTS.

The Congress of the United States passed an "Act (dated June 12, 1866) authorizing documentary evidence of titles to the owner of lands in the City of St. Louis." Under this act 109 decrees have been issued by the District Court of the United States at St. Louis.

Various acts have been passed by Congress, from time to time, ratifying or confirming claims made under the former acts, and also the claims of individuals to particular tracts.

At the present time, all legal principles regulating claims and titles have been thoroughly settled by the courts, and conflicting claims have been adjusted by compromise or court decisions; and, accordingly, very few spots are any longer in dispute. The facilities for examining land titles with accuracy and dispatch are so complete at St. Louis, that purchasers of property can readily satisfy themselves of the validity of their title should they wish to investigate the work of the abstractor.

LAKE AT ZOOLOGICAL GARDEN.

6

THE LIVRES TERRIENS, OR FRENCH AND SPANISH LAND RECORD BOOKS, PRESERVED "INTACT."

The Book of Registry of grants and transfers of lands at the village of St. Louis was called, in French, *the Livre Terrien.**

The "livres terriens," or provincial land records, together with all the documents and papers of the " archives," were handed over by the retiring Spanish Lieut. Governor to Captain Amos Stoddard, U. S. A., who represented the United States at Saint Louis, in March 1804, the date of the " Cession." The number of the documents, etc., exceeded three thousand, many of which remain on deposit with the Recorder at the present day. Books were provided in 1816, in which all these documents were transcribed, and they filled six large volumes.

All papers and documents of record were invariably executed in the presence of the Lieut. Governor of the Province (of Upper Louisiana), or of his official representative, and were deposited in his keeping. They were kept in the French language up to 1770, and afterwards in the Spanish.

An arpent or arpen comprised 192 feet, 6 inches each way, or 37.756 feet square, and about 85.07 of an acre English measure. A league square contained 7,056 arpens.

THE ARCHIVES.

The term "archives" from the Latin *depositorium*, originally signified a place of deposit for the safe keeping of official documents, and subsequently included the term "papers," or documents of esteemed value therein deposited.

Here at St. Louis, at the present day, when speaking of the French and Spanish "archives" of the early village,

---

*Note.—There were in all six books of "cap" paper bound in leather.—*Author.*

we apply the term to the *books* in which a large portion of their early documents were recorded. These were "concessions" or grants of lots and lands, leases, deeds, wills, inventories, powers of attorney, agreements, marriage contracts, and various ʼother documents of a miscellaneous sort relating to persons and things.

THE ASSESSOR'S LIST

Of real and personal property at Saint Louis, in 1811, covered only *sixteen pages of ordinary "fool's cap" paper*, but in the assessment for the year of 1888, the property required over seventy large books to set it forth.

THE REPUBLIC OFFICE.

CHAPTER VI.

THE EARLY COMMONS OF ST. LOUIS.

THE ORIGINAL "CONCESSIONS" WERE MAINTAINED BY ACTS OF CONGRESS AND THE FEDERAL COURTS. THE LANDS WERE UTILIZED BY THE CITY GOVERNMENT.

The "*Common Fields*" were four in number, viz: "The *Prairie des Noyer*," in the south-west original suburbs, beginning at or near Grand avenue on their east side. The grounds of Henry Shaw were a part of this prairie, including the Botanical Gardens and Tower Grove Park.

Next, the "*Cul de Sac*" *Common Fields*, which were situated a little north of Prairie des Noyer.

Then, the "*St. Louis Common Fields*," beginning, on the east, about Fourth street, and extending westward to Jefferson avenue. They embraced the territory bounded by Walnut street on the south, and Palm street on the north.

Lastly, "*Grande Prairie Fields*," bounded on the east by Grand avenue, on the west by Marcus, on the north by Florissant, and on the south by McPherson avenue.

The "Commons" were the public pasturing and haying grounds from the earliest settlement, but the best portions of them were cultivated for corn, wheat and vegetables. They aggregated 45,010.48 arpens, or 3,837.03 acres. They were "Conceded" by the French and Spanish Governments of Louisiana—for the use and benefit of the people of the town of St. Louis. To define, establish and confirm these grants, to the city of St. Louis, (and others to individual persons,) the Congress of the United States passed the following acts, viz:

March 26th, 1804,	April 21st, 1806,	March 3rd, 1813,
March 2nd, 1805,	March 3rd, 1807,	April 12th, 1814,
February 26th, 1806,	June 13th, 1812,	April 29th, 1816,

May 26th, 1826, and July 4th, 1836.

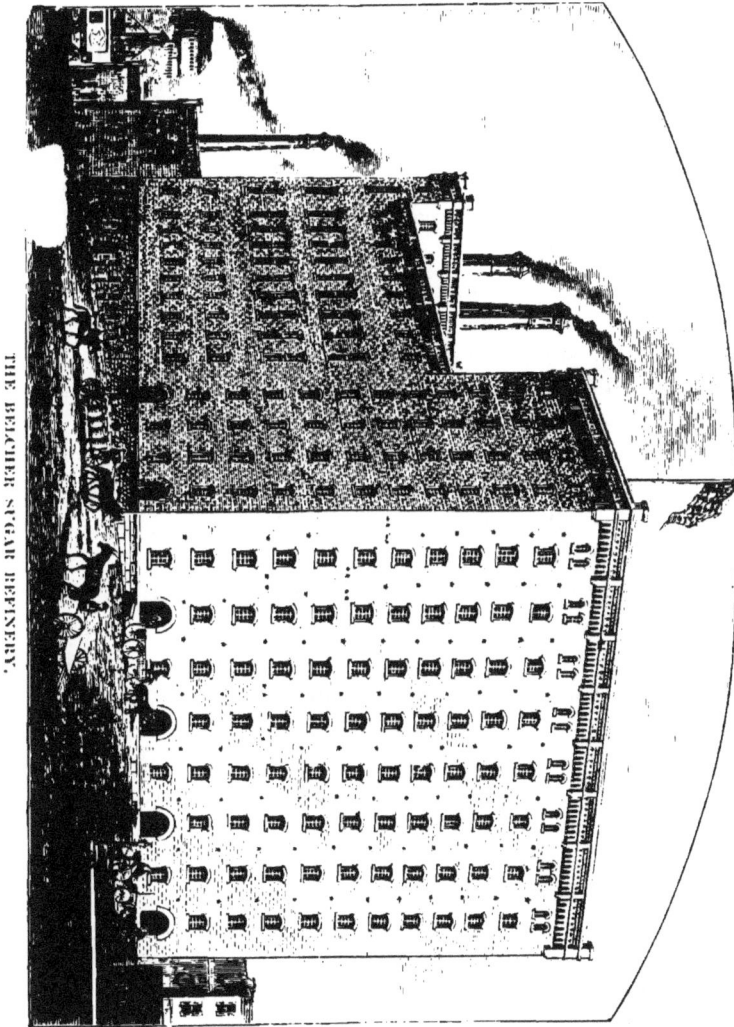

THE BELCHER SUGAR REFINERY.

These acts were in pursuance of Article III of the Treaty of Cession of the Territory of Louisiana by the French Republic to the United States. The "Text" of that article is as follows: "The inhabitants of the ceded territory shall be incorporated in the Union of the United States, and admitted as soon as possible, according to the principles of the Federal Constitution, to the enjoyment of all the rights, advantages and immunities of citizens of the United States; and, in the meantime, they shall be maintained and protected in the free enjoyment of their liberty, property and the religion which they profess."

These acts of Congress (mentioned in order of date), made for the purpose of ascertaining and adjudicating titles, were supplemented by acts of the General Assembly of the State of Missouri, which authorized the City Government of St. Louis to survey, subdivide and sell all the St. Louis Commons. The City availed itself of this authority, and the Council ordered, in March, 1835, a survey and sale thereof; and, accordingly, sold the entire Common Fields, (comprising 3,837 acres), for about the sum of *$400,000.00*. Very soon after these sales, many of the buyers became dissatisfied with their purchases, thinking that they had paid quite *too much!* and, great financial troubles coming on soon afterwards throughout the United States, the result was, that nearly every acre lapsed to the City for unpaid taxes, within a few years.

In 1854, or nearly twenty years thereafter, the City having meanwhile become repossessed of the greater part of the "Commons" under the tax laws, the municipality again advertised and sold the larger part of them, at public sales—during the years 1854-55-56 and 1858—for a sum aggregating $670,000.00. In 1859, what remained were sold. The prices ranged from $500.00 to $7,700.00 per front foot, and produced $80,601.00. So great was the public interest in these sales, that several hundred bidders were

present at each day of sale, and competing for the ownership.
The total sales amounted to $750,601.00.   Ten per cent. of
that sum was voted by the people into the Common School
Fund, and the remainder into the City Treasury and Sinking Fund.   The terms of these sales were one-sixth cash,
the remainder in five annual payments, drawing six per
cent, interest per annum.

INTERIOR VIEW OF THE CLUB HOUSE, FAIR GROUNDS.

CHAPTER VII.

THE OLD BUSINESS SECTION: WILL BE REVIVED.

As is well known, the improved property for twenty squares—between Franklin avenue on the north and Chouteau avenue on the south, and from Front to Fourth street—was almost the exclusive business part of this city, for merchants, manufacturers and offices, until shortly after the civil war. The first Lindell Hotel was built on Washington avenue just prior to the peace. Other large hotels were already established on and near Fourth street. Within a few years thereafter Barnum's and the Olive street hotels were closed. The German hotels on Second street, alone remained, and are still active. About the date of the completion of the Eads Bridge, all the more important hotels were located either upon or a square or two beyond the verge of the *old business limit*, at Fourth street.

Amongst the earliest to remove from the old limits, were jobbing and wholesale merchants; but, they went gradually, at first only a square or two, then somewhat further westward. That class of merchants continues to establish business still further in the same direction.

For a half century after Laclede's time, all the ground east of Fourth street was known as "under the hill." Originally, a bluff of limestone rock, of the height of thirty feet, beginning at Market street, and extending to St. Charles Road, occupied the line of Front, Commercial and Main streets. The "bluff" was utilized for its building stone, and houses were built where once it stood; until, as time progressed, the town extended to, and beyond the hill—spreading more and more—and, in 1876, the western boundary of the corporation was fixed seven miles west from, and nineteen miles along the River Front, where it has since remained. But, it was not until steamboats were largely superseded by railroads in the transportation of freight and passengers, that the moving impulse was felt injuriously to East-End property values. In 1874, upon the completion of the Eads' Bridge and Tunnel, the Union Depot for all the railroads entering the city was established two-thirds of a mile from the river, which greatly impaired the property valuations in the old district.

A somewhat similar movement occurred at the City of New York forty years since, and progressed rapidly for a few years; then, very gradually. At that city, the establishment of the railroad depots, and some of the largest and best hotels in "up town" localities, led to the exodus of the jobbing, importing and dry goods commission merchants from the old to new locations, and nearer the transient homes of their customers. At that day, New York did not possess any facilities of "rapid transit."

In the last particular, the case is different with St. Louis, since rapid transit is found to-day through several street-lines leading from the direction of, and near the East-End. Business men lose no time between their home and office, distant two, three, four and more miles. There is a still greater dissimilarity between New York city and St. Louis. The East-End stretch of this city is many miles in extent, whilst that of the former city is a slender *point* of land, from which the removal of business men dealing with the country merchants occurred. That the Merchants' Railway Bridge, with its terminal surface and elevated railway facilities, will be constructed at an early date is now an established certainty, which gives an entirely new aspect to the question of the eligibility of the East-End improved property. From this time there will be few removals on the part of those who have remained at the East-End; and fresh occupants of new warehouses will seek to be accommodated within the limits of the old district—whose restoration is only a question of a few years.

But, were the Merchants' Bridge and Terminals *never
to be built!* the East-End property would still be very
valuable. In what part of this city can be found property as suitable for dealers in all descriptions of heavy
and bulky goods, and especially of raw materials for
manufacturing, such as coal, ores, blooms and other
mineral products; lumber, timber, cotton, wool, hides and
grain, not to mention flour, meats and machinery?
The answer comes on the instant: "That *no other* location
will bear advantageous comparison with that of the East-
End in eligibility of situation, and in special adaptability to
all heavy lines of mercantile, manufacturing and commission business, including warehouses for goods and machinery."

Then, if this be so, the business property, not only
within the "old limits," but *all* property—both the improved and the unimproved—for several miles of river
frontage, possesses a high intrinsic value and fast-bound
quality, which is as enduring as the earth!

VIEW IN TOWER GROVE PARK.

THE CITY OF ST. LOUIS OF TO-DAY.

PART FOURTH.

CHAPTER I.

ST. LOUIS' AGRICULTURAL AND MECHANICAL ASSOCIATION. *

THIS has long been a favorite institution of the people of St. Louis, and of several of the surrounding states. It was founded in 1855, and held its first fair, October 1856. The fair was suspended during the civil war, but reopened October 1866. It has been continued annually ever since, and is likely to be, while interest in agriculture and the mechanic arts shall last. The area of the ground is eighty acres. All is inclosed, and improved with all needful buildings, conspicuous among which is the ampitheater, capable of sheltering one hundred thousand persons from sun and rain. The Zoological Gardens comprise numerous buildings, including the cages, dens and inclosures of a complete menagerie of wild animals, of all countries.

The annual exhibitions of machinery, implements of husbandry and products of the factory, farm, mine, etc., are

* NOTE.—Thirty-three years since, when the grounds of the Assoc ation were established at their present locality, they were in the remote s burbs; but now the Fair Grounds are within, and distant from the city limits two miles, and surrounded on all sides by costly improvements and a numerous population.—*Author.*

111

wonderful in extent and variety. The Fair attracts each
year hundreds of thousands of visitors during the five days
of the annual shows. The displays of live stock—cattle,
sheep, swine, horses and mules—are scarcely equalled in
any country for the variety and superiority of their valuable breeds.

THE ST. LOUIS JOCKEY CLUB, AND ITS EXCELLING "PLANT."

"How through his veins goes the life current leaping."— *Whittier.*

One of the other most attractive adjuncts of the Great
Fair is centered about the grounds of the Jockey Club Association, sixty-three acres in extent. Its magnificent Club
House, with its complete appointments, is the finest of
any of its sort in the United States. The Association has
semi-annual "meetings," in June and October, and is patronized from all sections of the Union. A very large capital is invested in extensive grounds and improvements, all
which have made this property the first of its class. The
Club, and its valuable properties in the plant, were the outcome chiefly of a laudable aim to promote and secure the
very highest improvement in the breed of trotting horses.

COAT OF ARMS, STATE OF MISSOURI.

CHAPTER II.

THE PERMANENT EXPOSITION AND MUSIC HALL BUILDING.

"Bids him forget what things have been,
        Life's toil and strain,"

The Exposition and Music Hall building is the largest and finest of all yet constructed in the United States for similar purposes; that of an annual exposition of improved machinery, and of inventions and designs; of mineral, agricultural and pomological productions, goods and wares; and of paintings and works of art in general. Beside these, are its unsurpassed entertainments in orchestral music. Hundreds of thousands of visitors, both citizens and strangers, visit and re-visit all these attractions during the usual autumnal term of six weeks.

The magnificent edifice occupies the area of two blocks of ground, and fronts on Olive street 332 feet, to a depth of 506 feet on St. Charles street, between 13th and 14th streets. The superficial area covered by the building is 280,000 feet. The ground was the original Missouri Park, of six and one-fourth acres, and was licensed by the Municipality to the incorporators of the Exposition for the term of fifty years, free of charges for ground rent and taxes (excepting only a tax on the boiler house). The incorporators are an enterprising company of citizens, who seek no direct profit from their investment, but whose design is to provide entertainments, instruction and

refined pleasure suited to the tastes and wants of the day
and age in which we live.

The grand Music Hall has a seating capacity of
four thousand persons, and standing space for half as
many more.

The splendid enterprise and talent of the Board of
Directors of this very popular institution, deserve from
citizens the fullest appreciation. Theory is now at an
end, and it is an established certainty that the views and
aims of the projectors and founders of this most popular
addition to the attractions centering at this city, have been
fully realized; and, that a foundation has been laid to
perpetuate the Exposition and its adjuncts. The very large
patronage of the public at home, and from the surrounding
states, voices the common sentiment of approbation and
of pride in these institutions.

THE GRAND OPERA HOUSE.

CHAPTER III

GRAND ANNUAL STREET ILLUMINATIONS AND PARADES.   THE
COMING OF THE VEILED PROPHET AND HIS SUITE.

"In Fairy-land, whose streets and towers
Are made of gems of light and flowers!"
—Lalla Rookh.

ILLUMINATIONS.

It has come to be an established custom, during each
fall season, to present to the public beautiful, tasteful and grand displays in processions and parades, accompanied with brilliant illuminations of gas jets, in
diversified colored glass shades—arranged in clusters
and arches spanning the streets—all which, together with
electric lights, give out such dazzling brightness and
beauty—through a number of miles of streets—as to be
truly magnificent!*

COMING OF THE VEILED PROPHET!

"THE GREAT MOKANNA! O'er his features hung
The Veil, the Silver Veil, which he had flung
* * * * * to hide from mortal sight
His dazzling brow till man could bear its light."
Veiled Prophet of Khorassan.

Upon a stated night, the Veiled Prophet, his embassa-
dors and their retainers—accompanied by the houri,† in
angelic attire—make their appearance on the streets—sitting and standing upon "floats" on wheels—in grandeur
of demeanor and dress—representing mythology, races of
men, individual characters and national customs—in *tab-
leaux*—resplendent in light and charming to the senses!
The pageant comprises a score or more of floats, each
accompanied by a band of accomplished musicians.

This pleasing, even instructive display to the masses, is
witnessed usually by a hundred thousand or more peo-

* NOTE.—Upward of one hundred thousand jets.
† "Nymphs of Paradise."—*Author.*

ple—and is obtained at a large cost in pains and money,
through the members of the Veiled Prophet Association,
including a few other individuals of taste and enterprise.
The procession ended, there follows a grand ball and reception, held in the largest and most eligible hall.

THE STATUES OF EMINENT AND FAMOUS MEN ERECTED IN PUBLIC PLACES.

The statues of eminent and famous deceased citizens,
and men of foreign birth, have been erected at different
times, and placed in the public parks: the last one is that
of Ulysses S. Grant, only recently "unveiled." It stands
in the center of the north-end of Twelfth Street Place.
All the statues occupy prominent localities, as follows:
that of Thomas H. Benton, in Lafayette Park; those of
Francis P. Blair and Edward Bates, in Forest Park; of
Columbus, Shakespeare and Von Humbolt in Tower Grove
Park; all are in bronze and of heroic size.

The statue of General Grant is by a St. Louis artist,
and the gift of the Grant Monument Association of this
city to the Municipality. The unveiling took place
October 20th 1888, and was attended with appropriate
ceremonies. The statue is in bronze, of heroic size, measures nine feet six inches in height, and weighs three
thousand pounds. It stands upon a pedestal of Missouri
gray granite, which has an elevation of ten feet, and rests
upon a terrace raised eighteen inches above the street level.
The height of all is twenty-one feet. On the south side of
the pedestal is a bronze group, in bas relief, representing
the Commander and his Staff at the battle of Lookout
Mountain. In the plinth above is the name, Ulysses S.
Grant, in letters of bronze. The statue faces the south.

This statue is the first yet erected in honor of the
"Great Commander." The eloquent orator of the occasion

remarked, that "it was becoming in St. Louis, of which city
he had been a citizen, to erect the first statue to his
imperishable fame!"

> "For thou art Freedom's now; and Fame's
> One of the few; the immortal names
> That were not born to die."—*Fitz Greene Halleck.*

BUILDING CORNER BROADWAY AND ST. CHARLES STREET.

CHAPTER IV.

THE PUBLIC PARKS, SQUARES, GARDENS, AND BOULEVARDS OF THE CITY OF SAINT LOUIS.

"How all the world is made for each of us!"—*Robert Browning.*

THE PARKS.

The Park system of this city is upon a scale the most liberal and happy in the distribution of the parks throughout the various parts of the city, and in extensive area. The four driving parks (Forest, Tower Grove, O'Fallon and Carondelet), are becoming more accessible to the people year by year; and, as a consequence, are more numerously visited, besides more highly appreciated and enjoyed.

Roads and avenues leading to them have been improved and adorned both by the city and interested owners. Several more charters for street railways, to be operated by different sorts of motors—for reaching all sections of the city—have been recently applied for. Also, the Municipal Councils have now under consideration an application for an extensive system of elevated railways. Each of these four parks can now be reached by street railways.

There are in all nineteen public parks, places and squares, including the Botanical Gardens. They contain in all 2155 acres, and are described in these pages with slight detail only. Several of the parks were made from grounds donated, others were reserved for park purposes from the original "Commons." But nearly all, and the large ones especially, were purchased by the city, and cost, including their maintenance up to the year 1880, the sum of $3,477,543,00.

The city constructed and finished the Boulevard on the north side of Forest Park, from Kings Highway to Union avenue, and between the Park and the finely improved grounds of Forest Park Addition. The city continues to plant trees in such of the parks as can still more be improved. The Nursery, situated at Forest Park, contains thousands of fine young trees, ready to be transplanted as the parks require. Several thousand deciduous and evergreen trees have been transplanted in the different parks and grounds of the public institutions during the past year. Special attention has been paid to the choice of the varieties of these trees, which consist of elm, sugar and silver maple, Norway maple, sycamore, ash, box-elder, birch, white oak, beech, burr oak, red bud, cypress, sweet gum, horse chestnut (red and white blooming), German and American linden, and varieties of pines and spruce.

The greenhouses in Benton and Hyde Parks have furnished a large variety of plants and flowers to all the parks, and in April, 1888, were stocked with fully eighty thousand plants for use during the year.

Picnics in the parks by schools, churches, associations, and families, have every facility offered them by order of the Park Commissioner, and during the year 1888, the permits granted for picnics numbered near two-hundred.

The parks are visited daily by large numbers of the people at all hours of the day, both week days and Sundays. Forest Park attracts thousands of visitors, principally ladies and children.

CHAPTER V.

FOREST PARK.

This Park contains 1,371 acres, and exceeds in size all the other parks of this city. It is admirably adapted by nature to the purposes of a rural pleasure resort, and as such is not surpassed by any other grounds for similar uses in the United States. As its name implies, it is *a forest of trees*. All the trees were deciduous at the first, but the park now contains a large number of evergreens, and is adorned with flowering shrubs and plants, grottos, lakes, bridges, etc. There are twenty miles of grand avenues, walks and drives. The tiny river Des Peres, meanders across the park from the north-east to south-west. The grounds cost $850,000.00, and up to August 10th 1877, there had been expended, including the improvements and embellishments, the sum of $1,385,120.16. Since that year, $30,000.00 have been expended annually in developing and beautifying the Park. It is on the western edge of the city, and is attracting about it a large number of costly family residences. Its surroundings on the west are still rural, while at the east end they are very urban. Visitors, who enjoy the salubrity of its atmosphere, may truly say: "God made the country, but man made the town!" The Park has a very fine and extensive oblong trotting course. Singing birds and squirrels are numerous, and the wildness of nature's scenery is still preserved on part of the capacious area.

Forest Park is approached from the east by Lindell and Forest Park Boulevards. The Park can be reached also via Olive street cable road, and other street railroads.

The improved drives are of a length of ten miles. Of summer roads there is an aggregate distance of thirteen

AMPHITHEATRE AT THE FAIR GROUNDS.

miles through overhanging shade trees, and surrounded by
beautiful artificial embellishments, which add to nature's
attractions. At the east side of the park are bronze
statues, of heroic size, of two of St. Louis' deceased citizens, Edward Bates and Francis P. Blair, the former distinguished as a statesman and jurist, and the latter famous
both in war and peace.

THE TOWER GROVE PARK, AND MISSOURI BOTANICAL GAR-DENS. (GIFTS OF HENRY SHAW TO THE MUNICI-PALITY OF SAINT LOUIS.)

"No thought nor care for gain,
   No foolish wish for glory's gilded letter,
Have brought these efforts of his heart and brain;
   But only that the world might be the better,
For one who has not spent his life in vain."

Henry Shaw was born in England, and settled at St.
Louis in the year 1819. He entered into the hardware
business and gave to it the most assiduous personal attention; closing it about 1840. He has ever since passed an
active out-door, yet retired life. Mr. Shaw never married,
resides in winter at his handsome house in the city, and
in summer sojourns at his tasteful dwelling in the "Gardens."

Mr. Shaw, who is as wealthy as he is munificent in
his gifts, long years ago selected grounds admirably
adapted to his proposed objects, namely, 190 acres of land
for a *Park*, and 50 acres for a *Botanical Garden*.
When verging upon three score and ten years (in the year
1868), he proposed to present to the municipal authorities,
the Park and Garden, on certain terms and conditions, which provided, that the municipality should ex-
pend the sum of three hundred and sixty-three thousand
dollars upon the Park grounds in improvements, and open
them to the public; that a strip of ground of the width of
200 feet on the four sides of the park, he would *reserve*,

but lease it to the city for ninety-nine years for a stated
sum of money, (as annual rent) to be devoted to the main-

VIEW IN LAFAYETTE PARK.

tenance of "Shaw's Garden:" and, finally in his "last will
and testament," he would bestow the Gardens to this, his
adopted city. The terms as proposed, were afterwards some-

what modified, and then accepted by ordinance of the municipal government. The Park was named *Tower Grove Park*,
from its vicinity to the "Water Tower." The city began
the work of improvement in 1870, and during the ensuing
five years, expended nearly a half million dollars upon the
Park. It is a parallelogram in shape, whose width is
1121 feet, and the length 6,163 feet. Mr. Shaw, a few
years since, erected at his own expense three bronze
statues of a men famous in their departments of discovery,
science and literature: Columbus, Von Humboldt and
Shakespeare. These are attractions to the visitor, but are
scarcely noticed amidst the magnificent scenery which
crowds upon the senses of the dullest observer as he strolls
through the embowered paths and dells, or drives
upon its spacious avenues. The Park is a gem of sparkling beauty—in spring and summer with its bowers and,
vine clad houses: its artistic bridges, pagodas, lakes,
fountains, and flowing freshwater springs: while through
all are set, by nature and art, beautiful evergreen and
deciduous trees, shrubs and flowers. The annual expense
of maintaining the Park is not less than twenty-five thous-
and dollars.

THE BOTANICAL GARDEN. *

Mr. Shaw began the improvement of his botanical garden many years since with the primary design of present-
ing it to the city. If the Park, as stated, be a *gem*, then
the Gardens are sapphires—in clusters of brilliant plants
and flowers both native and exotic, (including in the
latter a majority of all those found upon the globe)—and
resplendent with selections from nature's choicest beauty
in *flora*, spread over the entire fifty acres. But, the Garden
must be seen, to be appreciated. Mr. Shaw has added a
Museum of curiosities of considerable value from both the
animal and mineral kingdoms.

* NOTE.—Situated in South-west St. Louis.—*Author.*

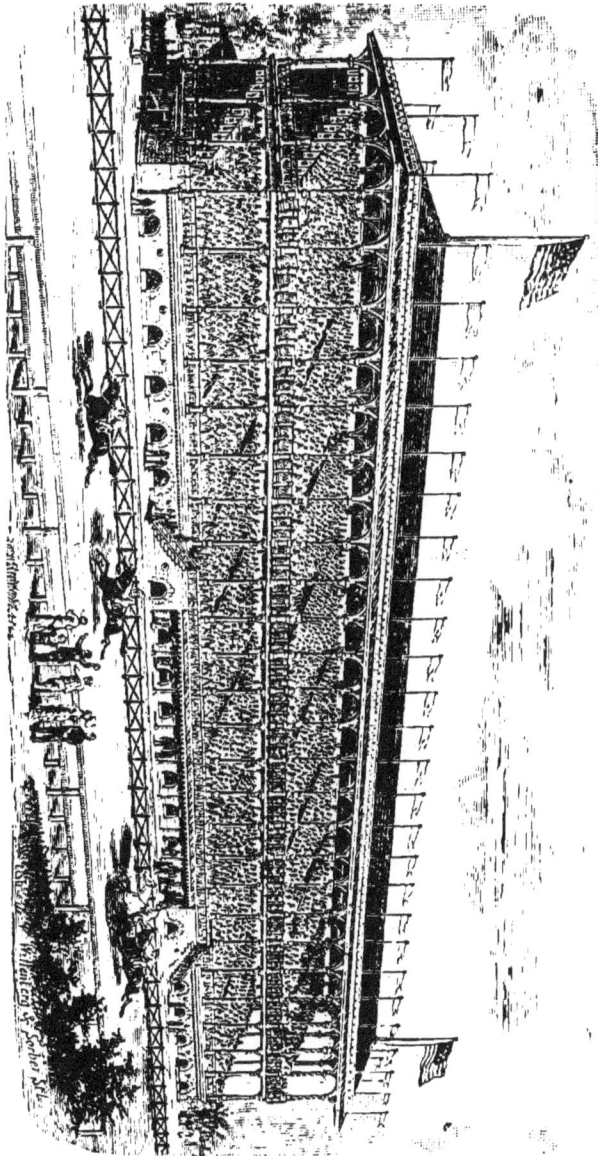

JOCKEY CLUB RACE COURSE, SITUATED IN NORTH-WEST ST. LOUIS.

The Garden, Museum and Park are open daily, and
may be seen and enjoyed—*without money or price*—by
strangers and citizens, it being free to all visitors under
reasonable regulations.

Mr. Shaw is in good health,* and in the possession of
a clear and active brain, at nearly ninety years of age!
He still takes special pleasure, and a deep interest in the
"children" of his life work: the Gardens and Park.

What other plans of munificence, or methods of benefi-
cence have been conceived and are in contemplation—if
not already formulated and resolved upon—by Mr. Shaw,
are unknown to the public. It is certain, however, that
his gifts or ultimate bequests, will be made in pursuance
of well considered resolutions, whose shape has been
moulded with special care and good judgment—after some
wise scheme of liberality toward the people of the city of
his adoption—and which shall carry his name down to
posterity with a sweet savor.

It may be hoped, that the life of this venerable philan-
thropist shall be   spared still longer,
and his remaining   days on earth continue to be passed   in peace and tran-
quility. That, final   ly, when he shall be
called from wearing   an earthly crown in
his paradise of   flowers, the sum-
mons shall be to a   heavenly home—
where only amaranthine flowers bloom—and *there* his brow
be decked with a chaplet of more enduring and unfading
verdure!

* At the present writing, February, 14th, 1889.—*Author.*

CHAPTER VI.

BENTON PARK

Is truly a masterpiece of landscape gardening, but possesses rare natural advantages. It contains miniature hills and valleys, a lake of two acres, together with facilities for boating, an attractive grotto, and a selection of the finest shade trees: whilst its beautifully undulating surface makes it appear double the actual area. Near this park is the so-called English cave. It is a natural cavern, two hundred feet in length, and thirty-five feet in width. It has special natural attractions, but it is adapted at the present time to utilitarian purposes of propagating mushrooms! It is in the hands of a company which employs a capital of ten thousand dollars.

CARONDELET PARK. (New Limits).

This is a picturesque natural park, with a diversified surface, upon which are well constructed winding roadways. A bright little spring of water flows out from a rocky source amidst grand old forest trees. These are intermixed with newly planted shade trees and evergreens, making a most beautiful and delightful combination of park scenery. In the western part of this park is a hill, which affords a magnificent view of the surrounding country. The park commissioner contemplates erecting an observatory on this hill, sixty feet in height, to enable visitors to realize the beauty of the outlying country.

LAFAYETTE PARK

Is a gem of natural and artificial beauty, and is one of the handsomest pieces of landscape architecture to be found in the United States. It is not a driving park, vehicles are

prohibited, and pedestrians only are given entrance.
During the summer it is crowded with delighted visitors.
A band of music is employed at the expense of the city, in

VIEW IN LAFAYETTE PARK.

summer, and on the days set for music, delighted throngs
of ladies and children are in attendance.

GRAVOIS PARK

Is one of the most beautiful of the promonade parks, and
is visited chiefly by the citizens of its neighborhood.

HYDE PARK

Is one of the best cared for and most freqented parks in the
city.   It is laid out handsomely, has a green house and an

BUILDINGS OF THE JOCKEY CLUB.

attractive fountain.   Its lawns and flower beds are unsurpassed in beauty.

LYON PARK

Is not completed, but is a delightful resort. The grounds are elevated, and covered with fine shade trees. It has a lake and fountain. Situated in a densely populated locality, where factories, forges, mills, etc., abound, it is most highly appreciated by the people of its portion of the city.

O'FALLON PARK.

This beautiful park has an area of 160 acres of ground, in fine elevations, from which perhaps the very best views of the city and its surroundings may be obtained. The park abounds with magnificent trees, whose foliage in summer and autumn presents a pleasing sight in contrast with the streets and houses. The park is a most popular resort in summer to large numbers of the people, who enjoy its privileges with ever increasing appreciation.

SAINT LOUIS PLACE.

This attractive spot of ground is not only the charm of its neighborhood, but one of special enjoyment and delight every fine day to the teachers and pupils of four public free schools situated in the vicinity. The place is divided into four sections, and is intersected by three streets. The two northern sections have fine lawns, shrubbery, trees and fountains. The two southern ones are not yet sufficiently advanced in their improvements; but will early become as attractive as the other two, and afford special benefits and pleasures to their neighborhood.

WASHINGTON SQUARE.

This pretty summer spot—in the heart of the city—has inviting shaded walks and lawns. It possesses a handsome fountain and *jet d'eau*. It is no longer a resort for ladies and children, but only for loungers.

THE OTHER PUBLIC GROUNDS

Of the municipality are Carr Square, Gamble Place, Jackson Place, Laclede Park, South Saint Louis Square, Exchange Square and Carondelet Park (·"old limits"). The last two are unimproved.

POLICE STATION, LAFAYETTE PARK.

THE CEMETERIES.

The boast of heraldry, the pomp of power,
  And all that beauty, all that wealth e'er gave,
Await alike th' inevitable hour,
  The paths of glory lead but to the grave.
                    —*Gray's Elegy.*

The burial grounds of the earlier days of St. Louis were gradually removed to remote rural spots and relocated on grounds most eligible and beautiful for their natural

scenery and shape. In the improvement and adornment of
these last resting places of the "silent," large expense has
been incurred, and all that fine taste and skill could do has
been done to render them pleasing and attractive. The
cemeteries are all easily approached. The two most
extensive are Bellefountaine, which contains 350 acres of

ground, and Calvary of 225 acres; the latter is owned by
the Roman Catholics, and the former by the Protestants.

Visitors from abroad, who have seen the cemeteries near
the Eastern cities, would be favorably impressed with a
sight of those of St. Louis.

A "CREMATORY"

Was completed early in 1888 at a cost of $20,000.00, and
built by a stock company. It is of one main apartment,
attached to which are two smaller rooms, and beneath is the
"furnace." The construction is after the most experienced
plans. Although recently damaged by an accidental com-
bustion, it was quickly restored to serviceable condition.
The crematory is on the edge of the city, five miles distant from the Court House.

The cremation "movement" is slowly progressing at
St. Louis, and is likely to obtain a larger following ere

long. During nine months, between April, 1888, and January, 1889, twenty-eight "incinerations" have taken place, of deceased persons, whose nationalities were as follows: American 7, German 13, French 1, Irish 1, Swiss 1, Austrian 2, unknown 3; showing that one-fourth only are known to have been of American birth. The few ounces of "ashes," found after cremation, are usually inclosed in a leaden casket, and deposited in a burial vault at a cemetery.

It seems as if "cremation"—ever repulsive to the taste of Christians from the earliest period of the institution of Christianity—may yet become popular, and be adopted as a sanitary measure for over-crowded populations.

IN THE CEMETERY.

CHAPTER VII.

THE MERCHANTS' BRIDGE COMPANY. THE TERMINAL RAIL-
WAY COMPANY. THE SWELLING VOLUME OF COM-
MERCE DEMANDS THEM TO-DAY.

Look! the lofty arches leap above the watery waste.

The construction of this most necessary additional
bridge, for which the Congress of the United States
granted a liberal and " self-protecting " charter, has been
commenced and will be pushed to completion within less
than two years, or earlier.

The confidence reposed in the ability of the officers of
the Merchants' Bridge Co. to carry out the expectations
which they had aroused in the community of the early
completion of their great enterprise, is now verified by a
most auspicious beginning.

The bridge is greatly needed to-day, its commencement
is hailed with delight 'by the business community. Its
construction will lead to the abolition of the present
"bridge arbitrary." and add millions to the wealth of St.
Louis. No enterprises could be as important, or produc-
tive of results so valuable to the commerce of St. Louis,
as the new Bridge and Terminal Railway. Indeed, their
need is of even greater importance, both at present and
prospectively, than the construction of the Eads Bridge
and Tunnel adjuncts were when begun twenty-one years
ago. The trade of St. Louis—so greatly enlarged during
the intervening period—will make a great leap when the

new bridge shall be opened to use, and will produce such an impulse to real estate values as has rarely been witnessed at St. Louis.

That the present bridge facilities, being entirely inadequate to the wants of the traffic of the present railroads, cannot, accommodate other roads—now building and projected—makes another bridge indispensable. It is not unreasonable to predict that in considerably less time than ten years from the completion of the Merchants' Bridge, another still will be required to meet the wants of trade and travel, which grow in the ratio of the great increase of this city, and the development of the vast surrounding territory.

The Merchants' Bridge will, in many respects, be a counterpart of the Eads Bridge, but will be capable of bearing one-third more weight to the square foot, than that bridge. At the period of the building of the Eads Bridge, a freight car had the capacity of only twenty thousand pounds, but now its size and strength is equal to forty and even fifty thousand pounds! Besides, the present locomotives are *giants* in contrast with the inferior weight and ability of engines twenty years since.

The cost of the Merchants' Bridge is estimated at from two to two and a half million dollars, a sum so much below the greater cost and expenditures of the Eads Bridge, as to render the building of the Merchants' Bridge comparatively a light work. It will be built and owned by St. Louis capitalists, who have taken the bonds of the company, and is satisfactory assurance that its utility will be preserved and maintained in the interests of the community. The lesser cost of a bridge similar to that of the Eads is to be secured, it is stated, through reduced cost in the rock foundations—owing to shallower depth—saving in damages and cost of ground; but, especially by economy and the reduced cost of materials and labor, as compared with their prices twenty years ago.

A NEW UNION PASSENGER RAILWAY DEPOT.

"Thus said the Duke, thus did the Duke infer."
—*Richard III.*

At length, it is declared intelligibly and authoritatively—at the headquarters of the Missouri Pacific Railway System in this city—that it has been definitely decided to build a new Passenger Depot, and to begin work without any unnecessary delay. The date named for its completion is September 1st, 1890. The period of eighteen months, which must intervene, will be found short indeed, in view of the pleasure flowing from the anticipation of such a boon. The advent of a new depot will be hailed with delight by the millions who travel to and from this city each year.

The estimated cost is one million dollars. The general plan of the new structure has been derived from mature experience, as to the sort of building, which a modern railway passenger depot should be—for comfort, convenience and elegance — to secure in its construction the highest demands of utility. But, it should be so planned, that safety to the traveling public shall be assured—at a great depot—where, at all times, surging crowds are hastening to and fro, almost unconscious of the surrounding dangers.

In view of security against accidents—from moving trains and trucks—the waiting and eating apartments of passengers will be *a story above the track level.* Different stairways will be used by the arriving and departing passengers, who will be conducted to their proper train without liability of mistake, and promptly from the cars.

The first floor of the new Depot will be on the plane of Poplar street, eighteen feet above the level of the railroad tracks of Mill Creek Valley. The grand front of the building will be on that street. The halls will be so spacious that ingress and egress—by separate doors—will be without jostling. The structure will have two additional stories—above the waiting and eating rooms—for the occupation of officers and employes. Every modern comfort, will be introduced in connection with good taste.

The materials used in the construction of this model depot, will be Missouri red and gray granite—both rock-face and polished—and St. Louis pressed brick, including those of ornamental forms. The Romanesque in architecture, will be adopted for the north and south fronts. The building will be fire proof, but as very great strength is not essential, the plan and details will secure—through their combination—greater elegance than can be obtained in a commercial structure.

The long "debated" question of the *location* of the new depot being now settled, it is interesting to know *precisely* where it will be built. Its site is between Twelfth and Fourteenth streets, and Poplar street and Mill Creek Valley. A portion of the high ground, together with the buildings yet standing, will be removed and the site adapted to its new uses. The width of Poplar street will be increased to 80 feet by adding 20 feet of the depot ground between Twelfth and Fourteenth streets, in order to secure ample space for travelers and carriages, but likewise to give finer effect to the front of the structure.

The length of the new edifice will be 450 feet, and its breadth 75 feet, which dimensions foreshadow the magnificence of its completed presence. The distinguished railway magnate, who controls great systems of roads centering at St. Louis, purchased, privately, during the past two or three years, all the ground needed for the site of the new passenger depot. Certainly, it is eligibly chosen, and fittingly suited to its purpose.

When the present passenger depot was built—nearly a score years since—it was both fine and commodious, but now it is wholly unsuited to the wants of the great public, who—cribbed, cabined and confined—chafe under the inflictions imposed upon them through contact with the present ineligible depot. The numerous railway companies using the Union Depot, can well afford to secure a new one, which shall be at once convenient, commodious and magnificent.

THE ROE BUILDING.

A FEW OF THE BUILDINGS COMPLETED DURING THE
YEAR 1888.

THE AMERICAN CENTRAL (THE "SINGER" BUILDING,
ENLARGED AND RECONSTRUCTED),

Occupies the N. E. corner of Broadway and Locust street,
and is eight stories in height. The original cost was
$225,000.00, and $200,000.00 more have been expended in

THE AMERICAN CENTRAL BUILDING.

the reconstruction. This splendid structure is strictly fire
proof. Not a single dark room is in the building. There are
several modern elevators which move 400 feet per minute.
The corridors are all wainscotted with fine Italian marble,
and the interior finish of the building is in solid quartered

oak, and the floors of marble. An iron and bronze stairway, leads from the basement to the top story, whose steps
are of marble. The entrance—corridor walls and ceiling—
are in panel work of marble. The lavatory is on the
eighth floor, finished in marble, brass and quartered
oak; in utility and taste it is not excelled. The American
Express Co., and the Wells-Fargo Express Co., have taken
a ten years' lease on the first floor, and use it as one general office. There are fifty office apartments in the five
stories next above the Express office, the rentals of which
amount to $25,000.00 annually. The American Central
Insurance Company occupies the entire seventh story,
which is splendidly lighted, and is the largest single office
occupied by any business concern in this city, if not in the
West. The building is thoroughly fire proof. Such
eligibility in the plan and beauty of details in an office
building are most creditable to the architect and builder.

THE BANK OF COMMERCE BUILDING.

This elegant and attractive structure, north-east corner
of Olive street and Broadway, was built and is owned by
the bank, which occupies the first floor. The sixty office
rooms—contained in the seven stories above—are convenient and tasteful. The building is of white marble, completely fire proof, and finished in antique oak. It is supplied
with Hale elevators, and is a model building. Its cost was
about a quarter million dollars.

THE COMMERCIAL BUILDING.

This grand and imposing structure, erected on the south-
east corner of Sixth and Olive streets, by the "Commercial
Building Company of Saint Louis," (a Chicago syndicate)
is eight stories in height, exclusive of basement. It has a
frontage on Olive street of 127 feet, and on Sixth of 116
feet. The construction of this building is of the very best
character in design, workmanship and materials, and is

suited especially for stores and offices, in accordance with the very latest improvements and requirements of such occupancy.

The exterior materials are polished and rock-face Missouri Syenite granite, and the finest quality of St. Louis

COMMERCIAL BUILDING.

pressed brick.   The sills, string courses, cornices, coping, bases and capitals are of Portage brown-stone.   Columns, (between each two piers), pilasters and lintels are of iron.

This building, in its fire proof qualities, and in all other respects—lighting, heating and ventilation, and perfect arrangement for the convenience of occupants—is unexcelled by any other yet erected in the West.   An inspection of its admirable construction is a treat to the visitor. The building is equipped with four swift-moving hydraulic elevators, made of iron and bronze.   There are three large store rooms and one smaller one on the first floor; and, on the remaining seven floors, there are 192 office rooms—of different sizes—and each furnished with a steel safe.   The corriders of first, second and third stories are floored with Georgia marble, and wainscotting of same material.   A broad, easy, iron staircase leads from the first to the top story.

The ground was leased at an annual rent for 99 years, and the cost of the building, the agent stated, was $600,000.00.

THE FAGIN BUILDING.

This magnificent structure—located at Nos. 806, 808, 810, 812 and 814 Olive street—wholly novel and unique in its style of architecture—attracts the general attention, being so unlike any other building in this city, whilst travelers, the world over, declare they do not remember to have seen any edifice resembling the Fagin Building!

The building is an *advertisement* in itself.   Since, should a stranger, who had once seen it and being desirous to return to its locality—not knowing the way—might simply enquire of a citizen the route to that wonderful "structure of *granite and glass!*" and, doubtless, would be referred unerringly to the proper one.

The facade—composed almost wholly of granite and glass from pavement to top—has an altitude of 152 feet, comprised in ten stories, the lower one being 21 1-2 feet in height. The granite is in four styles of work: polished, rock-face, ten line cut and pointed. The facade displays thirty-eight highly polished circular columns, of different dimensions. Over the central columns, are granite globes. The base of the columns rest upon blocks of pyramidal form, six feet in height and polished like a mirror. The glass is also varied in description: polished plate, discs and panes of cathedral, ondoyant and diamond star glass, the three last in tinted colors and several thousand in number. The plate glass is of unusual size, some being 110x194 inches, and contain 149 square feet. The columns vary in diameter from 15 to 30 inches. They are found, in their composite positions, the full height of the facade.

The *tout ensemble* of the front is picturesque and grand, whilst giving out the expression of great strength and beauty. Many blocks of rock-face granite in position, have a weight exceeding twelve tons.

The foundations of the building are broad and deep, constructed of stone from the noted Grafton quarries. The bottom courses of piers, columns and walls are of single stones, eight feet in width. Their superstructure is in accordance with the massiveness of the base. All are laid in cement mortar. So broad and solid are these foundations and so unyielding the earth at their foot, that, notwithstanding the great weight of the mammoth superstructure, there has not been any settlement. This is proved by the mark at the pavement line. No expense was spared in the construction, to gain the greatest strength, solidity and security.

The available space of the interior, is one million and fifty-two thousand feet, including the basement.

The style of construction adopted by the talented architect, has secured unlimited light, and is adapted to the highest demands of utility, whilst to the occupants it will be a perpetual pleasure. The stairways are constructed of iron, steel and slate. The building is equipped with two "Crane" elevators, of the latest description and improvements, enabling a speed of 600 feet per minute. Heating is by steam. The floors are of the modern "slow-burning" construction, walls stuccoed, and the entire building is denominated fire-proof.

The work of completion of the interior has reached a stage of advancement, where the proprietor rests, briefly, in order to adapt each story to the wishes or needs of tenants, who would lease for a term of years. The adaptations for use of this great building are various. It would compass the requirements of *one* large establishment in dry goods, fancy wares, hats, or other lines of business. Or for office rooms and halls. The top stories especially are magnificently lighted from the four sides, these—arranged in suites of apartments—would make the most eligible of "club" quarters.

The first, or lower floor, is a truly splendid store room, over twenty feet in height. The ceiling is in beautiful wood, elaborately carved, finished in oil, and, blending with the rest of the work of this elegant hall room—in harmony of materials and details—it is most attractive.

The location of the Fagin Building is among the most eligible and valuable of any on Olive street, directly opposite the grand structure of the National Government (Post-office, Custom House, etc.), which cost the sum of six million dollars, and occupies an entire city block.

Adjoining on the west is the superb building of the "Independent Order of Odd Fellows," just now being completed.

Olive street is in the heyday of prosperity, and the Fagin Building is another star in its decoration, but is a diadem in the crown of its enterprising owner, and the capstone of his monument! This costly building is a marked attestation of that public spirited push which distinguished him for the many years of his useful and honorable career when engaged in the commerce and development of this city.

THE LIONBERGER STORE BUILDING.

This building is one of the new structures erected for stores. It is not excelled by any, and equaled by but few. It is situated on the south-west corner of Washington avenue

THE LIONBERGER BUILDING.

and Eighth street. In all appointments which combine strength, utility and elegance it is admirable in a marked degree.

The architecture is "Romanesque," and the material brown "Kibbe" Massachusetts stone, rock-face and carved, of the fronts respectively on Washington avenue and Ninth streets. The building occupies 140 feet on the former, and 150 feet on the latter street. The front on St. Charles street is largely of St. Louis pressed brick. The height of the building is 100 feet, in seven stories, beside basement and sub-basement. The block is divided into two stores, one of 100x150 feet, and the other 40x150 feet.

The building is of the description styled "mill-construction." and "slow-burning," and is denominated fire proof. There are iron column "supports" in the first three, and wood column supports in the remaining stories. The iron columns are incased with hollow tiles. The floor is of three inch yellow pine, covered with water-proof paper, and one inch of maple or hard pine. The first and second stories are plastered, and the remainder painted. The roof is of composition materials.

The elevators and stairways are inclosed within brick walls, and the doors leading to them are fire proof. A water tank is located on the roof. "Fire" plugs are placed on each floor, besides a permanent wrought iron stand-pipe for ready attachment of hose, and a fire escape—conveniently placed, which are all valuable adjuncts. There are five freight and two passenger hydraulic elevators. The building is heated by steam, and lighted by both gas and electricity, or either separately. Lavatories are placed on each floor.

The cost of this admirable and model building completed was $350,000.00.

THE LACLEDE BUILDING.

This fine new building stands on the south-west corner of Olive and Fourth streets, has a frontage on the latter of 116 feet, and on the former street of 127 feet, and is eight stories in height. The materials are Missouri Syenite granite, (both rock-faced and polished), iron, and the finest brick. The interior construction is of wrought iron filled in with hollow blocks. The exterior walls are lined on the inside with hollow brick, as a protection against heat and cold. The hall walls are of polished Berdillo marble and

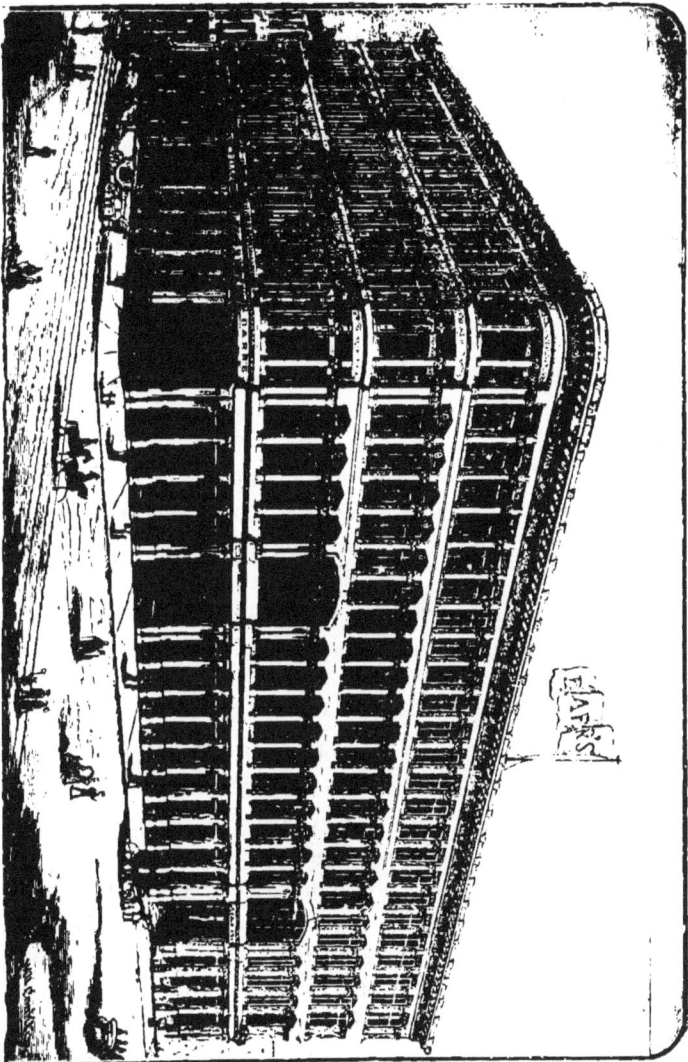

THE BARR BUILDING.

plate glass. The halls are arranged with ventilating shafts
for rarifying the air, and to maintain a regular current, but
modulated against draught. They are tiled with marble
throughout. And the ceilings in the halls of the lower
stories are of polished marble.

Many of the offices have handsome, open fire places.
Convenient lavatories are fitted in marble and porcelain in
each story. A telegraph station is on the first floor, and
four elevators, three of which are improved hydraulic.
The interior design and finish are replete in utility, taste
and elegance. In fine, the Laclede is one of the very best
office buildings in the country.

The Laclede Bank is located on the corner, ground floor,
and its spacious offices are fitted up in the most eligible
and superior manner. The Merchants' National Bank
occupies a portion of the Olive street front.

This splendid structure is a very marked feature of
Fourth street, and is a conspicuous adornment.

THE LIGGETT-MYERS BUILDING

Covers an entire block of ground. It fronts 270 feet on
Washington avenue, the same on St. Charles street, and
150 feet each on Tenth and Eleventh streets; it is seven stories in height above the basement, and so planned that one
tenant may occupy the whole as a single great establishment,
or that it may be divided into several stores, as occasion
may require. It is advancing towards early completion, and its
prestige is magnificent. It will be fire proof throughout.
The first two stories are constructed of Missouri Syenite
granite, and the remaining five of St. Louis pressed brick,
including those of diverse forms. The floor beams are of
steel, on which a floor of yellow pine will be laid seven
inches in thickness, and on top of that a covering of one
inch dressed maple. The number of spikes required for
this great floor is a quarter million of 7½ inches in length.

Massive cast iron columns (encased within hollow tile)
support the interior. The superior St. Louis-made plate
glass—not excelled in clearness and strength by the best
French make—fills all the window and door frames from
basement to top. The building is provided with fire-
escapes, numerous elevators and lavatories.

This great building will be heated by steam and lighted
by gas. The entire construction and finish of the massive
block is in a style of simple elegance, which adds greatly
to its attractiveness. The wealthy proprietors have been
unsparing of money in order to make of their block one
rarely equalled for utility and grandeur. The cost is estimated at $900,000.00. It will be ready for occupancy
the ensuing spring of 1889.

STAR PRINTING CO. BUILDING.

9

THE ROSENHEIM BUILDING.

This is a very fine wholesale business block, erected on the north-east corner of Ninth street and Washington avenue. It stands 130 feet on the former street, and 120 feet on the latter, and is seven stories in height. The materials used in the construction are Missouri Syenite granite, red sandstone and St. Louis pressed brick. The interior construction

ROSENHEIM BUILDING.

is of the description termed "mill-method," having no floor joists, but instead are massive yellow pine girders, which support cross beams running longitudinally, held by wrought iron stirrups and forming panels of 7x12 feet; the whole supported by strong and elegant pillars. The floor is of three inch tongued and grooved yellow pine, and, on top a covering of one inch maple. This forms an extremely rigid *roof-floor*, and would sustain a very great weight. This method of construction is styled *slow-burning*. This building presents a very handsome and imposing appearance. It may justly be considered one of the most tasteful business structures of the city, and is deserving the encomium of a Model Building.

THE GRAND BUILDING OF THE INDEPENDENT ORDER ODD FELLOWS.

This magnificent building is nearly completed. It is erected at the south-east corner of Ninth and Olive streets, and faces the national buildings on the opposite side of the latter street. It is eight stories in height. At the east corner of the main front a tower—of graceful proportions—rises to the height of 236 feet above the pavement. The exterior materials are, for the first story, Missouri Syenite granite, (in alternate rock-face and polished blocks, the latter are bright as a mirror), and the seven stories above are of the superior home red pressed brick. The interior supports are iron and steel pillars and girders. The ceilings and partitions are completely fire proof. The entire construction is of the most massive and enduring sort. The foundations are deep set with huge blocks of gray granite. They are capable of bearing greater weight than required by the superstructure. The edifice fronts 127 feet on Chestnut, and 112 feet on Ninth street.

A fine suite of rooms and Grand Hall of the Order, are on the top floor, and are as follows: Grand Hall, 60x100 feet floor space, and 27 feet in height, besides two rooms adjoining. On other floors are two Lodge Halls, each 40x60 feet, also four other Lodge Halls, each 30x40 feet, together with ante-rooms. On the second floor of the building is located the Library of the Order, a handsome apartment, 20x60 feet, adjoining which

is the office of the Grand Secretary of the Grand Lodge of the State of Missouri. There are also committee rooms. The building has in all seventy-two office rooms. The ground floor is divided into two magnificent store rooms. Two entrances to the upper stories are provided on first floor. There are four hydraulic elevators, and on each story a lavatory. The corridors are tiled with white marble, and the wainscotting is of Georgia gray and white marble. The building will be lighted by electric jets, and heated by steam. It will be ready for occupancy May 1, 1889. The cost of this magnificent building will be between $500,-000.00 and $600,000.00, exclusive of the ground, which is among the most valuable sites in the city.

NEW LOCATION OF BROWN, DAUGHADAY & COMPANY.

This superior structure, specially designed for a wholesale dry goods establishment, occupies the very eligible site on the south-east corner of Ninth and St. Charles streets. It is erected upon massive foundations, which were built, together with the elegant superstructure, and completed all within the short space of six months. The building occupies an area of 112 feet of ground on Ninth, and 76 feet on St. Charles street. It is seven stories in height above the pavement level, below which is a fine basement salesroom. The building is admirably arranged for light and convenience. Strength is a striking feature. The plan and materials of the interior construction is modern slow-burning — denominated fire proof. Two modern freight elevators are conveniently placed on the north side of the building, and one passenger elevator, on the east side, accommodates the current intercourse between the first and seventh floors.

The material of the basement and first story is rock-faced Missouri red granite. The additional six stories are of St. Louis pressed brick—including those of diverse and

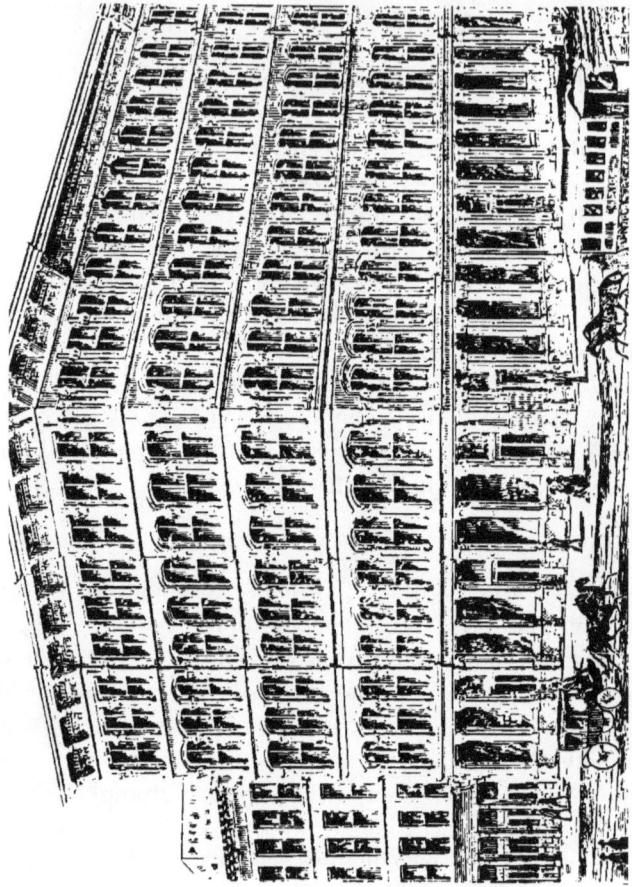

ornamental forms. The window caps and sills are red sandstone, carved and fluted. On the St. Charles street front,
iron columns are used in the second and third stories.

This admirable building—the last to be finished prior
to the recent New Year's day—of the considerable number
of fine business structures completed in 1888, and is a
striking ornament in the new business quarter.

THE PEPER BUILDING.

PUBLIC SCHOOL POLYTECHNIC BUILDING

THE CITY OF ST. LOUIS OF TO-DAY.

PART FIFTH.

CHAPTER I.

The Educational Institutions of Saint Louis.

THE Educational Institutions, including the Public
Schools of St. Louis, are not excelled by those
of any other city in thorough education, discipline
and general advantages. The pupil may pass
from the primary class through all the grades up to, and
through the high and normal schools without cost for
tuition.

The St. Louis system of Public Schools embraces a complete organization, beginning with the Kindergarten and
ending with the free High and Normal Schools.

There are seventy-seven school organizations in this
system, varying in size from the modest one-room school

157

to the schools which occupy stately and imposing three-story edifices—having from twelve to twenty-four commodious school rooms—with all the modern improvements for furnishing light, heat and ventilation. The Public School system includes four free Polytechnic evening schools, three of which have preparatory departments for instruction in the more elementary branches.

Nearly forty-nine thousand pupils were enrolled in these schools during the last scholastic year, and were instructed by eleven hundred and sixty-nine teachers.

These schools occupy in all, one hundred and six buildings, varying in size to suit their respective localities.

The lots of ground occupied by these buildings are estimated at $827,613.00, and the buildings and furniture $2,617,641.00, at moderate valuations. In addition, the Board of Public Schools controls realty valued at one and a quarter million dollars, held exclusively for the production of a permanent revenue. The income of that portion of this property which is leased, amounts to about sixty thousand dollars annually.

The total revenue for school purposes, including a four mill city tax and the state school fund, amounts to over one million dollars annually.

The course of study is broad and comprehensive, including within its requirements nearly all that can reasonably be expected; and, the methods of instruction and modes of discipline are such as have been generally recognized throughout this country as being among the best.

These schools aim not only to give the best possible intellectual, moral and physical education, but to furnish the information most needed for good and successful citizenship. That these schools are appreciated by all classes of citizens, is attested by the character of their patronage: the enrollment includes the names of children from fami-

lies provided with ample means, and from those in the
most moderate circumstances.

The school population June 1, 1885 (between the ages
of six and twenty), was 108,454, of which four and one-half
per cent. were colored. The increase in three years, to
June 1, 1888, is estimated to be 7,856, total 116,310.
Most pupils leave after a school attendance of four years,
and few attend who are over fifteen years of age. In the
last scholastic year, there were 20,558 children in attendance at schools other than public district schools.

FINANCIAL POSITION AND ENDOWMENT OF THE PUBLIC FREE SCHOOLS.

The President of the Board of Public Free Schools
published in November, 1888, the 34th Annual Report,
from which the following information is gleaned: The
estimated resources of the School Board for the current
year, which will end June 30, 1889, is ascertained to be
the sum of $1,047,000.00, and is derived severally, from
taxation $884,000.00; state school funds $95,000.00;
rents $58,000.00; and, interest on deposits and funded
securities $10,000.00.

From the revenue, the Board provided for the maintenance of the schools, (including 47 new school rooms
opened October, 1888); and besides added the sum of
$60,000.00 to the building fund. Further, the Board
retrenched expenses for the school year nearly $75,000.00,
and "without in any wise impairing the efficiency of the
schools."

The Board had under its control several valuable par-
cels of real estate, (which were not derived from the state
or national government); they were eligibly located, advancing in value, and yielding revenue. These the Board
deemed it advisable to transfer to the Permanent Fund,

but at a reasonable valuation, which aggregated the sum of $105,524.80. At the same time the Board possessed in its Permanent Fund and uninvested, upwards of one hundred thousand dollars. Also, the Board appropriated to its Building fund, from the revenues of 1887–'88, the further sum of $64,444.00.

The President states the very interesting fact, that the School Board is the largest single real estate owner in the city. Aside from its proprietorship of school lots, buildings and fixtures—which aggregate nearly five million dollars at the prime, or original cost, (but now of considerably larger value)—it is the owner of what is termed " revenue real estate," of an estimated value of $1,200,000.00, nearly all of which belongs to the Permanent Fund: the revenue only of which can be used for school purposes, since the principal sum is required, under the law, to be maintained without impairment.

In consequence of the movement of the resident population further westward, the Board is warranted in recommending the sale of several special pieces of property, which are near the east end of the city, and with the proceeds thereof to establish new schools in more convenient locations.

PRIVATE EDUCATIONAL INSTITUTIONS.

A few of these are named, as follows: Academy of the Christian Brothers, Loretta Academy, St. Joseph's Academy, St. Vincent's Academy, St. Louis University, Washington University, including Smith's Academy, Mary Institute, Henry Shaw School of Botany, School of Fine Arts, Law School, Manual Training School, College and Polytechnic School.

Concordia Seminary, American Medical College, Missouri Medical College, Missouri School of Midwifery, St.

Louis Medical College, St. Louis College of Physicians and Surgeons, St. Louis Post Graduate School of Medicine, St. Louis College of Pharmacy, Homeopathic Medical College of Missouri, Missouri Dental College, Mound City Commercial College, School of Short Hand and Telegraphy, Institute of Architects, Missouri School for the Blind, Women's Training School, besides numerous other Educational and training schools.

CONCORDIA COLLEGE.

ST. LOUIS UNIVERSITY.

CHAPTER II.

SAINT LOUIS UNIVERSITY.

This noted institution—the most venerable of the educational institutions of this city—was founded in 1829, and received its charter in 1834. The site of the university, prior to July, 1888, was on Ninth street and Washington avenue. The new site—two miles further west, following population—is grand for elevation and surroundings. It is upon a block of ground fronting on Grand avenue 446 feet, by a depth, on Lindell and Baker avenues, of 360 feet.

The institution is under the management of the Jesuit Fathers. In the course of studies, the ancient classics hold a prominent place. Mental philosophy, physics, chemistry, astronomy and surveying, are a part of the regular course, which comprises seven years. Lectures on the sciences are illustrated with experiments. An ample laboratory is provided for the students in chemistry.

A past-graduate department is connected with the institution. The lectures of this course are delivered upon evenings.

About 400 students are in daily attendance. Classes open at 9 o'clock A. M., and continue, with slight intermission, till 2 : 30 P. M. Since 1881, boarding students have not been received.

The Library and Museum halls are model apartments of their kind. The Library is 50 by 79 feet in length and breadth, and 67 feet in height. It comprises an open quadrangle, is covered by a glass roof; and has three wide galleries, which are reached by iron stairways. The Library is accessible from two floors of the building. It contains 30,000 volumes, many of which are rare editions of Latin folios, of the earlier years succeeding the discovery of the art of printing.

The Museum is a single hall. Its dimensions are 58 by 98 feet in length and breadth, and 52 feet in height. It is crowned by an elaborate roof, which affords suitable light. Costly paintings adorn its walls.

The corner of the spacious site, on Lindell and Grand avenues, was reserved for a church—Saint Xavier's. This edifice has not been completed, but services have been held in the ample basement since November, 1884.

The university buildings are admirably planned and constructed. Their appearance, on approaching them, is most imposing. They cost, without the ground, the sum of about three hundred thousand dollars.

S. W. CORNER ELEVENTH STREET AND WASHINGTON AVE.

WASHINGTON UNIVERSITY.

This institution—prominent among the educational foundations of this city—of distinguished merit and usefulness, was established in the City of St. Louis by Act of Incorporation of the State of Missouri, Feb. 22d, 1853. It intended to embrace the whole range of university studies, except Theology, and to afford opportunity of complete preparation for every sphere of practical and scientific life.

The following is condensed from the annual catalogue of the institution, and is of such special interest as to well deserve the space given:

THE UNIVERSITY
COMPREHENDS:

I. UNDERGRADUATE DEPARTMENT; INCLUDING THE COLLEGE AND POLYTECHNIC SCHOOL. II. HENRY SHAW SCHOOL OF BOTANY. III. ST. LOUIS SCHOOL OF FINE ARTS. IV. ST. LOUIS LAW SCHOOL.

"The following schools have also been organized under the charter of the University:

   I.   SMITH ACADEMY.

   II.   MANUAL TRAINING SCHOOL.

   III.   MARY INSTITUTE.

"The present members of the Corporation have no sectarian purpose to serve. They earnestly desire that the University shall attain a high moral and religious character, as a Christian institution in a Christian republic; but they equally desire that the narrow principles of sectarianism, and party spirit may never be allowed to enter. The exercises of the University are opened every morning in the chapel by reading the Scriptures and singing.

"On the 22d of April, 1857, the formal inauguration of Washington University took place with appropriate exer-
10

cises in University Hall. An oration was delivered by Hon. Edward Everett, in the Mercantile Library Hall. An advanced scientific class was organized at that time. The Academy had then been in operation about five years. The College and Mary Institute were organized in 1859, and the first Senior Class was graduated from the College in June, 1862. The Law School was organized in 1867.

WASHINGTON UNIVERSITY.   (ONE OF THE FIVE BUILDINGS).

The Polytechnic School was fully organized in 1870, the School of Fine Arts and the Manual Training School in 1879, and the School of Botany in 1885.

PRESENT FINANCIAL CONDITION.

"The financial condition of the University has been very materially improved during the past year by the addition to its various *permanent* funds of over $200,000.00. Its property now consists of real estate and buildings in actual use for educational purposes (unincumbered), costing over $625,-000.00; of Libraries, Scientific Apparatus, Laboratories, Casts, Architectural Models, Machinery and other personal property in actual use in the various departments costing over $160,000.00, and of investments for revenue in real and personal estate, derived from general and special endowments, amounting to over $650,000.00; giving an assured permanence to the Institution, and the guaranty of a wise, conservative, thorough and prudent administration of the trust which has been committed to the Board of Directors.

"Several departments of the University, however, are still inadequately endowed to meet the large demands of an institution of this character in the heart of the Mississippi Valley.

LAW SCHOOL.

"The Law Department of Washington University, also known as the St. Louis Law School, was opened September 16, 1867, and is now in its twenty-second year of successful operation.

"Its establishment was not only part of the necessary development of the University, but was deemed peculiarly appropriate to a great and growing city, offering through the number, variety and importance of the questions adjudicated in its tribunals, unsurpassed advantages for combining practical instruction with theoretic study of the law. During nine months in the year, beside the ordinary municipal and inferior courts, are in almost uninter-

rupted session the Circuit and District Courts of the
United States, taking cognizance of questions in Admiralty,
Revenue and Bankrupt Law, beside causes at Common
Law and in Equity; also the Circuit and Criminal Courts
of the State, and the St. Louis Court of Appeals—in one
or other of which are constantly illustrated the learning
and practice of every department of American jurisprudence.

"The school is open upon equal terms to students from
all parts of the United States, and the course of instruction
is intended to prepare them for the practice of the profes-
sion in any part of the United States. Beside the doc-
trines and principles of law applicable alike in all the states
and territories, it will embrace pleading and procedure in
the Federal as well as State courts, and under the common-
law system and that of the new codes, in all their general
features.

"Students who have already determined the State in
which they expect to practice will receive assistance, if desired, in studying the procedure and statutes of that State
in connection with the general course of study. It is be-
lieved that such attention to positive law, in any form in
which it is actually administered, not only will not interfere
with the study of principles, but will be a great assistance
to that end, and for that reason we recommend students to
pursue it whenever possible.

"It is the single aim of the Law Faculty, and of the Directors of Washington University, to make this Law School
a true School of Jurisprudence, to which none shall be disposed to come except those who earnestly seek a thorough
elementary knowledge of the law, and from which none
who may come with that purpose shall go away disappointed.
To ensure the perpetual maintenance of its course, and by
the generous public spirit of a few friends, an endowment
now amounting to *seventy-seven thousand dollars* has been

given, and invested in good securities in the name of Washington University, in trust for the perpetual support of the Law Department; the interest of such fund to be used for that purpose. It is hoped that this fund will be enlarged by other gifts until a complete endowment of one hundred and fifty thousand dollars is obtained.

"The Directors of Washington University, have met this noble gift in a like spirit, by formally dedicating to the use of the Law Department rent free, forever, the building now occupied by the Law School. No. 1417 Lucas Place, standing upon its own grounds, with a frontage of one hundred feet upon Lucas Place, the most convenient and pleasant location in the city for such an institution."

ST. LOUIS SCHOOL OF FINE ARTS.

REORGANIZED MAY 22, 1879.

"The establishment of an Art School upon a broad and permanent foundation has always been a part of the plan of Washington University. For twenty-five years art instruction has been embodied in the course of study. In 1875, special students were admitted to the Drawing Department, and class and public lectures were given on Art History. The same year an evening school was opened.

"On May 22d, 1879, the Directors of the University adopted an ordinance establishing a Department of Art in Washington University, from which the following extracts are taken:

"'A Department of Art is hereby established as a special Department of Washington University, to be known as THE ST. LOUIS SCHOOL OF FINE ARTS.

"'The objects of said Department shall be: Instruction in the Fine Arts; the collection and exhibition of pictures, statuary, and other works of art, and of whatever else may be of artistic interest and appropriate for a Public Gallery or Art Museum; and, in general, the promotion by all proper means of aesthetic or artistic education."'

"The rooms are open for the study of drawing, painting, and modeling, every day from 9 A. M. to 5 P. M., and for the study of drawing from the antique and life, mechanical drawing, and modeling, three evenings in the week, from November to May.

"The school furnishes instruction in Drawing, Modeling, Painting, Artistic Anatomy, Perspective, Composition, and Architectural and Mechanical Drawing.

"Students may enter any class upon submitting examples of work showing the necessary skill. Applicants for admission to the evening Life Class must submit a drawing of a full length figure from the Antique or Life.

"The school is fully equipped with models, casts from the Antique, etc.

"There are seven fine studios, all well lighted, and excellently adapted to the purposes of the school.

"The artists connected with the school as teachers have received their training in the Art Schools of Europe.

"Instruction in all classes of the school is individual. Advancement of each student depends on the degree of proficiency only. Students are at liberty to work as much or as little as they desire between the hours of 9 A. M. and 5 P. M.

"Tests of the students' progress are held at the end of each semestre; students are required to make a drawing within a limited time from subject assigned, and without the assistance or advice of instructor. These test drawings are submitted to the examination of a committee of competent judges appointed for the purpose, who decide upon the merits of each individual drawing.

"The museum of the school, in its various collections, affords rare opportunities for study. The sculpture galleries contain examples of work illustrating the different periods of art history, from Egyptian art at the time of Amenophis III, to Italian art at the time of Michael Angelo.

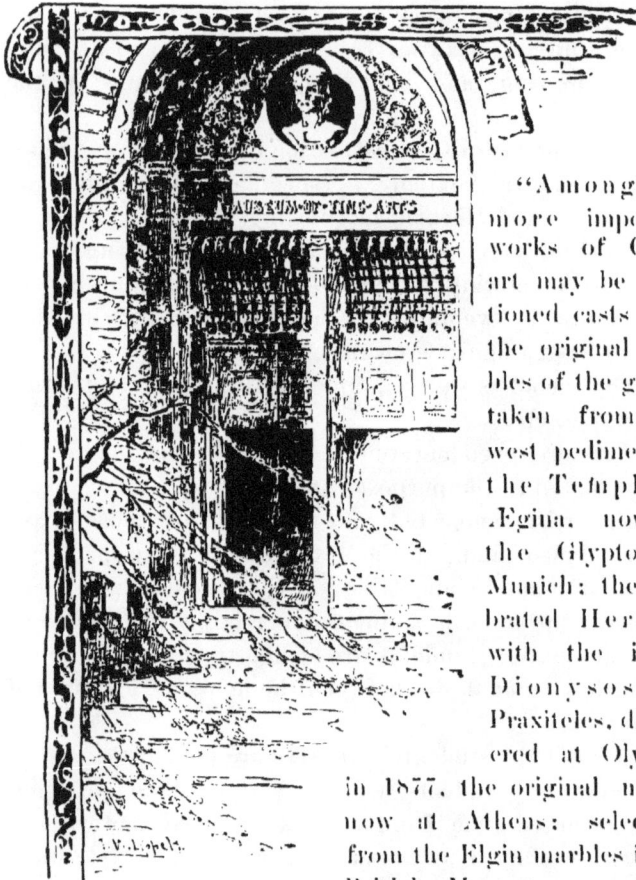

"Among the more important works of Greek art may be mentioned casts from the original marbles of the groups taken from the west pediment of the Temple of Ægina, now in the Glyptothek, Munich; the celebrated Hermes, with the infant Dionysos, by Praxiteles, discovered at Olympia in 1877, the original marble now at Athens; selections from the Elgin marbles in the British Museum, comprising the Frieze of the Parthenon (west side), a Caryatid from the original taken from the Temple of Pandrosos on the Acropolis at Athens, and the Metopes from the Parthenon; the Flying Victory, original

ENTRANCE TO MUSEUM.

now in Athens, discovered at Olympia in 1875; and the Laocoon group.

"German art of the XV century is represented by the masterpieces of Peter Vischer and Veit Stoss. The great work by Peter Vischer, the Shrine of St. Sebald, in the Church of St. Sebald, Nuremberg, is represented by a cast from the original, and is the only reproduction of this great work in America. The justly celebrated statue, The Praying Mary, by Veit Stoss, in the Germanic Museum, Nuremberg, is among the most refined works of German art of this period.

"Italian art of the Renaissance period, is represented by works of Donatello, Michael Angelo and Ghiberti. The Gates of the Baptistery at Florence, the greatest work of Lorenzo Ghiberti, are placed near the Shrine of St. Sebald to afford the student an opportunity of comparing the two works of art in metal by these masters of the Italian and German schools.

"Michael Angelo is represented by the well known figures of the two slaves, from the originals in the Louvre, the Madonna of Bruges, and the unfinished bas-relief of the Virgin and the Child, taken from the original work in the Royal Academy, London. Donatello's St. George and the

BELL PULL WROUGHT IRON; XVI CENTURY.

Singing Children represent an earlier phase of the Italian
school.

"The museum and school collections of casts combined,
number three hundred and forty-five
pieces, and are supplemented by a
series of plates (numbering 1041)
made from the collections of the
British Museum described more fully
elsewhere.

"The collection of oil paintings in
the picture galleries includes Harry
Thompson's "Shepherdess," Luigi
Loir's "End of Autumn," Beyle's
"Parting Kiss," Vely's "Love and
Riches," Washington Alston's "Paul
and Silas in Prison," several works
by Charles Wimar, the celebrated
painter of Indian life, and many other
works. Besides these, there are
always on exhibition many works lent
by friends of the institution.

"The picture galleries also contain
a collection of modern works in water
color, and black and white. In the
latter class the museum is especially
fortunate in possessing a collection of
works selected by Mr. W. Lewis
Fraser, showing the various methods
employed by well known American
artists in illustrative work.

"Several hundred autotype reproductions from sketches, studies and
paintings, by celebrated masters,
from the XV Century to the present time afford
students ample opportunity to familiarize themselves with

CLOCK CASE AND DIAL—
XVI CENTURY.

the leading characteristics of the various schools of painting.

"The northern galleries contain many objects of art workmanship in wood, iron (both wrought and cast), bronze, gold and silver, ivory, glass, and examples in various wares.

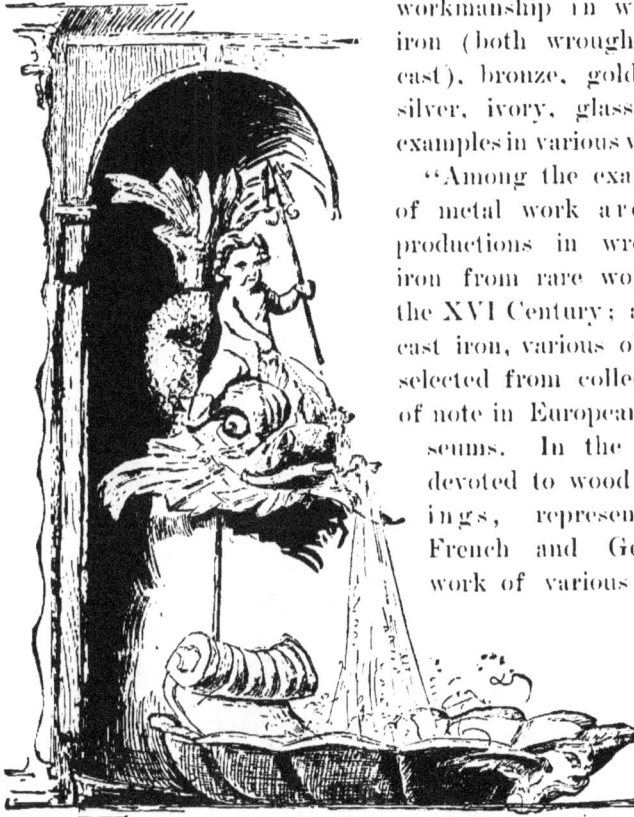

"Among the examples of metal work are reproductions in wrought iron from rare work of the XVI Century; also in cast iron, various objects selected from collections of note in European museums. In the room devoted to wood carvings, representative French and German work of various peri-

HAND BASIN—XVI CENTURY.

ods, original and reproduced, show to the student methods of applying art knowledge to objects of every day use."

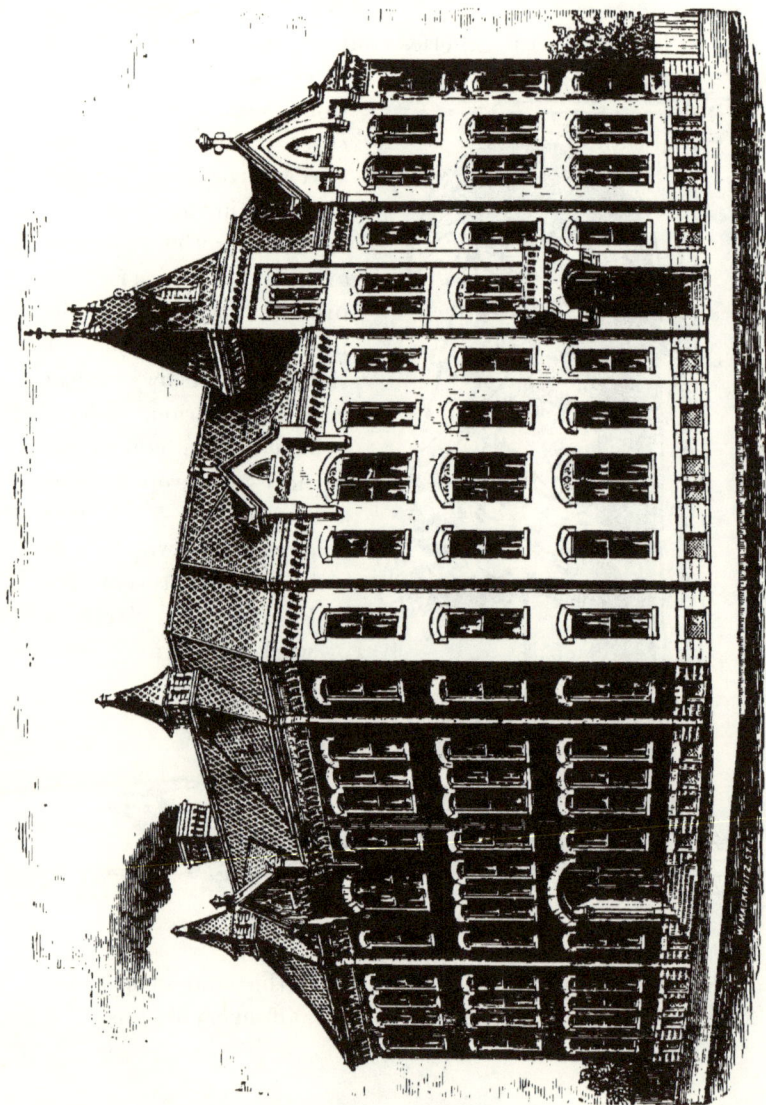

MANUAL TRAINING SCHOOL, ST. LOUIS.

MANUAL TRAINING SCHOOL.

ESTABLISHED JUNE 6, 1879.

" Hail to the skillful cunning Hand!
Hail to the cultured Mind!
Contending for the world's command,
Here let them be combined!"

The Ordinance establishing the school, declares:

" " Its object shall be instruction in mathematics, drawing, and the English branches of a high-school course, and instruction and practice in the use of tools. The tool instruction, as at present contemplated, shall include carpentry, wood-turning, pattern-making, iron chipping and filing, forge work, brazing and soldering, the use of machine shop-tools, and such other instruction of a similar character as may be deemed advisable to add to the foregoing from time to time.

' " The students will divide their working hours, as nearly as possible, equally between mental and manual exercises. They shall be admitted, on examination, at not less than fourteen years of age, and the course shall continue three years.' ' '

SCHOLARSHIPS.

" The founders of the school desire that the advantages of this school shall be within the reach of boys from every class in the community. From fifty to sixty free, or partially free, scholarships will, therfore, be kept filled. It is desirable that they should in general be given as rewards of merit to promising boys in straitened circumstances.

" Boys who can produce records of good character and scholarship, but whose circumstances render it practically impossible for them to pay the tuition fees of the school,

are invited to write the Director, or to get some friend to
write for them. In such cases the occupation of the
father should be given. It must not be assumed, however,
that because application is made a scholarship will always
be given: the number of scholarships may be full, or it
may be thought that the applicant is not entitled to special
consideration.

" Persons desiring to found scholarships are referred to
the members of the Board of Managers, or to the Directors.

FROM REGULATIONS.

" Boys are expected to be earnest, faithful, truthful and
polite. Every one is expected to do his best promptly and
cheerfully under all circumstances.

" Pupils whose influence is found to be bad are dismissed;
and those who fail to make good progress in their work
after reasonable trial are required to withdraw.

THE WORK.

" *All shop work is disciplinary; special trades are not
taught, nor are articles manufactured for sale;* as a rule,
the products of the shop have no value except as exercises,
illustrating typical forms and methods.

" The object of the school is education, and none of the
class exercises, whether in the shop, the drawing or the
recitation room, can be supposed to have any pecuniary
value. The most instructive tasks have no outcome except
in the intelligence and skill of the student himself.

" The shop training is gained by regular and carefully
graded lessons designed to cover as much ground as possible, and to teach thoroughly the use of ordinary tools.
This does not imply the attainment of sufficient skill to

produce either the fine work or exhibit the rapidity of a skilled mechanic.

DIGNITY OF INTELLIGENCE IN LABOR.

"One great object of the school is to foster a higher appreciation of the value and dignity of intelligent labor, and the worth and respectability of laboring men. A boy who sees nothing in manual labor but mere brute force, despises both the labor and the laborer. With the acquisition of skill in himself, comes the ability and willingness to recognize skill in his fellows. When once he appreciates skill in handicraft, he regards the skillful workman with sympathy and respect.

"Again, it is highly desirable that a larger proportion of intelligent and well-educated youth should devote their energies to manual pursuits, or to the development of mechanical industries, both for their own sakes, and for the sake of the occupations and society.

THE RESULTS OF EXPERIENCE.

"The school is now in its tenth year. From the start it has been well patronized, and vacant seats have been few. The enrollment shows a steady increase. The zeal and enthusiasm of the students have been developed in a most gratifying degree, extending into all the departments of work. The variety afforded by the daily program has had the moral and intellectual effect expected, and an unusual degree of sober earnestness has been shown. The wholesome moral effect of a course of training which interests and stimulates the ardor of the student is most marked. Parents observe the beneficial influence of *occupation*. The suggestions of the day fill the mind with healthy thoughts and appetites during the leisure hours. Success in drawing or shop-work has often had the effect of arousing the

ambition in mathematics and history, and *vice versa*. Gradually the students acquire two most valuable habits which
are certain to influence their whole lives, namely : precision
and method.

"Finally, the school has served to demonstrate the entire
feasibility of incorporating the elements of intellectual and
manual training in such a way that each is the gainer
thereby. Lastly, it is most gratifying, that this school
has met the public demand for such an education which,
while it insures the most valuable mental discipline, im-
parts at the same time knowledge and skill of great intrinsic worth."

COURTS OF CRIMINAL CORRECTION.

CHAPTER III.

THE LIBRARIES OF SAINT LOUIS.

Open treasure houses of pure gold!

THE SAINT LOUIS PUBLIC LIBRARY.

"All that mankind has done, thought, gained or been—it is lying in magic preservation in the pages of books."—*T. Carlyle.*

The Public Library is a public treasury and fountain from which all may partake and become opulent in wisdom. St. Louis is fortunate indeed in the possession of such a library. It ministers daily to the needs of a hungry population pining for knowledge, and whose thirst is assuaged at its well-spring. This library was founded by the Board of Public Schools, and it exists and flourishes under the same fostering care. The library contains seventy thousand volumes of choice books in every department of knowledge, science and literature.

The Juvenile Department is a special feature. It comprises 4,000 volumes by the best authors, selected with a view to aid in the mental and moral development of children. A taste for good reading in childhood and youth, cannot fail to develop a higher standard of character and usefulness in mature life.

11

The Reading Room is supplied with 55 newspapers from all parts of North America, and important points in Europe, Asia, Africa and Australia, and 115 other periodicals, including the illustrated weeklies, the most attractive journals, and the best scientific and literary magazines, domestic and foreign.

The membership fee is the nominal charge of $1.00 per year to pupils of the public schools; $2.00 to residents of the city, and $3.00 to non-residents. Strangers may call for any book in the library and consult it there free of charge. The public reading room is free to all persons, whether citizens or strangers. The library is well conducted, and courteous attention is extended to all callers.

The Public Library is kept in the Polytechnic Building, which occupies the south-west corner of Chestnut and Seventh streets. This fine structure is owned by the Board of Public schools, and is the headquarters of the Board. It was completed in 1867 at a cost of $450,000.00.

The Librarian, Mr. Frederick M. Crunden, who is an accomplished scholar, says in his report for 1887: " Very aptly the Public Library is termed the People's University. It takes students of any age or stage of advancement, it has courses adapted to the varying needs and capacities of every man, woman and child. By its aid the poor boy who is compelled to leave school at 12 years of age, may be at 25 a better educated and better informed man than the majority of college graduates. Having acquired the barest rudiments and a desire for knowledge, the Public Library provides him with all facilities for a thorough education at an inappreciable cost to the State. That school curriculum is incomplete which does not embrace some introduction to the best literature, and that teacher falls short of his highest usefulness who does not show his pupils that there are other books than those of their task-work, who does not inspire them with a love for good reading, who does not lead them to the door of the Public Library and explain to them that the highest aim of their school course is to give them the keys to that treasure house of knowledge and power."

The same authority, speaking of the Public Library, in his report for the year 1888, issued in December, says: " The Public Library, in short, is being more and more recognized as an essential adjunct and supplement to the common-school system, as an important factor in civilization, and as one of the most potent agencies in the enlightenment of the people, on which must depend the safety of the State, and the welfare of its citizens."

THE MERCANTILE LIBRARY ASSOCIATION

Has ever been an object of deep interest, and has received the most devoted care, involving the active and liberal support of merchants and other citizens, from its earliest inception and founding to the present time. On January 8th, 1889, the forty-third anniversary was held in the new library building—just completed and opened.

Mr. John M. Dyer, the able and efficient Librarian, most devoted to his task of transferring the treasures under his care to the new library, was greeted by the President and Board with high commendation for his excellent work.

It was the most enthusiastic assembly known to the friends of the library in many years. Their delight grew from the cheerful outlook, since never in the history of the library has it been so pronounced.

The Mercantile Library Association was formed—under its present name—April 9th, 1846. A few months later it was organized under a constitution, and opened with a

MERCANTILE LIBRARY BUILDING.

library of 1,680 volumes, since when it has grown to seventy-one thousand! The Association possesses a number of valuable works of art in paintings, statuary and basso relievos.

In 1851, the Association purchased the present site, upon which they early erected a building of large size and special utility for those times. It served its purposes until no longer suited to the rapidly growing needs for more space, and for the preservation of its treasures of literature and art within the walls of a fire-proof structure. The Association is now in full occupancy of its new library building, erected upon the original site at a cost exceeding $350,000.00. That portion not occupied by the Library Halls, yields an annual rental of forty thousand dollars.

The edifice is six stories in height above the pavement, and the basement is profitably utilized. The architecture is Romanesque; the exterior walls are of Missouri red granite, St. Louis fine pressed brick—plain and ornamental—and presents a very handsome appearance. The building fronts 128 feet on Locust, and 114 feet on Sixth street. It is fire proof, and first-class in all materials and construction. The library halls are of a height of twenty feet. In appearance they are most inviting, and are both grand and beautiful. In plan, arrangements and furnishings they are adapted to convenience and eligibility in every particular; in ventilation and light they are admirable, whilst at night they are illuminated with the most approved electro incandescent lights.

The favored fortunes of this popular institution have followed it closely down to the present era of the inauguration of its magnificent new home, which in size will accommodate the wants of another generation. The original site cost $25,500.00, about thirty-five years since, and is worth to-day, without the improvements, fully three hundred thousand dollars.

OTHER LIBRARIES.

The libraries of Washington University and St. Louis University are extensive and very valuable: besides, there are others of value belonging to literary and other societies.

The library of the "St. Louis Bar Association" contains 12,000 volumes of standard authors. Of private libraries belonging to citizens of culture and literary tastes, it is estimated there are one hundred of note, some of which are extensive and very valuable.*

LIST OF LIBRARIES AND THEIR LOCATION.

The Mercantile Library Association, Sixth, corner of Locust street.

Public, Polytechnic Building, Chestnut, corner of Seventh street.

Law Association, south wing of the Court House.

St. Louis Law School, 1417 Lucas Place.

St. Louis University, Grand avenue, opp. Pine street.

St. Louis Diocesan, 1519 Chestnut street.

St. Louis Turnverein, Turner's Hall, Tenth street, between Market and Walnut streets.

The Odd Fellows' Association, Chestnut, S. E. corner of Ninth street.

The Young Men's Christian Association, Circulating, 2835 Pine street.

The Young Men's Sodality, Washington avenue, corner of Ninth street.

The Young Ladies' Sodality, Washington avenue, corner of Ninth street.

St. John's Circulating, Sixteenth, N. W. corner of Chestnut street.

National Library Association, 304 N. Eighth street.

Slavansa Lipa (Bohemian), 1811 S. Eighth street.

* NOTE.—The sense of appreciation of the eligibility of St. Louis for holding national assemblies, is being constantly attested by the large number of conventions held at this city. And, now it is the "Annual Conference of the American Library Association," which embraces all the Libraries of note in the United States and Canada, will be held here in May next, 1889.—*Author.*

CHAPTER IV.

LITERATURE, AUTHORSHIP AND ART AT ST. LOUIS.

" Our echoes roll from soul to soul,
And grow forever and forever."—*Tennyson.*

In St. Louis a very marked proclivity toward authorship in literary work has obtained in later years, and the
number of cultured writers is not inconsiderable in general literature, the sciences and fiction; the larger number are essayists and writers for magazines. A few
of these are notable, but a small number have gained
celebrity.* Within fifty years this city has developed as
many as five hundred writers and authors, some of whom
were, and are above mediocre ability.

THE SCHOOL OF FINE ARTS

Has a large patronage. Its yearly work developes an increasing taste for art culture among the people of this city
and surrounding territory, and draws numerous delighted
pupils.

THE MEMORIAL ART BUILDING

Was built by a munificent merchant, now deceased, who
dedicated it, together with treasures in art, to the
memory of a favorite son, who died early. It contains a
large number of rare works of art, in statuary and paintings, etc., selected from different schools and periods of
art history, many of which were obtained at a large cost.
These attractive galleries are open daily to the public. On

---

* NOTE.—In fiction, the most noted author is Miss Murfree.—*Author.*

Saturdays and Sundays, from one o'clock P. M., they are
free. The memorial art building is on the north-east corner of Lucas Place and Nineteenth street. This handsome
structure is of Missouri gray granite, fire proof, and cost
$135,000.00, including the site.

ARTISTS, AND ART COLLECTIONS.

St. Louis has given birth to, and been the adopted
home of a number of painters and sculptors of distinguished merit,* some of whom survive and are still residents. A few private collections—owned by citizens of
taste and wealth—contain rare paintings of great value.

NEWSPAPERS AND PERIODICALS OF ST. LOUIS.

" Beneath the rule of men entirely great,
The pen is mightier than the sword,
The arch enchanter's wand—"
                        —*E. Lytton Bulwer.*

ENUMERATION OF NEWSPAPERS AND PERIODICALS PUB-
LISHED AT THE CITY OF SAINT LOUIS
IN THE YEAR 1889.

There are of daily publications, 11; of weekly, 62;
of semi-weekly, 3; of tri-weekly, 1; of semi-monthly, 4;
of monthly, 42; and of semi-monthly, 2. Whole number, 125.†

* NOTE.—Miss Sarah M. Peale was a popular painter of portraits at St. Louis
from 1847 to 1878. Portraits of Daniel Webster and Thomas H. Benton, from her
pencil, are in the collection of the Mercantile Library. And, Miss Harriet Hosmer
may be claimed as belonging to the Art History of St. Louis, having been a student
here when in her nineteenth year. Two beautiful works by her are to be found in
this city: Œnone, and Beatrice Cenci, one of them owned by the Art Museum, and
the other by the Mercantile Library Association.
    Robert M. Bringhurst is yet a young man, but is of recognized ability in painting
and modeling. His latest work is the statue of Gen. U. S. Grant, in this city.—*Author.*

    † NOTE.—Several of the daily newspapers publish weekly, semi-weekly and tri-
weekly editions of their paper, all which are counted as distinct publications.—
Author.

Of these, 105 were in the English language; 18 in the German; 1 in the Spanish; and one in Bohemian.

Many of these publications are devoted to advertising, politics, home and general news, and some exclusively to literature. But, 21 were published in the interest of religion, 1 in the interest of the colored race; 7 were devoted to medicine, 1 to medicine and surgery, 1 to surgery, 1 to homœopathy, 1 to dentistry, 2 to law, 1 to music, 3 to education, 1 to photography, 1 to mining, 1 to iron products, 1 to lumber, 1 to shoes and leather, 2 to furniture, 1 to machinery, 1 to farm machinery, 3 to agriculture, 3 to flour milling, 1 to merchandise, 1 to groceries, 1 to drugs, 1 to tobacco, 1 to stoves and hardware, 1 to jewelry, 1 to trade and traffic, 1 trade record, 1 to building trades, 1 to building associations, 1 to insurance, 1 to railroads, 1 to sporting news, and 1 to poultry raising.

Many of these journals hold a high rank in their respective spheres of work. The editorial ability employed upon the journals published here, is equal to that of other cities, which alone is sufficient commendation. But, the active enterprise of the conductors of several of the daily newspapers of this city, surpasses that of almost any other city of the United States, especially in the size of their daily editions and volume of distribution.

CHAPTER V.

THE CHURCH DENOMINATIONS OF SAINT LOUIS.*

Most of the denominations of Christians found in other American cities, are represented here. There are of the Baptist denomination, 22, three of which are German, and seven colored; Christian, 4; Con-

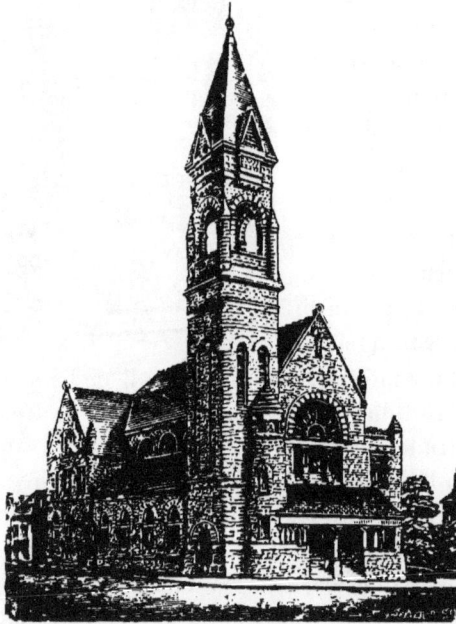

TEMPLE ISRAEL.

gregationalist, 13; Episcopalian, 15, one of which is colored; German Evangelical, 14; English Evangelical Lutheran, 1; German Evangelical Lutheran, 12; Methodist Episcopal, 17, of which 3 are German and 1 Swedish; M. E. Church, South, 8; New Jerusalem, 3; Presbyterian,

* NOTE.—In various portions of this book may be found plates of numerous church edifices.—Author.

23, of which 2 are German; Cumberland Presbyterian, 3, of which 2 are German; Reformed Presbyterian, 1; United Presbyterian, 2; Roman Catholic, 47, of which 15 are German, 1 Bohemian, 1 Polish, 1 colored, and one German and English; Unitarian, 3; Miscellaneous, 18, 3 of which are colored. The edifices devoted to the worship of the Almighty number over two hundred and twenty, of which 8 are Hebrew. The rabbis are able teachers.

The clergymen of St. Louis, without regard to sect or denomination, have from an early period been distinguished for piety and zeal, as well as for eloquence and marked ability. A few of them have spent a lengthened life in this city—devoted to the moral welfare of its people.

The French Roman Catholic missionaries were the earliest to bring the institutions of Christianity to the aborignees of the Mississippi Valley, and subsequently to the French colonists. The curates were distinguished for zeal. The earliest "tabernacle" in Laclede's time, was a tent of poles and boughs of trees. The Catholics built the first brick and stone church erected in St. Louis, about seventy years since.

Many of the church edifices of this city are large and costly. For tastefulness in archictecture they will bear comparison with the structures of other cities. Some are superb, and others grand.

SOCIETIES FOR MORAL AND RELIGIOUS

Improvement are numerous, and are found amongst all the denominations, Protestant, Roman Catholic and Hebrew. Some of them are prominently identified with works of special social improvement. The Young Men's Christian Association has several branches, including one for young colored men. Their German branch is specially active, and raised the full cost of a separate home, a handsome new building recently completed. All these societies have the active sympathy of community, and are useful in their spheres.

THE HOTELS

Of St. Louis are numerous and well appointed. Some, for size and elegance, are not inferior to the best of other cities,

THE SOUTHERN HOTEL.

and whilst in comfort and viands are equal to such, their charges to guests are less.

The hotels of this city have been found equal to the task of caring for the numerous great assemblies of people from the country at large, gathered here within a few

years past, notably amongst which were the triennial con-
clave of Knights Templar, annual assembly of the Grand
Army of the Republic, the convention to nominate a
President of the United States, and the National Sænger-
fest. The central position of this city, the hospitality
of its citizens, agreeable climate, and the reasonableness
of the prices of its hotels—all combine to make St. Louis
a popular and favorite spot for the holding of conventions
by organized bodies of men.

But, each autumn, during the forty days of the annual
Fair, Exposition, Musical Entertainments, Illuminations,
etc., this city entertains daily, without crowding, many
times ten thousand strangers.

BATHS—NATATORIUM.

A natatorium of ample area is maintained during the
summer season. It is liberally patronized by bathers and
learners of the art of swimming. Bathing establishments
are numerous throughout the city, some of which furnish Turkish baths. But, a city situated on the banks of a
great river, might well afford baths at all seasons for the
populace. Disease would be diminished, and health promoted.

FREE PUBLIC BATHS.

The completion of the new water works, in 1893, is
likely to be a fitting era for the adoption by municipal
legislation of a general system of free bathing, or public
baths at a merely nominal charge, yet equaling only the
current expenses. The municipality will then be able to
furnish fifty million gallons of water daily, and the authorities might well favor the establishment of a popular plan
of free, or cheap bathing in each ward of the city.

THE DRAMA AND OPERA.

The people of St. Louis are liberal patrons of the
drama and opera. They have ever been specially devoted

to art music in vocalization, and this city has given birth
to a number of distinguished singers. There is an increasing
taste for music in all its forms among citizens, which is a
sure indication of growth in refinement.

There are a number of theatres and opera houses, to
which the leading "stars" and their troupes draw crowded
audiences.

The musical societies of St. Louis are numerous, and
their amateur performers have high merit; whilst, from
these schools of vocal art, has come forth an occasional
pupil, bringing credit to the city and celebrity to the artist.

BASE BALL CLUBS.

Among a considerable class of citizens a great fondness
for athletic sports prevails, and has developed—during several years—until attendance upon base ball playing has
become a popular pastime of the patrons of this rage.

OPPORTUNITIES FOR OUT-DOOR ENJOYMENT.

Few other large cities are as amply provided with free
grounds, open daily to the public, in charming and delightful parks, gardens, squares and boulevards—spacious
enough for a much larger population—and where all may
find pure air, and freedom for relaxation. Besides these,
are beautiful and refreshing drives through streets and
avenues lined with the most tasteful improvements, and
where—in spring, summer and autumn—many of both
sexes may be seen walking or riding horseback.

Each year has not failed to add new means and methods, through which the public has found opportunities for
rational and health-giving enjoyment.

ASSOCIATIONS, CIRCLES, CHAPTERS, CLUBS, LEAGUES, LODGES, ORDERS, SOCIETIES, ETC.

The number of organized bodies in force at St. Louis
is *legion*. It exceeds eleven hundred! Their objects and pur-

poses cover almost the whole ground of rational views and desires. The most prominent only of which need be mentioned, *namely:* Those for social enjoyment; for mental, moral, intellectual, physical, musical, dramatic and religious culture; for objects benevolent, charitable, mutual aid and protection, etc. A stranger coming to the city to remain, and wishing to attach himself to some organization, could scarcely fail to find one to suit him, and friends willing to take him cordially by the hand.

Among the very prominent *clubs* are the following: Mercantile, Marquette, McCullough, Dramatic, Germania, Harmonie, St. Louis, Elks, Hendricks, Sketch, Jockey and Calumet.

The Knights of St. Patrick meet quarterly.

The Caledonia Society has an annual dinner, toasts, speeches and songs.

Societies of Members of Grand Army of the Republic are numerous. Also, an *Ex-Confederates Association*.

The Missouri Historical Society, organized in 1866, makes yearly progress in membership, and in the number and value of its collections.

The Southern Historical and Benevolent Association is enabled to help needy ex-Confederates, and gather contributions for its archives.

ST. LOUIS' CHARITY TO THE POOR. MUTUAL RESPECT BE-
TWEEN EMPLOYER AND EMPLOYE. PROFIT-SHARING.
NO DISCONTENT AMONGST MECHANICS AND
LABORING MEN. STRIKES NOT PROBA-
BLE. NO ANARCHISTS IN
SAINT LOUIS.

In no other city is more kindly and compassionate work done for the poor and needy, through organized and systematized relief associations, or by individual acts of benevolence. Charity, as an active sentiment, is broad in this community. It is apt to observe the injunction of the

Divine Teacher, that "the poor are always present." In the hot season, considerate citizens provide delightful free steamboat day-excursions on the River, for poor mothers and children. Enlivening music and abundant food and drinks, are superadded to the fresh air and incidental diversions. To those for whom provided, these are only transient, but not unforgotten joys.

At the last Christmas (Dec., 1888), fifteen thousand poor children were entertained at Exposition Hall with music and merriment — including a visit from "Santa Claus"—and accompanied with the bestowment of (to them) rare gifts. All which carried good cheer to thousands of darkened hearthstones.* But this was *one* only of similar entertainments provided for the needy and cheerless on Christmas Day, at public and private institutions, and of charity and liberality—flowing freely—toward such as needed relief and help.

POST-DISPATCH BUILDING.

The rich and comfortable men and women of the city were not unmindful of the wants of the poor and less favored. These simple, yet gracious acts, carried satisfaction to many dissatisfied hearts, and joy to cheerless homes.

But, such special acts, in conjunction with general benevolence, do not end simply in bringing pleasure to the

*NOTE.—The fund raised for this *fête* from citizens, amounted to between eight and nine thousand dollars. It originated with an associate manager of one of the popular daily newspapers, and by whom it was carried through. This paper paid all the attendant expenses, including rent of hall, etc.; the amount of which exceeded one thousand dollars. A balance of the fund remained—after the bestowment of the gifts of "Santa Claus"—of about five thousand dollars, which was expended in shoes and clothing for the most needy and worthy of the boys and girls,—*Author.*

givers, and comfort to the recipients, but they go much further. They are satisfactory assurances to many that not *all* of the rich are sordid; but, on the contrary, are open and expressed friends and benefactors. It is apparent, that a generous and wise consideration suitably demonstrated by the rich and well-to-do citizens toward the masses and laboring classes—unfurnished in luxury's good things—is what impresses them with satisfaction, if not with content. This feeling is prevalent amongst them, and daily noticeable in their ranks.

There are not only no riotous assemblies, and no anarchial gatherings here, but not any appearance of discontent amongst the working classes. In general, they find ready employment, and at fair wages. It is also proof of the prevalent prosperity at this city.

Whilst some attempts are being made to abbreviate the daily working hours, the "wage" rates—paid to mechanics and day laborers—seem to be satisfactory. The plan of *profit-sharing* has been adopted by several firms, and has worked satisfactorily. The system is to be recommended, not only because it produces a more cordial feeling between the employer and employed, but it leads to greater industry and a stronger interest in the success of the business. It goes further still, in preventing "strikes," and in increasing the profits of the establishment. And, at the "annual reckoning," whatever it be, both parties start afresh with renewed zeal.

Amongst the many thousands of workmen and workwomen in this city, there is not the slightest dissatisfaction apparent, nor is there likely to be any other feeling than that of the general opinion, that the employer pays all the wages he can afford. Besides, manufactures, buildings and all works and enterprises, progress freely and are undisturbed by fears of strikes or riots.

PAY, FREE, CHARITABLE AND BENEVOLENT INSTITUTIONS OF ST. LOUIS.

What provision is made at St. Louis for the sick, diseased and destitute may be seen by examination of the list given of

ASYLUMS, HOMES, ETC.

'Deaf and Dumb Asylum and Half Orphan's Asylum for girls; Blind Girls' Industrial Home; Girls' Industrial Home; Old Ladies' Home of the Friendless; Insane Asylum; St. Vincent's Institution for the Insane; St. Ann's Widows' Home; Infant Asylum, and Lying-in Hospital; Home of the Good Shepherd; House of Protection for servant girls out of situations; Little Sisters of the Poor, a Home for indigent and aged people; St. Joseph's Female Night Refuge; the Babies' and Children's Receiving and Distributing Home; Working Women's Home; Women's Christian Home; House of the Guardian Angel; St. Elizabeth's Institute; Home of the Immaculate Conception; Home for Aged and Infirm Israelites; Orphans' Home; the Baptist, Episcopal, German Evangelical Lutheran, German General Protestant, German Protestant, Methodist, Mullanphy, St. Louis Protestant, St. Bridget's (half-orphan), St. Philomena, St. Joseph's Male, St. Mary's Female, and St. Vincent's (German) Orphan Asylums and Homes.

HOSPITALS AND INFIRMARIES.

Alexian Brothers' Hospital and Insane Asylum; Augusta Free Hospital for the children of St. Louis; City's Free; Evangelical Lutheran; Female (Hospital and Industrial Home); German Evangelical Lutheran (Hospital and Asylum); Good Samaritan; Lying-in; United States' Marine; Missouri Pacific Railway; Private Hospital for Ladies; Pius; Quarantine and Small Pox; St. John's; St. Louis, and Children's Hospital; St. Louis

Female (Infirmary); St. Louis, Iron Mountain and
Southern Railway Employes' (Home); St. Louis Post
Graduate; St. Louis Mullanphy; St. Luke's Episcopalian;
St. Mary's (Infirmary); and Protestant Hospital Associa-
tion of St. Louis.

GRAND TOWER BLOCK, N. E. CORNER FOURTH AND MARKET STREETS.

CHAPTER VI.

THE RAILWAYS ENTERING ST. LOUIS.

THOSE FROM THE EAST ARE

The Wabash, (Eastern); Vandalia and Terre Haute; St. Louis and Indianapolis, (Bee Line); Ohio and Mississippi; Chicago and Alton; St. Louis, Alton and Terre Haute; Terre Haute and Indianapolis, via Vandalia; Toledo, St. Louis and Kansas City; Illinois and St. Louis; Louisville and Nashville; St. Louis, Arkansas and Texas; Venice, Marine and Eastern; St. Louis and Central Illinois; Mobile and Ohio, (via St. Louis and Cairo); St. Louis and Paducah; Chicago, Burlington and Quincy; St Louis Bridge Company.

AND, FROM NORTH, SOUTH AND WEST.

South Western System, of seven great railways—with the Missouri Pacific at its head—comprising upward of seven thousand miles of road, but connected with, and operating upward of seventy-five branch roads; St. Louis and San Francisco, (Frisco Line); Wabash Western, including nine branches; Chicago, Burlington and Quincy, including its northern and western connections of great extent of mileage.

OFFICES OF THE NATIONAL GOVERNMENT AT ST. LOUIS.

The offices of the United States *civil service* are the following:

Assayer, Circuit Clerk, Custom House, Collector of Customs, Commissioners, District Attorney, Engineers, Internal Revenue, Inspector Post Office Department, Jury

Commissioner, Light House Inspector, Light House Engineer, Marine Hospital Service, Mississippi River Commission, Masters in Chancery, Marshal, Post Office, Signal Service, Supervisor of Education, Secret Service, Railway Mail Service, Registers in Bankruptcy, Treasury Department, Examining Surgeon's Office, Special Examiner, Pension Bureau, Inspector of Steamboats.

ARMY DEPARTMENTS.

Cavalry Depot, Pay, Subsistence, Recruiting Office for Infantry, Recruiting Office for Cavalry, Clothing Depot, Medical Purveyor's Depot, Quartermaster's Department.

JEFFERSON BARRACKS—ARSENAL.

The department of war established a military station near St. Louis at the period of the cession of the territory of Louisana, in 1804, and has maintained it ever since. Jefferson Barracks was built upward of sixty years since, and the Arsenal soon afterwards. The original purpose was the maintenance here of a *corps de reserve* of the army. Few other army posts have been found as pleasant to the army officers, in consequence of the agreeable climate and social advantages of St. Louis.

THE UNITED STATES COURTS, AND SUPREME COURT OF MISSOURI.

U. S. CIRCUIT COURT.

The regular term begins in Saint Louis annually on third Monday in March and September, held by Hon. Samuel F. Miller, Associate Justice of the U. S. Supreme Court, allotted to the Circuit (8th Judicial); or by the

Circuit Judge residing in the circuit, or by the District Judge of the Eastern District of Missouri, acting as Circuit Judge, or either of said Judges.

U. S. DISTRICT COURT.

The regular term begins on the first Monday in May and November. Return term on first Monday of each month.

SUPREME COURT OF MISSOURI.

The regular term begins on first Monday in April and November.

FOREIGN CONSULS RESIDENT AT ST. LOUIS,

For the countries following, to-wit: German Empire, France, Austro-Hungary, Italy, Spain, Netherlands, Belgium, Denmark, Sweden, Norway, Switzerland, Brazil, and Mexico.

EXPOSITION BUILDING.

CHAPTER VII.

ST. LOUIS A CENTRE OF MINING CAPITALISTS.

St. Louis is headquarters for nearly all of the mines of Lead, Zinc, Copper, Iron and Coal in the State of Missouri, and of the coal output of south-western Illinois. It is headquarters for a number of the valuable mines in the precious metals of Old and New Mexico, Arizona, Colorado, Montana, etc. Some fortunate investors of this city have, within a few years, added to their exchequer an amount of wealth rivalling the rich returns of the early days of the California finds.

THE MINING STOCK EXCHANGE,
NO. 312 NORTH THIRD STREET,

Was organized November 10th, 1888. The officers chosen were as follows: J. D. Abeles, *President;* Joe J. Mullally, *Vice-President;* Page McPherson, Treasurer: Albert Singer, Secretary: S. A. Abeles, Ass't Secretary.

The Constitution and By-Laws—carefully and rigidly prepared—were unanimously adopted. The organization provides for a membership of one hundred persons, divided equally between active and associate members. Each active member is entitled to a representative on the floor of the Exchange. Rates of commission on sales were established, together with initiation, monthly and annual fees of members. Rules were adopted, among which was one to prohibit "wash" trading.* Any violation of this rule by members, is followed by liability of expulsion.

---

*NOTE.—A term given to unreal (false) sales, but reported as if they had actually occurred.—*Author.*

Trading *outside* of the Exchange is disallowed. A mine may be "listed" upon the application in writing of the officers of any mining company, and the payment of a fee of fifty dollars.

The Exchange holds two sessions daily: from 11 A. M. to 1 o'clock P. M.; and from 3 to 4 o'clock P. M. A "call" is held at 11:30 A. M. daily. The hour of the delivery of stocks, is 2:30 P. M. on the day succeeding their sale.

ST. LOUIS SAMPLING AND TESTING WORKS, (NEAR UNION DEPOT) UNDER THE CONTROL OF DEPARTMENT OF MINING AND METALLURGY, WASHINGTON UNIVERSITY.

These works—most creditable to St. Louis, and convenient and advantageous to miners and investors in mines—are available to citizens and strangers at all seasons of the year.

"These works are supplied with a full line of machinery and appliances for crushing and sampling ores, etc., and testing ores by any process of milling or concentration, for ascertaining by practical working tests the average value of ore, the best method for its treatment, and the commercial results to be expected from such treatment.

"To meet these requirements the machinery employed is the same as that in actual practice, and is of the most improved pattern. It includes: One rock breaker, 10x4. Two sets of rolls, 10x16. Automatic sampler and feeders. One battery of three 650 lbs. stamps, with inside and outside copperplates for gold milling. One battery of five 650 lbs. stamps, with amalgamating pans and settler for silver milling. One full-sized Frue vanner. One "Golden Gate concentrator." One reverbratory roasting and chlorodizing furnace. Leaching and precipitating tanks.

Four sizing screens. Six jigs, hydraulic separator, pointed boxes and Evans buddle.   One coking oven.

" The building is 60x139 feet, equipped with a 30 horse-power engine, and a 60 horse power boiler, thus affording ample space and power to carry on the work, and also make special trials of new machinery or appliances relating to mining or treatment of ores.

" Well appointed assay and chemical laboratories are connected with the mill for the assay and analysis of ores, fuels, furnace products, etc." *

* NOTE.—This description of the " Sampling and Testing Works" is condensed from Catalogue of Washington University.—*Author.*

COURT HOUSE.

THE CITY OF ST. LOUIS OF TO-DAY.

PART SIXTH.

CHAPTER I.

Commercial and Manufacturing Growth.

THE large trade enjoyed by this city with the extensive and populous territory of which it is the centre, continues to increase and its area to expand yearly in a volume corresponding with its gigantic surroundings. The active growth of commerce—represented by the aggregate money value, as well as by the volume—and the large demand for manufactured productions, is indicative of a healthy condition of trade, and of uninterrupted prosperity.

The popularity of St. Louis as a trade centre is not at all likely to diminish, but continue to increase. This city has gained the good will of the traders and people of the Great Valley and countries beyond it, by fair dealing, liberality and enterprise—all which have entitled it to appreciation and patronage. As a centre for the distribution of commodities, merchandise and manufactured products, its geographical position was a primary factor only, its active citizens developed and confirmed the advantages flowing therefrom. But, of all the business men, of every large

and prosperous city, the jobbing and wholesale merchants
are the most influential—as they are the most conspicuous
in trade—through their constant and intimate intercourse
and contact with the dealers who come from every section, and to whom is imparted the spirit, and often the
characteristics, of the men of the commercial metropolis.

The merchants and manufacturers of St. Louis have
cultivated with diligence and energy the great and fertile
field lying around, and opened invitingly to them, that
they might put their hand to the plow. But, a large
measure of credit for the popularity of this city for fair
and honorable dealing, is due to that large class of intelligent and deserving men, the traveling salesmen—
"drummers"—and for spreading the reputation of St.
Louis' business men. These men are the most powerful factors in creating and maintaining established trade and commerce. Upon them, in a large measure, depends the extension of the fame of this city as a most desirable market
—deserving of the general favor.*

THE SCOPE OF TERRITORY WHICH TRADES DIRECTLY WITH ST. LOUIS.

"Let us, then, be up and doing,
Still achieving, still pursuing."

—*Longfellow.*

Adam Smith, the very able Scotch political economist,
in his talented work entitled "The Wealth of Nations,"
states it as a clear and practical necessity, that "the valuable trade of any spot is that commerce which is carried on
between the inhabitants of the town and those of the

* NOTE.—See Appendix: Commercial Traveling Men.—*Author.*

country." St. Louis trades directly, and through its commercial travelers, in a greater or lesser degree, with a very large proportion of the States and Territories, the whole number equals thirty. The great South, Southwest and Northwest are increasing annually in a greater ratio than other parts, as is well known, and it would not be extravagant to accord to them two-thirds of the whole population of the entire Union at the close of the century.

The territory with which St. Louis enjoys commercial intercourse embraces the following States, namely: Illinois, Kentucky, Tennessee, Mississippi, Louisiana; nearly all of Missouri, Arkansas and Texas; a large part of the Territories of Arizona, New Mexico, Montana, Idaho, Utah and Indian (Territory). Also, of the States of Wyoming, Nevada, Colorado, Kansas, Nebraska, Iowa, Minnesota, South Dakota and North Dakota. Besides, some firms send their travelers into, and sell to the States of Ohio, Indiana, West Virginia, North Carolina, Georgia, Alabama, Florida and Wisconsin.

New railroads, and extensions of others already built, are annually constructed, connecting with this city, both directly and indirectly, and they constantly swell the volume of trade which pours into the lap of St. Louis.

Two new railway connections with St. Louis have recently been completed, and opened, namely: That of the Chicago, Burlington and Quincy Railway—in combination with its great lines and their branches in Missouri, Iowa, Nebraska, Kansas and beyond. The other road has made direct connection with this city, starting from Paducah, Kentucky, and from thence south and east with the extensive system of the Chesapeake and Ohio, Louisville and Nashville, and other leading lines to the Gulf and Atlantic seaboard. These connections were completed and consummated in December, 1888.

THE MANUFACTURING INDUSTRIES OF ST. LOUIS.

MANUFACTURES IN IRON AND STEEL.—Car wheels, chains, counting-room safes, scales and balances, steam-boilers, steam engines, shovels, mill saws, files, vises, iron-wares, granite ironwares, steel wire rope, fence wire, baling ties, iron and steel wires, wire goods, general hardware, iron working in general, steel jail works, water pipe, cutlery, etc.

METAL AND BRASS GOODS, lead pipe, gas pipe, sheet and bar lead, lightning rods, architectural and ornamental iron and zinc works, etc.

AGRICULTURAL IMPLEMENTS, continuous hay presses, wagons and carriages, car building, chairs, household furniture, office furniture, refrigerators and ice chests, stoves and ranges, saw mills, steam and wood pumps, lamps and lanterns, wood mouldings, picture frames, mantels, etc.

PLATE GLASS of all descriptions, window glass, ornamental glass, druggists' glasswares, etc.

CHEMICALS, fire clay products, photographers' dry plate, terra cotta, sash, doors and blinds, packing boxes, cooperage, wooden and willow ware, show cases, counting room desks, etc.

WHITE LEADS, paints and colors, castor and cotton-seed oils, soaps, candles, fertilizers, glucose, glue, lubricating oils, etc.

BAGGING, bags, rope and cordage.

ELECTRIC LIGHT PLANTS, electric engines and lights, optical instruments, artificial limbs.

POWDER, fire works.

ENGRAVING on steel, copper and lithographing..

PIANOS, organs, billiard tables, solid silver and plated wares, jewelry, gold pens.

SHOES AND BOOTS, hats, clothing, fur and knit goods.

SADDLERY AND HARNESS, machine belting.

BLANK BOOKS, roofing and sheathing paper.

PRINTING, in all departments, book binding.

BRICK MAKING, granite and marble working.

TOBACCO MANUFACTURES.

BEER BREWING.

WINES from native grapes, sparkling champagnes, still wines, whiskies, cider, vinegar.

COMPLETE OUTFITS FOR DAIRIES.

MISCELLANEOUS.

Also, manufacturers in other, and different products, in part as follows:

Furnishings for merchant and grist mills; middling purifiers; grain elevator machinery; mill machinery; mining and coal-pit machinery; miners' supplies; wood and iron working machinery; rock drills; well boring drills and apparatus; house elevators, and elevating machinery; power and hand corn shellers; copper stills, and distillers' outfits; ice machines, and implements; soda water supplies; railway supplies, and refrigerating machines.

FIRE-CLAY AND ITS PRODUCTS.

It is conceded, that the fire-clay deposits at this city are of finer quality than those of foreign countries. The following analysis of Missouri, German and English clays, is of value for comparison:

ANALYSIS.	ENGLISH.	GERMAN.	MISSOURI.
Silica	63.03	48.79	63.25
Alumina	23.03	28.50	23.20
Oxide of Iron	1.92	4.20	1.75
Magnesia	.20	.45	.06
Lime	.14	.10	.09
Soda	....	.06	.08
Potash	.18	.22	.07
Hygroscopic water	2.10	3.50	2.15
Water of composition with organic matter	9.40	14.18	9.35
	100.	100.	100.

From this analysis it will be seen, that in that element which is the most essential for a useful, tractable fire-clay, viz: silica, the Missouri clay is better provided than the English, and very much better than the German.

The proof of the great value of the fire-clays of this vicinity is the very large and growing demand for them for shipment to other places to be manufactured, and the extensive demand for the products of the several extensive works of this city.

The earliest discovery of fire-clay, at Cheltenham, (4 miles from the Court House), was made in 1838; not until years thereafter was it utilized, or its superior quality understood: its products have been found preferable in Canada to the famous Stonebridge products (England). St. Louis also supplies Pennsylvania, New York, New Jersey, and many other sections, and including entire districts.

For a long period the New Jersey products held the market—until the St. Louis wares came to be appreciated at their full value—but our productions are now first in amount and value, and for quality as well, in the United States. The following are a part of the articles manufactured:

Sewer and drain pipe—from 4 to 24 inches, and upward in diameter—crucibles, chimneys, fire-brick, paving-brick, (stands to the heaviest hauling), the Livessy-Somerville Refrigerator Furnaces, silica fire-clay cement —extensively used where great heat is to be resisted—furnace linings, glasspots, gas retorts, and pots for corroding white lead.

Terra Cotta Lumber is also made—a mixture of fire-clay and sawdust—and its properties are very remarkable: indestructible by fire, water, frost, gases, acids or age, a poor conductor of heat, dampness, sound or electricity, it neither expands nor shrinks under extraordinary or sudden changes of temperature, and will resist the hottest flame: its weight is half that of brick, two-thirds of granite or marble, and one-seventh iron, besides it is not costly.

The sales of the fire-clay products of St. Louis are most extensively spread; they find a market in Old Mexico, California, New Orleans, Boston, Philadelphia, Pittsburgh, and nearly every large city and manufacturing spot in the United States. Linings for blast furnaces are sold to Alabama, Tennessee, Virginia, Pennsylvania and Michigan; and their Bessemer Tuyeres to Troy and Pittsburgh. The glass works and iron furnaces in all parts of our country use almost exclusively the heat resisting fire-clay products of the St. Louis manufacturers.

The manufacture of fire-clay wares at St. Louis was begun in 1856, in a moderate way, and gradually grew to the present great proportions. The capital employed in this valuable industry is not less than two and a half million dollars, and the annual products are equal to six million dollars in 1888.

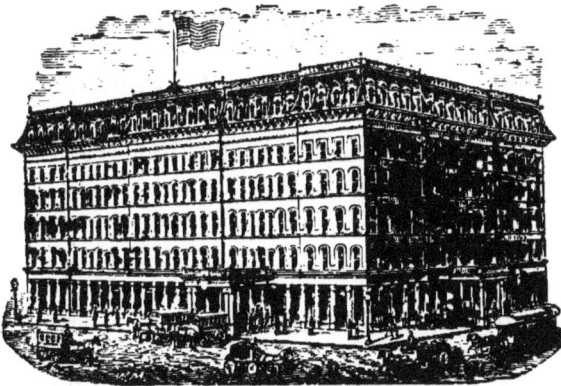

LACLEDE HOTEL BUILDING.

DESCRIPTION OF A FEW OF THE LEADING MANUFACTURING PLANTS OF ST. LOUIS.

MANUFACTURES IN GLASS.

Neither Pittsburgh, Wheeling, or New Albany, have advantages equal to those of St. Louis and its suburbs, for the manufacture or sale of glass goods; not only on account of the cheapness of its fuel, and centrality of its position for distribution, but in the great abundance and rare quality of the chief constituent of glass—the sands. In this department of industrial production, St. Louis might well be proud of its factories, since they vie with all others in America or Europe in the excellence of their wares, especially in plate glass, which in strength, purity of tint, and general excellence, is not only equal, but even superior to the best of French production. The superior quality of the St. Louis plate glass is appreciated throughout all the territory of the Great Valley and at the East. It is utilized in the finest residences and business buildings.

Window glass, druggists' and bottlers' goods, rough and ribbed plate glass, rolled cathedral and undoyant glass, crown discs, etc., are also products of the nine plants of this city.

One of the plate glass companies began in 1872, with a capital stock of $250,000; two years later it was doubled; and in 1880 it was increased to one million dollars. Three years later the capital was raised to $1,500,000. The plant comprises 5 melting furnaces, 94 annealing kilns, 22 circular grinders, 50 smoothers, 36 polishers, and 20 steam engines, together with all else to make up an establishment complete as any in Europe.

The capital invested in the glass industry aggregates six million dollars.

The best and most desirable descriptions of sand for the manufacture of plate glass and glass ware, are found in unlimited quantities near St. Louis.

Superior glass sand is sold and sent from St. Louis to factories at Pittsburgh, Steubenville and Wheeling in large quantities. One firm alone ships annually upward of a thousand tons.

CHEMICAL WORKS.

There are at St. Louis five or six chemical plants which are extensive and varied in their productions—one is confined to sal soda; another to ammonia for druggists' and chemists' use, and refrigerating purposes; another to pharmaceutical specialties exclusively for physicians; another for druggists' and distillers' fruit essences, and other specialties required by the trades. And yet another manufactures a full line of pure chemicals for medicinal and photographic purposes, embracing over three hundred articles. This extensive plant makes a number of technical products, amongst the most important of which are aqua-ammonia and anhydrous-ammonia, of which large quantities are shipped to all parts of the country, for the cooling of breweries, the manufacture of artificial ice, etc.

Some idea may be formed of the great establishment last mentioned (which covers two entire city blocks and employs two hundred workmen), when it is stated, that its products are made in tons' weight, many of them high priced, but some of which cost several dollars per ounce. This company sells its goods in nearly every part of the United States, and exports them to foreign countries. The superior quality of these goods gives them quick sale over a wide field of distribution.

GRANITE IRON-WARES.

St. Louis possesses one of the greatest manufacturing plants of this description of wares in any country. A beginning was made in a small way in 1859, until the buildings now cover an area of two city blocks of ground.

The body of granite iron-ware is made of sheet iron of superior quality, of a description which formerly was made only in England. But, by experience, it was found that the quality lacked uniformity of grade, and in order to obtain the required standard, the St. Louis manufacturers undertook to make it themselves, contrary to the opinion of sheet-iron manufacturers, who said such iron could not be made in this country. Notwithstanding, they purchased five acres of land within the city limits, built a rolling mill, and completed it in 1870. And, by skill and energy, they were early rewarded by making the desired quality of sheet-iron.

This mill is capable of producing twenty tons of sheet-iron daily. The process of the manufacture of granite iron-ware is briefly described as follows: The coating of sheet-iron is a highly vetrified glass, insoluble and impervious to vegetable acids, and approaches in this respect the properties of earthern, or porcelain wares. Granite iron-ware is preferable to earthern in all the qualities of strength, durability, non-breakableness, lightness, and cheapness; besides, its appearance is not injured by heat.

After various experiments, this enterprising firm produced their first perfect iron ware in 1874. Since then, their wares have been received with acceptance wherever they have been introduced in this country, or in foreign markets. The annual sales are very great, and the use of granite iron-ware is destined to become indispensable to many households.

U. S. INTERNAL REVENUE COLLECTIONS—IN THE FIRST DISTRICT OF MISSOURI. (ST. LOUIS.)

FREEMAN BARNUM, COLLECTOR.

DESIGNATION.	1884.	1885.	1886.	1887.	1888.*
Lists (chiefly banks)	5,955 04	1,345 25	5,702 98	4,424 74	3,700 26
Spirits Stamps . . .	1,879,372 50	1,923,295 90	2,063,721 10	1,847,665 80	1,335,410 10
Tobacco " . . .	1,818,562 27	2,231,705 78	2,484,204 41	3,222,774 00	3,200,714 26
Cigar " . . .	131,213 29	121,510 57	130,759 09	140,198 93	141,883 16
Snuff " . . .	3,863 00	3,322 28	3,589 80	3,777 56	4,045 16
Beer " . . .	995,694 13	975,222 81	1,116,817 34	1,293,945 51	1,379,425 75
Special tax Stamps	129,040 60	124,891 42	118,932 36	123,184 05	141,431 52
†Oleomargarine stps	. . . .	. . . .	. . . .	42 18	. . . .
Totals	4,963,700 83	5,381,294 01	5,923,727 08	6,636,012 77	6,206,640 21

MANUFACTURED TOBACCO.

St. Louis holds the first place—as the largest manufacturer of tobacco in the world! The amount on which tax was paid in the First Missouri District (of which St. Louis produced 96 per cent) in 1887, was 40,284,675 lbs., representing a value of $15,000,000.00, against 32,448,936 lbs. in 1886, valued at $11,500,000.00.

The total output of the United States for the fiscal year ending June 30, 1887, was 199,937,743 lbs., of which the First Missouri District produced 34,057,743 lbs., equal to 17 per cent. The increase over the year ending June 30, 1886, was 14,511,550 lbs., of which St. Louis produced about 30 per cent.

* NOTE.—The falling off in the revenue for 1888, was occasioned by the reduction in the output of highwines and whiskies, as will be noticed. The receipts of revenue on spirits stamps was $512,255.70 less than for 1887, otherwise, the total receipts, instead of being less, would have exceeded those for 1887.—*Author.*

† NOTE.—No oleomargarine factories here; the collections made were on illicit goods seized at this point, and released under compromise.

FIRST INTERNAL REVENUE COLLECTION DISTRICT,
Of which 96 per cent belongs to St. Louis.

CALENDAR YEAR.	Tobacco Manufactured. Lbs.	Amount Tax Paid.
1878	5,990,801	$1,440,716 84
1879	8,670,466	1,477,899 00
1880	12,889,784	2,063,549 45
1881	17,234,869	2,751,307 06
1882	17,170,190	2,728,525 82
1883	23,835,720	2,219,433 19
1884	22,631,104	1,818,562 27
1885	28,517,401	2,235,028 06
1886	32,448,936	2,484,204 41
1887	40,284,675	3,222,774 00
1888	40,060,020	3,200,774 26

FROM THE REVENUE OFFICE, WASHINGTON, D. C.
INTERNAL REVENUE RECEIPTS ON MANUFACTURED TOBACCO, FOR JANUARY, 1888 AND 1889.

DISTRICTS.	1888.	1889.
First Missouri, (St. Louis)	$ 240,561 05	$ 274,921 51
Fifth Kentucky	79,190 73	89,543 78
First Michigan	63,070 00	86,415 48
Fifth New Jersey	131,807 98	176,075 83
First Ohio	70,989 86	83,055 84
Second Virginia	130,702 00	123,640 42
Sixth Virginia	101,407 64	120,073 77
State of North Carolina	128,274 43	147,011 73

From which it will be seen that St. Louis manufactures more tobacco as the three States of Ohio, Kentucky and Michigan combined.

The manufactures of tobacco for 1884, 1885, 1886, 1887 and 1888, are classified as follows:

	1888. Pounds.	1887. Pounds.	1886. Pounds.	1885. Pounds.	1884. Pounds.
Plug Chewing..	35,543,164	35,491,829	27,916,690	23,809,253	18,488,399
Fine Cut	217,104	314,702	240,567	301,676	330,137
Smoking	4,249,035	4,478,144	4,291,679	4,364,394	3,763,226
Snuff	50,717	47,219	46,919	42,078	49,342
Totals	40,060,020	40,331,894	32,495,855	28,517,401	22,631,104

CIGARS.

CALENDAR YEAR.	Manufactured.	Amount of tax Paid.
1884	41,327,500	$121,094 40
1885	41,466,220	121,510 57
1886	43,586,363	130,759 09
1887	46,732,973	140,198 93
1888	47,294,380	141,883 16

THE BREWING INDUSTRY.

There are twenty-two breweries, whose great output is indicated by the revenue receipts, which amounted, in 1887, to $1,293,945.51 (paid as revenue tax); and, the number of gallons produced exceeded forty-three million![*] The capital employed in the brewing industry is several million dollars. The works give employment—inside and outside the establishments—to many thousands of operatives. Of all industries, the manufacture of beer affects more diversified interests than any other. Barley, hops, cooperage, bottles, coal, ice and water supply, men, horses, insurance, ships and railroads, are all necessary adjuncts. In 1887, 1,383,361 barrels were required for the output, and the export trade of bottled beer was beyond twenty-five million bottles.

THE ANHEUSER-BUSCH COMPANY.

The *export trade* is chiefly enjoyed by the Anheuser-Busch Company, which uses a process for the preservation of beer in all latitudes. The sales of this firm equaled a half million barrels in 1887. Its annual product exceeds all of the great single breweries of Europe or the United

---

[*] NOTE.—The number of gallons of beer produced in 1888, was 46,710,815.—*Author.*

States. This establishment consumes in barley annually over one million bushels, and three-fourths of a million pounds of hops. It uses a half million bushels of coal, and employs fifteen thousand cars annually in receiving and forwarding products and supplies. The freightage paid by this firm is a very large sum.

The "register" indicates the consumption of twenty-five million gallons of water used yearly in beer brewing, cooling and washing by this single company. They use twenty-five thousand tons of ice, notwithstanding the establishment is cooled by refrigerating machinery. The area of ground covered by the works of this company, comprises thirty acres, or one and a quarter million superficial feet of space. The wages paid exceed a half a million dollars annually.

Other establishments are not so large, but great, nevertheless. Some adequate idea may be formed of the money value of the brewing industry from a reference to *one* brewery only. A noted man in London—over one hundred years ago—looking upon a single brewing establishment, was asked, "why he took so much interest in it—not being an owner?" He replied, "because, sir, I see in and around me the potentiality of great riches!" Of a truth, then, the golden environment of St. Louis' twenty-two breweries possesses a value almost incalculable.

It is an interesting fact, that an English "syndicate" has purchased, at large figures, a number of *brewing plants* in different cities of the United States. Recently (February, 1889), its agents have made proposals to buy several of the great breweries of St. Louis, and, it is publicly stated, that all *refused to sell*, including the largest one of them all, which declined an offer of seven millions of dollars!

AMOUNT OF BEER MANUFACTURED IN ST. LOUIS, ANNUALLY,.
FOR TWELVE YEARS.

YEAR.	Barrels.	Gallons.
1877	471,232	14,608,192
1878	521,684	16,172,204
1879	613,667	19,023,677
1880	828,072	25,670,232
1881	959,236	29,739,313
1882	1,069,715	33,661,165
1883	1,100,000	34,100,000
1884	1,122,265	34,790,215
1885	1,086,032	33,666,992
1886	1,280,091	39,682,821
1887	1,383,361	43,575,872
1888	1,482,883	46,710,815

The exports direct to foreign countries during the year
1887, was equal to 1,924,108 quart bottles, of a value of
1887 $300,000.00.

WINES, THE PRODUCT OF MISSOURI VINEYARDS.

THE AMERICAN WINE COMPANY, ST. LOUIS.

This company—celebrated for its pure wines of superior
quality—was established in 1859, by Isaac Cook. It is
still continued in vigor and prosperity through the able
management of its president, a son of the founder. This
wine plant has become a leading one of the United States.
It associates St. Louis with the celebrity of the products
of the American Wine Company. Its "Imperial Sparkling Champagne" is celebrated both in Europe and
America. And, scarcely less noted is its "Boquette"
brand. The wine vaults of this company are 40 feet in

depth, and cover an area of 100 by 200 feet. They have a storage capacity of 150,000 gallons.

Another, the Stone Hill Wine Company, makes wines of the purest and most generous quality, from grapes of the vineyards of Hermann, Missouri. Still another, the "Sect Wine Company," makes all its wines from selected grapes. And, its champagne, "Koehler's Sect," and "still" wines, are widely known. The storage capacity of this company is 80,000 square feet, at their vaults, Nos. 2814 to 2824 South Seventh street. In addition to these there are several other wine companies.

MANUFACTURE OF CIDER AND VINEGAR.

There are six establishments engaged in the making of cider and vinegar; whose trade covers many States and Territories. Their cider especially has a very extensive sale.

A SUBURBAN RESIDENCE.

CHAPTER II.

THE ADVANTAGES OF ST. LOUIS AS A MANUFACTURING SITE FOR COTTON AND WOOLEN TEXTILE FABRICS AND FINE POTTERY WARES, PAPER, ETC.

In most of the productions of mechanical skill—known to other large manufacturing cities—St. Louis is found to be eminent, and in some pre-eminent, as a producer. It excels is tobacco, beer, fire-clay, white lead, shot, saddlery and harness products, and perhaps in a few others. But, in iron, lead, and other mineral productions, and in engines, boilers, water-pipe, fence and other wires; varied machinery, furniture, carriages, chemicals, and glass wares: besides, the results of many other valuable industries, St. Louis is a stalwart rival of other manufacturing cities in all the lines mentioned.

Nevertheless, in a few of the industries which flourish elsewhere, this city is deficient, especially in manufactures of cotton and woolen textile fabrics, fine pottery and paper. These are wanting, not because they *cannot* be made here cheaply, and sold profitably; but, in consequence of the need of the requisite skill and capital for employment in such valuable industries; any or all of which might be incepted, developed and conducted under conditions the most favorable and profitable.

The crude materials are to be had here at prime cost and in unlimited quantity; superadded is a great and growing *trade centre*, which affords facilities for the sale and distribution of many millions of dollars in value annually of such staple manufactures.

In the Seventh Part of this treatise, statistical tables may be found of the quantity of cotton and wool staples—raw materials—received annually at, and shipped through

this city to more distant parts, including cotton to Canada
and Europe, and wool to Philadelphia and Boston. These
great staples are sent here to be handled, as to their primary market, direct from the cotton fields and sheep ranges.
It will suffice to state, that for the last cotton year, ending
August 31st, 1888, two hundred and fifty million pounds
of cotton were sold at, and shipped through St. Louis. Of
wools for the calender year, ending December 31st, 1888,
there were received here to be sold on commission, exceeding twenty million pounds, not including through shipments of the staple.

But, since the sources of supply of cotton and wool
are so near at hand, the quantity available may be increased to any degree demanded for the supply of manufacturing plants, should they be established at St. Louis.

This city is a large market for paper, both in its consumption and distribution. A vast quantity of paper stock
is gathered in this city, and received from a wide range of
territory outside, sent hither to be marketed. Wood-pulp,
which enters so largely into paper making, might be obtained—delivered at this city—much cheaper than at any
other locality—East or West. It would be derived from
the extensive forests South and West.

In pottery clays and kaolin, the most vauable varieties
and qualities—pure and plastic—are found convenient to St.
Louis. Competent judges consider these clays equal to
the best European. Some descriptions, other than kaolin,
are as white as wheaten flour! They are quite accessible,
and in unlimited quantity.

The supply of labor available for cotton and woolen
mills is adequate. But, if once established, the supply
would not be limited either to the city or suburbs; it could
be drawn from numerous surrounding villages and towns,
and at justifiable "wage" rates. Ground for manufacturing
plants, and homes for a large number of operatives could be

had at reasonable valuations. Such measure of intelligence in the operatives—as is required in cotton and woolen mills—could readily be obtained, and trained up to the required standard.

Yet, when it is considered, how large a part of the work done in a modern manufactory is performed by machinery, the number of human hands and eyes to a thousand spindles or a hundred looms, is inconsiderable. In a modern factory, human labor and skill is reduced to a *minimum*. Invention has given to machinery such ability as formerly was possessed only by trained minds and able bodies.

At St. Louis, within easy reach of the raw materials and every other auxiliary for cheap production, to establish factories of cotton and woolen textiles, and mills for making paper and pottery, all that remains to be supplied are, *First*: enterprise and skill; *Secondly*: the requisite knowledge and capital. These, if suitably applied, and the existing advantages be ably availed of, success is reasonably assured.

The scale is weighted down on the side of St. Louis whenever any manufacturing enterprise is in contemplation requiring a convenient site and commanding home market, or both at the same time; but, where are also found, cheap fuel, abundant supplies of raw materials, and adequate labor in skill and volume.

ST. LOUIS UNITES IN ITS SINGLE SITE, THE POSSESSION OF
ALL THE RAW MATERIALS AT ORIGINAL COST,
THE ADVANTAGES OF THE FIVE GREAT MANU-
FACTURING SPOTS OF GREAT BRITAIN,
NAMELY: MANCHESTER, ROCHDALE,
BIRMINGHAM, SHEFFIELD AND
STAFFORDSHIRE, ONLY IN
A HIGHER DEGREE.

It can be truthfully said, that nature, which has provided a site so eligible, and furnished means and materials

of such magnitude, as are found at this city, for PRODUC-
TION and CONVERSION in so many departments of human
skill and industry, including artificial facilities and adjuncts
for their sale and distribution—all concentrated at a single
point—is a very rare spot in any country.

The natural gifts alluded to, joined to an extensive system of transportation, and inter-communication, have provided such facilities for the exchange and distribution of
products as to give this city most excelling advantages.

But, to some it will appear a large and questionable
statement to aver, that St. Louis unites in its site and surroundings most of the advantages in manufactures
that are possessed by the five great manufacturing spots
and places of Great Britain. Yet it is true! Manchester, Rochdale, Birmingham, Sheffield and Staffordshire are meant. But, in respect to *accessibility to the raw
materials*, both Manchester and Staffordshire have inferior
positions compared with this city. The first obtains its
cotton staple from distant foreign countries, and the latter
does not possess the number of varied and valuable clays
that are found at St. Louis and vicinity, but obtains material from the continent (of Europe). Rochdale also draws
its chief supply of wools from other countries.

It is well known that these five cities and localities
have been the great centres of the leading manufactures of
Great Britain, if not of all Europe and the world, for
many years past. Manchester chiefly in *cotton*, and Rochdale in *woolen textile fabrics;* Birmingham and Sheffield in
*cutlery, machinery, and in all the productions of iron,
brass, etc.;* and Staffordshire—an extensive area of factories—in *pottery* productions.

Only one of these cities exceeded in population the city
of St. Louis, namely: Manchester, which by the last
British census, 1881, contained a population of 517,649,
including the inhabitants of its twin sister, the town of

Salford, situated on the opposite side of the river Irwell. According to the same census, Rochdale had a population of 68,866; Birmingham of 343,787; Sheffield of 284,508, and Staffordshire, in a number of manufacturing towns— much scattered—an aggregate manufacturing population of about one hundred thousand.

St. Louis possesses within easy reach an unlimited supply of the best varieties of iron, lead, zinc, and manganese ores, besides fuel in coal and fuel-gas. Cotton and wool are obtained at home, and not from foreign and distant countries.

Wherefore, what should hinder the establishment at St. Louis of factories for the making of cotton and woolen textile fabrics, cutlery and pottery wares? Might not these manufactured goods pay as well as others which flourish here?

Hence, if the natural advantages found existing at St. Louis, are so freely offered, and the crude materials are so abundant and cheap, no further invitation or incentive to outside manufacturers and capitalists is necessary. Investigation would lead to knowledge, thence to action, and the latter to results. The intelligent man of business needs just sufficient information to enable him to find the road, then, he himself will gain all the knowledge required to accomplish a safe and satisfactory journey.

Capable men, who shall be led to make inquiry into the inducements offered for the establishment of cotton, woolen and paper mills, and potteries at St. Louis, will—if residing abroad—come and make thorough personal examination of the field. The field is most inviting, and worthy of the most careful investigation and complete consideration, by men of experience and skill in the manufacture of cotton and woolen textiles, pottery and paper.

To citizens, capitalists and owners of the real estate of this city, a simple word need only be addressed: Is it not a fact, that the rapid rise and progress of your city, as a great seat of commerce and manufactures, is to be attributed, not *too much* to its grand natural site and magnificent surroundings of rich and populous territory, but chiefly to the foresight and energy of its active men, who founded, first the factories, and then built the railroads to carry, spread and distribute their manufactured products into all the country around, and to numerous distant points.

We should not be willing simply—under the compulsion of increased demand—to enlarge existing manufacturing plants, but to create *new* ones, and especially in those lines—*made to our hand*—in the industries named and advocated.

Further, to the *great variety* of the manufactures and products of the mechanic arts, of this city, is to be attributed that celebrity which it enjoys as a manufacturing centre. In the days of the long range squirrel gun—suited as well for the red-skinned foe—the " Hawken" rifle, made at St. Louis, led all other arms in the equipment of the early pioneers of the great West. But, since that period, a hundred other instrumentalities of hand-craft and machinery, have been potent factors in laying the foundations and building the superstructure of St. Louis' greatness.

Now, at this favorable period, may not cotton, woolen and paper mills and potteries be added? They will help to hasten the full fruition of that period in the history of this city, spoken of in the inaugural of its first Mayor, two generations since, as the era " *of its mighty futurity!*" *

---

* NOTE.—Address of William Carr Lane to the " Aldermen," in 1823.—*Author.*

CHAPTER III.

THE MISSISSIPPI RIVER: ITS GREAT AND LASTING VALUE,
IN CONNECTION WITH AN ISTHMUS ROUTE TO THE
WEST COASTS OF NORTH AND SOUTH
AMERICA AND EASTERN ASIA.

" Upon the threshold now we stand;
    What shall the record be?
The future stretches far beyond
    Our vision's wildest sea.

*   *   *   *   *   *   *

" Thus, when we meet the problems
    Of our city's weal or woe,
We must meet them single handed—
    We must conquer as we go.

" Time waits for no man's hand to turn
    The furrow with the plow;
The future fades beyond our sight,
    In the 'eternal now.'"
                        —*Russell R. Dorr.*

THE "INLAND SEA." ITS FORCES BRIDLED, ITS POWERS IMPROVED—
AS EXPERIENCE AND SCIENCE DIRECT—THEN, ITS UTILITY
AS A NAVIGABLE HIGHWAY WILL BE REGAINED.

The averments of the caption are not novel, but refer
to a practical work and its grand results. They suggest a
theme, than which few could be as big with importance or
money value. They recall the priceless utility of the Mississippi prior to the building of railroads, and the falling
away of its use since the construction of those swift and
direct means of transit—the railroads—which carry the
freight and passengers of great districts of country many
times the traveling population and tonnage of forty years
ago. But, the river remains: the same mighty flood continues to flow, and is still capable of carrying the commerce of a continent! Shall this magnificent stream—the

14

match of which the globe does not furnish—traversing a
country so rich in resources of wealth, beauty, and rational enjoyment as alone could make life worth living—
lapse into a *water-shed*, mainly? Or, shall it be utilized as
the cheapest outlet for the farm products and the manufactures of the great valley, seeking a European, or Spanish American market? The answer loudly comes—"Use
it! Restore the prestige of the Mississippi; bring back
the former days of the river's 'glory,' only with brighter
effulgence!"

Not all the old boatmen, nor the thoughtful men, allow
of despondency, but see that "the coming event casts its
shadow before," when the King of Rivers shall resume his
sceptre! It is asked by the doubting, "when will that
great event come?" It will come when the Mississippi
River Commission—of able and scientific engineers—have
finished their work from the Missouri's mouth toward the
Gulf, or even sooner, when *direct* trade shall be opened
with Spanish America. But, it will flow in a mighty
stream when *an Isthmus route* for ships is accomplished.
Then, from all Pacific Ocean countries—including Asia—
will come that commerce which, before the Christian Era,
enriched Tyre and Alexandria. And, centuries after its
commencement, gave great opulence to Venice, Lisbon and
Genoa; and, later, to Amsterdam and London. We, of
St. Louis, can have the same priceless trade, only vastly
enlarged, provided, *we seek it*. But, it will be found by a
shorter and swifter route: Not by toiling caravans of
camels, or slow sailing ships requiring a year "in doubling
the Cape" and returning, but, by steamships, each month,
bringing and taking the commodities offered in exchange,
of which the other has not, and desires to possess, instead
of that of which either has too much.

The traffic of the globe *demands* a passage through the
narrow neck joining the two continents, just as the Suez

Canal became a necessity when the long voyage, via Good Hope, could no longer be afforded by the world of commerce.

It is not disputed, that there is sufficient enterprise and ready capital to construct both an Isthmus Canal and Railway, at an early day. The indications are encouraging that one or two through routes between the two great oceans will be opened prior to the commencement of the twentieth century, now only a decade distant.

Did not Columbus sail westward, expecting to find (not a midway continent, but) *a passage to Asia*, and to realize the old legend of an open sea (via an equatorial line), and the wishful dream of Europeans, who sighed that *thence* they might reach the " Far Cathay." *

Almost two hundred years had elapsed, after LaSalle planted a column at the Delta of the Mississippi, and proclaimed possession of the country on behalf of Louis Quatorze, in 1682, but still the same shallow mouths of the Mississippi remained. The delay in the settlement of the great valley was due, in larger part, to the too early day, and the effete Spanish and French governments dominating the region. But, when the period of Anglo-Saxon ownership arrived, in the purchase of "Louisiana," in 1803; Florida, in 1819; all the vast countries from Mexico, under the treaty of Guadaloupe Hidalgo, in 1848, and of the Gadsden purchase in 1853— at once the people and government of the United States took active measures for settlement of the Mississippi Valley, including the development of the Great River. And, in less than twenty-five years after the last mentioned acquisition of territory, the National Government, undertook to adapt the river at the mouth to the largest of marine ships with full ocean cargoes. Then, the "Jetties" were constructed at the Delta;

---

* NOTE.—The name given to China at and before Columbus' time.—*Author.*

and, by 1878, a permanent channel of thirty feet depth was successfully accomplished.

Cheap carriage of the cereal crops, destined for Europe from St. Louis, via New Orleans, by barges of *double* the present capacity, the transfer of manufactures and productions from ships at that port, to and from Spanish America, (and ultimately with the countries on both sides of the Pacific ocean, via Isthmus routes), are prospective means destined to become great factors of wealth, and of which St. Louis may avail by the use of ready skill and enterprise. A small beginning would shortly grow to large proportions, and hasten the fulfillment of St. Louis' great destiny as the foremost city of the mighty West! In fact, this city has the greatest possibilities in the heart of the Great Valley. It is necessary only to stretch out active and able hands to gather in greater wealth—through the interchange of our manufactures for the commodities of those countries—than all the treasure in the precious metals that has ever been, or shall yet be obtained from South, Central and North America combined!

The award by Congress of two million dollars—to the "Mississippi River Commission," in 1888, is indicative of no cessation of the interest felt by that body in the great work of improvements. But, much *larger annual appropriations* are needed to hasten its completion, and to adapt the character of the improvement to the necessary requirements of barges of double the present tonnage draught (for carrying grain enroute to Europe), and for marine ships, as well. The *suitable* improvement of the Mississippi, from the mouth of the Missouri or Illinois down, would make it—all things considered—the most valuable of all navigable rivers!

It is important, that a heartier interest—in and out of Congress—be aroused to give a greater impulse to this invaluable national work. The ablest of the nation's representatives, without regard to party, having always favored it, and even declared, that not the national *interest* only, but national *pride* demanded the doing of the work: therefore, it seems to be necessary only to make a vigorous appeal to Congress.

Whilst the River Commission is expending the appropriations *just as they are granted*—their work goes onward too slowly, and (for the want of larger annual awards) with only moderately beneficial results. Shall not enlightened representatives in Congress take special and favorable action tending to larger annual appropriations looking to the early completion of the work. Let the millions of people, who inhabit the vast territory drained by the Father of Waters, and are dependent upon cheap freights to the Gulf (and beyond) for their great cereal crops— be remembered! Railroads cannot, and never will compete successfully with an *improved* river in cheap freights on grain destined for European ports.

Science is yearly discovering, experience and observation are noting, besides new plans and instrumentalities are being devised—for the accomplishment of great works in engineering. Then, surely, the deepening and improving of the channel courses of the Mississippi only await their consummation—with the assurance of the desired utilization—by those means and methods which both science and experience shall prove the best.

It is assumed that, as problems in the task of river improvements come to be better understood, that the Mississippi shall be made to *dig out its own channel*, (as at the Jetties), and so deep as to carry its floods freely and harmlessly to the sea. If so, then hurtful inundations will be unknown, and thirty thousand square miles of cultivatable land— rich as that of old Egypt—will be reclaimed. But the grandest achievement of all will be direct trade with Span-

ish America, China, Japan, and all the Eastern countries
opened to Commerce.*

SHALL TRADE BE OPENED BETWEEN SAINT LOUIS AND SPANISH AMERICA?

"From India, from the region of the Sun,
    Fragrant with Spices,—that a way was found,
A channel opened, and the golden stream
    Turned."   —Samuel Rogers.

Through the splendid enterprise and adventurous hero-
ism of the Portuguese navigators and merchants, who
"doubled" the Cape of Good Hope, with their pioneer
ships, about the end of the fifteenth century, and
introduced to their city of Lisbon the priceless "India
Trade." This they accomplished against great opposition
of jealous Mohammedan opponents and native rulers. And,
the prize was only obtained after fearful losses of life and
capital in the value of ships—lost and destroyed in battle
and storms of the seas—during twenty years of the
contest, which ended in establishing a trade that enriched
Portugal and ultimately all western Europe!

After the lapse of four hundred years, as rich as a
prize awaits the aroused ambition and enterprise of the
manufacturers and merchants of St. Louis, in the Spanish
American trade. They are not required to fit out armed fleets,
at great expense, filled with fighting men and their costly
outfit. They are not compelled to wait a score of years
before laying hands on the prize to be obtained only after
huge sacrifices of men and money. They are not obliged
to make a voyage of twenty thousand miles—twice round-
ing a stormy cape—and consuming a year nearly in the
circular voyage. They are not constrained to lose a year's

---

s NOTE.—The American diplomatic representative (Mr. Childs, of Missouri)
to Cochin China, has only recently told us, that country "uses an immense quantity
of wheaten flour, and is very favorably disposed to trade with the United States."
                                                            —Author.

interest on the capital invested, nor to send coined money with which to purchase the desirable commodities which they need!

On the contrary—under conditions the most favorable and inviting—the merchants and manufacturers may send their goods, wares and machinery in lieu of money, and find it more acceptable *in barter* than cash could be. They are required to consume not more than one-sixth to one-twelfth the time in the round voyage—the distance being in similar proportion less—and with only slight loss in interest on the capital invested. They are not compelled to equip armaments, nor fight battles, nor to wait many years until rewards shall come and profits flow into their treasury!

How different the conditions under which St. Louis may be enabled to grasp a prize greater than that which the hardy and hopeful Portuguese risked their lives and money! The people of Spanish America are not enemies, they are friends. No hostile hands are raised to repel, but friendly ones are extended to receive and welcome our mariners, supercargos and goods. They are anxious to obtain our manufactures, and to open reciprocal trade—upon terms so favorable, that it is surprising to find them offering *rewards*—in subsidies of money and exceptional commercial privileges—as inducements; and, as if to *constrain* us to visit them and to establish mutual relations of friendship and trade.

MAY NOT THE MISSISSIPPI BE NAVIGATED BY MARINE STEAM-
SHIPS IN TRADE WITH MEXICO, CENTRAL
AND SOUTH AMERICA?

The Great River has been appropriately called an " Inland Sea!"* in consideration of its mighty volume of water.

---

*NOTE.—That distinguished and able man, John C. Calhoun, was chosen presi-
dent of a Convention, held at Memphis, in 1836,—composed of delegates from all the
Valley States, to urge upon Congress the improvement of the water courses of
the great district; and, in his speech, he called the Mississippi the " Inland Sea."
Mr. Calhoun, although voting in Congress against the " Cumberland turnpike road"
bill, advocated large appropriations for the improvement of the Great River,
and branches.—*Author.*

Therefore, marine ships may navigate it—as well as any
other sea—provided, that their draught does not exceed the
channel depths. A marine vessel, constructed to navigate
the open sea and inland seas or rivers as well, will be a
steamship, but mast rigged, as is customary. Yet, if built
after the ordinary models of inland steamboats, it would
not be adapted to marine navigation.

Nevertheless, it is claimed by Andrew H. Lucas, of
St. Louis, that he has by his invention of a double, or
cloven hull, and an adjustable keel, accomplished the necessary conditions in the construction of a river-marine
steamship—adapted at once to river and ocean service.
He cries Eureka! and promises with his ship to make round
voyages between this city and Spanish America, and to
calculate with certainty dates for regular departure and
arrival.

A company has been formed by Mr. Lucas and his
friends, who are actively striving to build a trial steamship of one thousand tons carrying capacity. They wish
to construct the vessel during the ensuing twelve months,
that she may enter the trade in the spring of next year,
1890. The company has obtained the offer of a valuable
subsidy in money from the Argentine Republic, together
with the most encouraging inducements in special commercial privileges. And, not alone from that republic, but
from Mexico and several other governments of Central
and South America, offers of both subsidies and privileges,
most rare and valuable, have been received by the company,
which has availed of direct and influential correspondence
with those enterprising states.

The question of *direct trade*—by water—between St.
Louis and Spanish America is of such commanding importance to the manufacturers and merchants, as to be
supremely worthy their attention, to the end that a thorough and complete investigation of the subject, in all its

bearings, be made. What more engaging visions of wealth could be presented to the thoughtful investigator, and enterprising man than through *direct trade* with Spanish America—a country so rich in the rarest and most desirable natural productions? These, St. Louis buys in immense quantity, and pays the profits of two or three middle men. This city also loses the profit on its manufactures, which could be bartered for the productions of that country, besides having the carrying both ways.

There is more wealth to be acquired in this trade than the Spanish invaders obtained from the accumulated wealth of the Incas, which once obtained, ended forever! While trade with Spanish America would flow toward us in an unceasing golden stream!

THE LUCAS STEAMSHIP: IS THE COST OF AN EXPERIMENTAL SHIP JUSTIFIED BY THE VALUE OF THE SPANISH-AMERICAN TRADE IT PROPOSES TO REACH?

The Lucas invention is of St. Louis birth, and, as such it deserves friendly consideration. Its novelty and grand pretensions, have attracted the curious attention of citizens at large, including citizens of other states, and of foreign countries. It has drawn the gratified attention and consideration of the Mexican, Central and South American Republics. But, few persons have undertaken to express any opinion of its adaptation to the peculiar field of navigation it proposes to enter—that of river-marine service, as a carrier of freight (and passengers, the latter at first incidentally) between this city and Spanish-American ports —assuming to occupy the place of the *pioneer* in trade with our rich neighbor lands.

No competent critic has yet been found to deny that it has merit, and no one has yet pronounced adversely upon its adaptation to accomplish the results it claims to be able to secure. Therefore, both the public and private opinion

is in abeyance, but with a preponderance decidedly in favor
of the Lucas ship.

Nevertheless, no person who is unacquainted with ship-
building, or the special requirements of a steamship
—suited to the trade of those parts of Spanish-America
with which St. Louis desires to trade—is able to give

"THE LUCAS MODEL SHIP."

any reliable opinion relative to the merits of the St. Louis
invention. And, such persons scarce dare venture to ask
the question: Is the Lucas ship worthy, does it deserve
encouragement and a trial? These, however, are perti-
nent questions, just at the present time, when the mind
of many persons is turned, not only inquiringly, but
solicitously toward Spanish-America, as a most promising
Eldorado!

The prevalent opinion is that the Lucas steamship
would be an *experiment!* Let that opinion be admitted,
in order to follow the inquiry to a satisfactory conclusion.
Then, on the other hand, it may be asked of a doubter,
whether he has any *other* plan, or, has any other model of a
steamship been offered for trial? Has another man a different and better plan of a ship by which to secure the *desideratum* of a combined marine-river ship, and one capable of
carrying an adequately paying cargo to the tropics, and
return from thence with a corresponding load of paying
freight volume?

The answer is: "No man has any substitute for the
Lucas model!" Then, in view of the possibilities and
known facts, the expenditure of a sum necessary to build
a steamship on the Lucas model is both desirable and justifiable. It could not fail wholly of success, and if it
succeeded in part only—it is most worthy a trial. And, if
the money invested in a steamship on the Lucas model
were to be a total loss, (which is impossible), still the
investment would be a proper business adventure, in view
of the great probability of its success. It would be a
grand event if, through its instrumentality, a priceless
trade should be gained, whose extent and value would
yearly increase and continue during the lives of at least
the present generation, if not for all time!

CHAPTER IV.

TRADE BETWEEN SAINT LOUIS AND SPANISH AMERICA BY STEAMSHIP.

"Others, like merchants, venture trade abroad."—*Shakespeare.*

"He set himself wholly to mind the East India trade."—*Burnet.*

The sailing ship, as a carrier of commerce, was employed hundreds of years prior to the Christian Era, by nations engaged in foreign trade. The "caravan" of laden camels, was admirably suited for inter-traffic by land routes, as between Tyre and Persia and countries beyond. Also, between Carthage and the interior parts of Africa.

Tyre, Carthage and Alexandria were the principal maritime cities of that early period. It is presumed, if not conclusively known, that the ships sent by Hiram, King of Tyre, and Solomon, King of Jerusalem, made their voyages to "Ophir," via the route of the present Suez Canal — reconstructed by the enterprise of DeLesseps — and, *coasting* the countries they visited, returned by the same route, after a "voyage of three years." At a later period, under conditions of improved construction, the Tyrean and Carthagenian ships were the "best sailors afloat." The admirable model of the Carthagenian ships, having been copied by the Romans, they were enabled to assail Carthage successfully, by utilizing their own sailing squadrons. The fine model of the Roman vessels encouraged

Cato to pronounce his famous fulmination — presaging war — "Carthage must be destroyed!"

The adventurous Phœnicians, with a commendable zeal to extend their commerce and enrich themselves, sailed out of the Mediteranean Sea and into the Atlantic Ocean, "*without a compass*," and with rudder only!

Are the merchants and manufacturers of St. Louis less adventurous and enterprising than the Phœnician "merchant princes," after the lapse of more than two thousand years, and having the use of all the improvements and discoveries of the intervening period—including steamships—a thorough knowledge of navigation and the mariner's compass? They would not admit any personal inferiority, while rightfully claiming superiority!

Then, shall not the merchants and manufacturers of St. Louis imitate, and outdo, the successful Tyreans? And shall they not declare after the manner of the Roman Senator, whilst (not "carrying a war into Africa," but) sending their ships with peaceful intentions to Spanish America, "*the trade, it must be established!*"

No great improvement was made in the model of sailing ships until after the discovery of the Mariner's Compass. But, shortly after that event—coming near the period of the discovery of the art of printing—it ushered into the field of commerce a fresh impulse of adventurous enterprise, (just as printing developed a new era of intellectual light!) The Portuguese, in 1497, (under the famous Vasco de Gama, with his ships), "doubled" the Cape of Good Hope, reached the "farther Inde," and returned to Lisbon, bringing the wealth of the "East."

That wealth—in the rare and costly fabrics in silks, fine muslins, stuffs and shawls of Persia and China ; and the spices of the East Indian Archipelago and Arabia—the opulent city of Venice (the "*lady* of the Adriatic"), had long been accustomed to monopolize. Her ships and "supercargos," or agents, regularly met the caravans from Eastern and Central Asia, at the ports of Asia Minor and Egypt. But at length, the pre-eminence of Venice is about to depart and the golden tide to be turned into a port of western Europe. Her opulence and commanding influence are to become only traditions of her mighty past!

> " Thus did Venice rise,
> Thus flourish, till the unwelcome tidings came,
> That a way was opened, and the golden stream
> Turned to enrich another. Then she felt
> Her strength departing, and at last she fell."
> —*Samuel Rogers.*

Columbus, guided by the compass, sailed confidingly westward, seeking a more direct water route to " India." At the present day, we are certain to reach the country we wish, and know the route where to find unmeasured wealth.

Fulton's successful experiment, in 1807, with his ship, the Clermont, the first complete steamboat, was a great surprise—even to his friends—to whom he had made known his plans and confident belief in the perfection of his steamboat.

But, it was not until thirty-one years later, that the ocean steamships, the Sirius and Great Western, reached the city of New York from England, having been the earliest steamships to cross the Atlantic. At the present day, steam has largely superceded sailing ships, especially between distant parts of the globe. Steam vessels have been adopted by every commercial nation, now that speed has become the prime element of success.

Steamships are employed in the navigation of the great rivers of all countries. Only such as are of shallow or light draught can enter the smaller rivers, or cross the " bars " at the entrance of greater rivers, upon which some of the most important cities of commerce are located; and, whose surrounding country is amongst the richest of any, especially upon the continent of America. The more profitable carriers of passengers and freight—the larger steamships—are enabled to enter only the bays and great rivers of the Atlantic coast and Gulf of Mexico, and are mainly employed in ocean navigation.

The improvements in the model of ocean steamships—since the first successful attempt to cross the Atlantic—consists chiefly in means of propulsion, economy of fuel and greater speed. Eighteen to twenty-one days were employed in the earlier years for the transit of the best steamships between Europe and America, whilst seven are now sufficient for the passage.

The steamship demanded at the present period, should be one of such model, that whilst uniting speed, strength and large carrying capacity, shall also be adapted to enter the smaller rivers, cross bars at the mouth of rivers, and serve the purpose of marine and river navigation—all without "lighterage" of cargo. Such a steamship is the *desideratum* of our day! The *size* of such a ship must be determined by the voyage and ports she is intended to "make." For such trade as St. Louis would seek earliest in Spanish America, the size would probably be one thousand tons carrying capacity; and, the ship would visit such ports as should enable her to make monthly round voyages.

Some one will inquire, "Can such a novel or useful steamship be constructed, and is it reasonable to suppose that inventive genius could accomplish such a wonder in river-marine ship architecture?" A suitable answer might be, that the wonders accomplished in mechanics in the construction of the *land plow*,—including mould board and coulter—within the last generation, would encourage the expectation of a great improvement upon the model of ships with which to *plow the waters!*

The improvement must be in the *keel* of the ship. It was *that* which enabled the American yacht, at the last

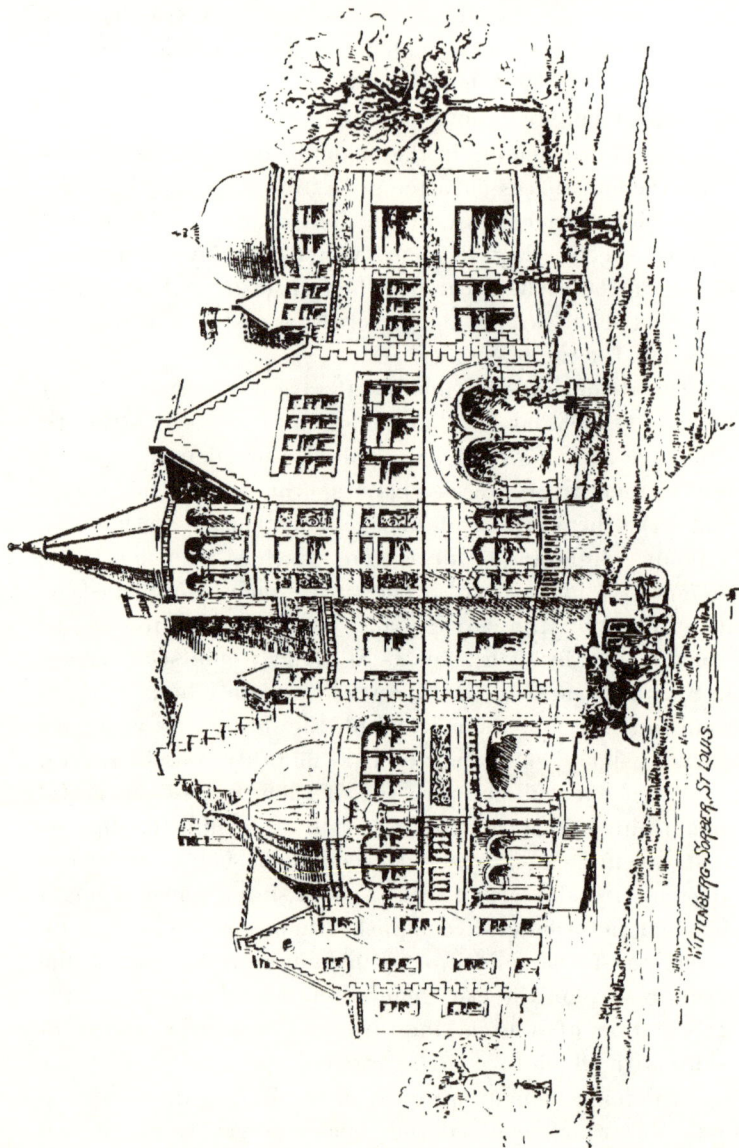

RESIDENCE OF MR. JOHN W. KAUFFMAN.

trial of speed with her British rival, to still maintain the supremacy—leaving the latter far in her wake!

It is in the keel, that Andrew H. Lucas claims to have found the key to unlock the shallow waterways of the continent, and to cross bars at the mouth of bays and great rivers—with a steamship carrying an ample cargo.

If he has truly solved the problem, which has hitherto been sealed and beyond the "ken" of ship builders, then, wealth in the commerce of nations will be increased a thousand fold! And, some of the most valuable productions of the interior of continents, which now perish to the value of millions annually, will be saved!

GERMAN PROTESTANT ORPHANS' HOME.
TAKES CHILDREN WITHOUT REGARD TO NATIONALITY, OR CREED OF THE PARENTS.

15

CHAPTER V.

A DESCRIPTION OF THE MISSISSIPPI AND MISSOURI RIVERS.

> " Beautiful, sublime and glorious:
> Mighty, majestic, foaming, free—"
> —*Bernard Barton.*

Well might the Mississippi be called the Great River, or the " Inland Sea," in consideration of the mighty volume of its waters which flow in ceaseless majesty ever onward to the ocean! But the great magnitude of the Missouri and Mississippi rivers are worthy of special mention.

The Basin of the Mississippi, of which St. Louis is the key, comprises an area of 2,455,000 square miles. It extends through thirty degrees of longitude and twenty-five of latitude, an area greater than that of all Europe, when Russia, Sweden and Norway are left out of the account.

The basin of the Upper Mississippi has an area of 169,000 square miles, and a height of 1,680 feet above the sea level.

The Mississippi at 1,330 miles above its mouth, or at the confluence of the Missouri, has a width of 5,000 feet, and a mean discharge of 105,000 cubic feet per second. The Missouri is 3,000 feet wide at its mouth, with a mean discharge of 120,000 cubic feet per second, and the area of the basin is 518,000 square miles. The Lower Mississippi has a width of 2,470 feet, at its mouth, and its basin comprises an area of 1,244,000 square miles. Its mean discharge per second is 675,000 cubic feet. The Mississippi and its tributaries afford an internal navigation of 9,000 miles for steamboats, and 6,000 miles more for flat boats and timber rafts. The main stream, from its mouth to St. Paul, is 1944 miles, and from St. Anthony's Falls to Sauk Rapids, 80 miles. The Missouri is navigable at ordinary water to a point 60 miles above the mouth of the Yellowstone, distance 1,894 miles, and at high water to Fort Benton, 2,644 miles, from its confluence with the Mississippi.

THE DELTA OF THE MISSISSIPPI.

The mighty flood, flows in silent majesty ever onward!

Don Alonzo Alvarez Peneda coasted the Gulf of Mexico with his ships, in 1519, and discovered the mouths, or Delta of the Mississippi River, which he named the Rio Grande del Espiritu-Santo, (or River of the Holy Ghost).

The story of the Chevalier La Salle's expedition from Canada, in batteaux, with a small party, the first to descend the Mississippi to its mouth, his arrival at the Delta, in 1682; the planting of the Cross, and taking possession of the country in the name of his sovereign, Louis XIV, King of France, is familiar to all readers. But, it remained for later Frenchmen to explore and survey the Great River at its mouth. This was done in 1720, and a description of the Mouths, or "Passes" was then given, but not accurately until in later years.* The three principal Passes are known and designated as the South-West

---

* NOTE.—Mons. Panger, a French royal engineer, in 1720, by order of the Governor, (Bienville), made a survey of the Delta of the Mississippi, and of all the passes, bars and channels below the (present) site of New Orleans; by which it was determined that the site selected by the Governor might be made a commercial port of the province, and shortly afterwards the principal Depot and Offices of the "India Company" were established at that site, to which was given the name of New Orleans.—*Author.*

THE ROE BUILDING.

Pass, South Pass, and Pass a'Loutre. From skillful surveys, by order of the United States, it was found, that the first and last named discharged each forty-five per cent, and the South Pass ten per cent of the volume of the River into the Gulf; that the depth of water on the bar at Pass a'Loutre was about twelve feet, at South Pass eight feet, and at South-West Pass fifteen feet. These surveys were made prior to the commencement of the building of the "Jetties," which were constructed by that able and distinguished engineer, Captain James B. Eads, of St. Louis, and completed in 1878. The year following it was ascertained, that the depth of water in the South Pass—improved by the construction of the Jetties—was increased to thirty feet seven inches, and now—after the lapse of ten years—the depth is no less.

Near the Pass a'Loutre is the site of the old " Balize " village, (settled by the French more than one hundred and fifty years since). After that name, that Mouth, or Pass of the River, has always been designated and called the " Balize."

The Delta of the Great River is full eleven hundred miles—by the devious windings of the stream—from Cape Girardeau, Missouri, which is fifty miles above the confluence of the Ohio with the Mississippi. Scientists have confidently asserted, that at a remote period in the ages past, the Delta of the Mississippi existed no lower down than at, or just north of the present mouth of the Ohio. Probably it was near the "Cape," (at which point the level of the River, at low water, is 285 feet above the sea at the Gulf), and, that then — when the ocean extended north to *that* point—the waters of the Mississippi must have fallen over rocks one hundred feet higher than the Falls of Niagara!

Rocks have been located and found *in situ*, by competent civil engineers, on both sides of the Mississippi, twenty

miles below the mouth of the Ohio. Trees and logs have
been found, by boring and excavating, at great depths in
numerous places along the course of the Mississippi towards
the Gulf; and it has long been known, that a vast volume
of drift in trees, logs, etc., find lodgment at the Delta, and
—together with millions of tons of soil in solution constantly descending the mighty River—they gradually form
in compact masses of solid land, and thus extend the Delta
further and further into the Gulf of Mexico. In the same
manner it is claimed, that the soil of the Great Valley was
gradually formed during the long years of the past.

HURST'S HOTEL.

CHAPTER VI.

THE GREAT STEEL BRIDGE SPANNING THE MISSISSIPPI AT SAINT LOUIS.

The bridge when it was completed, fifteen years since, ranked amongst the few great steel arched bridges of the world, and received the universal admiration. Some details of this magnificent structure might interest the general reader and others who have had only a " passing " sight of the bridge. Two towering piers rise out of the water— between the abutments on either shore of the "Father of Waters,"—all are of hewn stone. Three graceful arches of steel span the intervening spaces, each 520 feet in length. The huge piles of masonry rest upon the solid rock, which underlies the river bed. The west pier is planted a depth of ninety-one feet. The foundation of the east pier is one hundred and twenty-seven feet below high water. The great iron "caisson," at its bottom, was sunk eighty-two feet to the solid rock, and in it was built the foundation—of cemented stone. The abutments are one hundred and thirty-five feet below high water. The masonry in the bridge measured sixty-nine thousand cubic yards; the iron weighed six million three hundred thousand pounds; and the steel arches drew four million seven hundred and eight thousand pounds. The bridge is of two stories, and the great arches carry two double railway tracks. Over all, is a highway of seventy-five feet width, for carriages and foot passengers. The bridge is without roof, and its top elevation affords a fine view of the river and surroundings. The length of the bridge between the abutments is 2,225 feet. The clear " headway " is fifty-five feet above ordinary high water. This magnificent

work—of skillful engineering and mechanical ability—required seven years in its construction, and was finished in 1874. The distinguished builder, James B. Eads, also constructed the "Jetty" system, at the Delta of the Mississippi, under contract with the National Government. The well deserved fame of that eminent citizen has served to heighten the reputation of St. Louis for producing capable and noted men. The achievements of James B. Eads, as a practical engineer, affords a conspicuous illustration that the acts of a useful citizen raises both himself, and the community in which he lives and labors, to a higher plane of honor and distinction.

But, great credit is due to all the other promoters and builders of this great railway bridge—the municipality and public spirited private citizens. Citizens devoted a munificent share of their private fortunes in taking the stock of the bridge company, and looked beyond their personal interest in order to serve the interests of the community. These citizens deserve to have their names cut upon a monumental shaft—in testimony of their splendid enterprise, and in grateful attestation of their self-devotion to the interests of their fellow citizens.

CITY OF EAST SAINT LOUIS, (ILLINOIS).

The young City of East Saint Louis, is situated on the east side of the Mississippi river, in the county of Saint Clair, and State of Illinois. It lies directly opposite the City of St. Louis, and was, previously to twenty years since, known as Illinois Town. The two sides of the Great River are connected by several steam ferries, and the magnificent steel railway bridge. The latter will shortly be supplemented by another similar structure, only of even greater strength. The new bridge will cross the Mississippi, two miles north of the present bridge, at Venice, situated in Madison County, State of Illinois, to Ferry street, St. Louis.

The numerous railways, which approach St. Louis from the East side of the River, pass through East St. Louis — to cross the Great Bridge, thence via the Tunnel to reach the Union Railway Depot in St. Louis. The distance, from the Eastern approach of the bridge to the end of the Tunnel at the depot, slightly exceeds two miles.

East St. Louis has a municipal government similar to that of St. Louis, and is a rising town. It is specially mentioned in this treatise in order to state, that it is *no part* of the city of St. Louis, but it has a most intimate relation to the great city on the opposite side of the river, and its low topography strongly contrasts with the elevated site of this city. A bluff of limestone rock, formerly skirted a portion of the river front, near which commence a succession of grand plateaux—reaching far back into the country, and extending many miles up and down the stream—giving grandeur to the elevated site of St. Louis. The interests of East St. Louis are closely identified with those of its greater neighbor—much like Jersey City towards New York City.

East St. Louis sits on a part of the river front of the great "American Bottom" of alluvial land, and was subject to an annual inundation prior to the construction of a *dyke* at the edge of the river. But, its street level required, (and still requires) to be *raised*, in which respect it resembles the original surface of Chicago. East St. Louis has a very promising future.

THE RAILWAY TUNNEL—CONSTRUCTED BENEATH THE MOST POPULOUS PART OF THE CITY.

A description of the bridge would be incomplete unless accompanied by another of the tunnel, which is the indispensable adjunct of the former and supplies all the requisite facilities of transit through the city without interfering with the use of the streets. This was accomplished by cutting below the apex of the bluff, which fringes the river to the height of thirty feet above the level of Front street. The elevation of the bridge above the surface of "high water" is at the *minimum*, with a suitable regard to navigation. The tunnel commences at the western end of the bridge, at Third street, follows Washington avenue to Seventh street, then turns toward the southwest to Eighth street, and pursues the line of the latter to Clark avenue, at which point a short *open* cut brings it to the level of the railroad tracks (at the Union Depot), which are laid upon the depression of what was formerly " Mill-Creek " valley.

The length of the tunnel is 4,886 feet. Its construction was accomplished by cutting downward from the street level. A wall of massive masonry was built on either side, and one in the center, over which two parallel arches of brick, of great strength, were constructed, each from the center wall. Finally, the earth was replaced, and the top surface reconstructed in the best manner. The tunnel has two tracks, with a massive division wall. A collision of trains is an impossibility.

The quantity of earth which was removed in digging the tunnel, measured two hundred and fifteen thousand cubic yards. The walls required fifty thousand cubic yards of stone, and the arches thirteen million bricks. The height of the tunnel is sixteen feet, six inches. Its length from the southwestern end—including the bridge—to the level of the railway approach at East St. Louis, is two miles and a twelfth.

The cost of the bridge and tunnel construction, was six and a half million dollars; but, through the accrued interest, damages, etc., the amount was swelled to nearly ten million! The time occupied in the construction of these gigantic works was seven years. The bridge is a marvel of modern engineering. It is claimed, that no other bridge of the arch or truss pattern, will bear comparison with it for strength, and beauty!

CHAPTER VII.

THE PRESENT PROSPECTS AND FUTURE OF EAST END IMPROVED PROPERTY.

It is a question that has been fruitful of earnest discussion and debate in community—especially by the much interested owners—what shall the future be of the old East End real estate? Once the seat and center of all the wholesale and retail business of this city—in all departments of merchandise and manufactures—shall it continue to decline in income value, or does it possess an intrinsic quality—ever clinging to it—which, together with active effort favoring, shall prove the possession of a vital power that shall raise it up again to special usefulness and much greater value?

It is, however, a fair opinion—based on knowledge and observation — that the old East End improved property reached its lowest point of practical valuation in 1888; and, that during the current year of 1889, this opinion will be conclusively justified by its rising appreciation.

No *dislike* prompted the earlier and later removals from the old district; but the dealers in dry goods, clothing, boots and shoes, hats, etc., required more capacious and eligible buildings — suited to the times and a rapidly expanding trade, which demanded the change. The growth of the trade of this city still requires many more stores and warehouses than the old business section supplied or could ever furnish.

It is certain, however, that the movement westward to larger and more eligible buildings would not have commenced as early and been so generally followed by those

classes of merchants, had suitable accommodations in store
buildings been offered by property owners in the shape of
new stores and warehouses. They would, in numerous cases,
have remained.   And, at the present time, it is incumbent
on owners of East End property for their profit, more than
property salvation, to reconstruct and rebuild their stores
— such as shall conform to the present greatly improved plans, including modern conveniences, taste and
strength.

The eligibility of situation of East End property can not
be taken away from it.   It possesses advantages for certain leading lines of valuable business—than which no other
locality is as suitable—and, the location will continue to be
preferred.   But, a necessary condition attaches, that new
and enlarged buildings of modern descriptions shall be
reared upon the foundations of the old buildings, which
forty years since were large, strong and fine enough, but
are no longer adequate to the business requirements and
tastes of the present day.

ST. PAUL'S GERMAN EVANGELICAL CHURCH.
NINTH ST. AND LAFAYETTE AV.

THE CITY OF ST. LOUIS OF TO-DAY.

PART SEVENTH.

CHAPTER I.

THE MERCHANTS' EXCHANGE OF ST. LOUIS.

"The busy mart, let Justice still control
Weighing the guerdon to the toil."—*Schiller.*

OFFICERS OF THE MERCHANTS' EXCHANGE, FOR THE ENSUING YEAR—
FROM JANUARY 9th, 1889.

At an election held at the Merchants' Exchange, January 9th, 1889, the following gentlemen were elected for the ensuing year:

CHARLES A. COX, *President.*

ALEXANDER EUSTON, *First Vice-President.*

HUGH A. ROGERS, *Second Vice-President.*

DIRECTORS:

1888-'89.	1889-'90.
FRANK GAIENNIE,	CHARLES F. ORTHWEIN,
CHARLES P. BURR,	I. B. AMBS,
HENRY W. CHANDLER,	JOHN B. GONDOLPHO,
ISAAC M. MASON,	R. M. HUBBARD,
JOHN C. FEARS.	C. H. SPENCER.

Twelve gentlemen were appointed to the Committee of Appeals, and ten to that of Arbitration.

And, GEORGE H. MORGAN was re-appointed *Secretary and Treasurer.*

This important body of business men are the representatives of every branch of the commerce, manufactures and business of St. Louis. Their influence is com-

mensurate with all the great interests of the city. The
Merchants' Exchange is not solely devoted to the promotion
of the private and personal business of its members, but,
it originates and engages in works and measures of great
importance looking to the advancement of the public welfare. The membership of the Exchange numbers nearly
thirty-three hundred, and comprises men of the highest
standing for character, ability and wealth—accustomed
to enterprise, activity and push. In energy and intelligence, they are not surpassed by any similar organization,
and keep fully abreast-of-the-times!

The Exchange Building is situated at Third, Chestnut
and Pine streets. It fronts 187 feet on each of the last
two streets, and has a grand frontage of 233 feet and
main entrance on Third street.

A portion of the basement on Third street is utilized
for eligible offices. Three lofty stories rise above, and are
also occupied for offices—on either side of ample hall-
ways. At the north end, are the offices of the board of
directors, secretary and treasurer. The reading-room
adjoins these, and contains files of the leading commercial
journals of the United States and foreign countries.

A spacious double stairway—constructed of massive
black walnut in elaborate carved work—leads to the entrance of the Grand Hall of the Exchange. The Hall is
221 1-2 feet in length, 92 feet 10 inches in width, and 80
feet in height. An elevated gallery occupies the four sides
of the hall. The lofty ceiling is finished in elaborate fresco
work and paintings in panels. In their general details
these are strikingly elegant, but the *tout en semble* is grand!
The chandeliers and jets, when lit at night, give out the
appearance of such splendor as to bring to mind the palaces
in the "Tales of the Arabian Nights!"

Few public halls in the United States are equal to the
Merchants Exchange in size and splendor. The west

half of the building accommodates the Grand Chamber above, and below, a spacious hall of entrance and exit from, and to Pine and Chestnut streets. It comprises all the ordinary adjuncts found in other halls and offices which such great public commercial edifices require.

Daily sessions of the Merchants' Exchange are held in the Grand Hall during 'change hours, which open at 11 o'clock A. M., and close at 1:15 P. M. Visitors to the floor are only admitted through a member.

The entire cost of the Exchange Building, including the grounds, was eighteen hundred thousand dollars ($1,800,-000.00). Its exterior walls are principally of Warrensburg, Missouri, sandstone. It was completed and opened for use in December, 1875. Well may this large, active and able body of the business men of Saint Louis be proud of their grand and useful structure!

THE DECORATION OF THE GRAND HALL OF THE MERCHANTS EXCHANGE.

The ceiling, including the cornice and border, is 99 by 215 feet, but, exclusive of them, is 50 by 179 feet, and is divided into three compartments or panels, each containing a beautiful painting in colors.

The figures of the centre panel are emblematic of St. Louis—surrounded by typical groups of the agricultural, mineral and industrial products of the Mississippi Valley. The groups of figures at the north end of the hall are representatives from the four quarters of the globe — bringing their various offerings to the Great West; and, with arms outstretched, they offer their products in exchange. The two figures, below these groups, are representatives of the West and include the Mississippi River.

The other two panels are in divisions, each containing four smaller panels—with paintings, etc., representing the industries of the State of Missouri, in basso-relievo.

The nationalities represented in the north panel, are characteristic types of European nations—England, Germany, Italy, France, Scotland, and Ireland—and form a central group. Russia, Switzerland, Spain, Sclavonia, European Turkey, and Greece are represented by the surrounding groups.

The south panel partly represents characteristic types of Asia and Africa, including Arabia, Egypt, Judea, China and Japan, which form the principal group, and are surrounded by Ethiopia, Caucasia, India, Persia, Abyssinia and Mongolia.

The cornice of the ceiling, (including the spandrels and lunettes over the windows), forms a border twenty feet in width, and contains the names of the States of the Union, together with the merchant flags of the Nations in panel work.

ST. MARK'S EVANGELICAL LUTHERAN CHURCH.
(REV. M. RHODES. D.D.)

CHAPTER II.

THE SAINT LOUIS COTTON EXCHANGE.

OFFICERS FOR THE YEAR TO END, OCTOBER 1889.

GUSTAV ROSENBERG, President.

T. C. WITHERSPOON, Vice President.

C. W. SIMMONS, Secretary.

H. W. YOUNG, Assistant Secretary.

DIRECTORS:

J. N. STEGALL,	WM. M. SENTER,
AUGUST TAUSSIG,	JEROME HILL,
THOS. H. WEST.	J. H. COGSWELL.
E. BAKER.	

Saint Louis is the largest *inland* cotton market in the United States. The St. Louis Cotton Association was organized, October 17, 1873. During the following year, it was noticeable that the organization exerted a very practical influence on the cotton trade of this city. On the 4th day of August, 1874, a new charter was adopted, and the name changed to "Cotton Exchange." At this period, the membership was small; but, it soon increased in numbers and efficiency. Prior to 1872, the "fleecy" staple was received only in moderate quantity at St. Louis, but, in less than six years—from the organization of the Exchange—the receipts reached, in the season of 1879–80, the number of 480,000 bales. The membership, in less than eight years, had increased to upward of three hundred active and influential men, engaged in the cotton trade, including some from the Eastern States, and Europe. The business had now grown to such proportions as to

demand more eligible accommodations for the transaction
of the business. At this period the present handsome and
capacious Exchange Building was erected. It was opened
with special eclat, on the 4th day of May, 1882, and the
occasion was accompanied with speeches and music. The
Exchange Hall is of fine dimensions, tasteful in frescoes
and embellishments, whilst the location is most eligible.

The Cotton Exchange has continued to prosper, and is
a most valuable adjunct to the commerce of this city. It
has aided very powerfully to bring the cotton States in
closer fellowship with, and to buy from St. Louis a much
larger part of their "supplies"—in merchandise and manu-

COTTON EXCHANGE BUILDING.

factures, machinery and utensils. Besides, the cotton
trade has given profitable employment to the existing railroads, and demanded the building of more. These have
greatly increased the direct trade with the southwest—
in a constant and swelling volume. The cotton received,
comes chiefly from the States of Arkansas, Texas, and
from Indian Territory; but, also in a moderate degree from
Tennessee, Mississippi and Southeast Missouri. Great
credit is due to the officers and membership of the Cotton

Exchange for their enterprise; and to the cotton factors for their liberality to consignors in drought years. Just weight and fair dealing—are marked characteristics of the factors who receive the cotton coming to this city.

The cotton year closes annually the last day of August. The following figures show the business of the year, ending August 31, 1888:

STATEMENT.

TOTAL RECEIPTS COTTON, 1887-88.	BALES
Gross Receipts	527,900
Through "	271,091
Net Receipts	256,809
Shipments	528,135
Stock on hand September 1, 1887	4,140
Receipts for year	527,900
	532,040
Shipments for year	528,135
Stock on hand September 1, 1888	3,905

C. W. SIMMONS, *Sec'y.*

COTTON COMPRESSES.

There are two compress companies: FIRST —

THE ST. LOUIS COTTON COMPRESS COMPANY.

This great establishment covers an area of five entire city blocks. having a total frontage of 1,748 feet. and occupies fifteen acres of ground. Its two stories make *thirty* acres of floor surface. There are, in all, nine fireproof buildings—having brick walls and iron doors. Throughout all the warehouses the best and most modern safeguards against fire have been provided: fire extinguishers, and pipes to throw a five-inch stream of water, etc. The capital stock of this company is $625,000.

THE PEPER COTTON COMPRESS

Is not so large as the other compress, but is furnished with two powerful hydraulic presses, and is amply provided for a large business and safety against fire. The capital stock is a quarter of a million dollars.

The aggregate capacity of the two Compress companies is as follows:

For Storage...............................310,000 bales of Cotton.
For Compressing daily...................... 7,500 " "

COMMERCE IN COTTON AT ST. LOUIS TO THE END OF THE LAST "COTTON YEAR", AUGUST 31, 1888.

The business of the last cotton year represents the trade in this great staple to be in a very satisfactory condition. The gross receipts were 527,600 bales, and the largest of any year since St. Louis became a cotton market. Although the increase over preceding years, was mostly in through cotton, and the increase in cotton handled only 12,738 bales greater than the previous year, still the fact remains, that there is an annual increase in the staple seeking an outlet through St. Louis, and illustrates the advantages of this city not only as a point of sale and distribution, but a direct through route to the seaboard. It seems to be settled, that this city shall become the principal interior point for storing, compressing and shipping cotton, destined both for home and foreign markets. The centering of numerous railways at St. Louis, makes it most accessible to buyers from the east and Europe.

To March 1, 1889, the receipts of cotton at St. Louis were about nine thousand bales in excess of those for the year 1888; and, it is estimated, that number will be increased to about twenty thousand bales.

The shipments for the year reached 528,135 bales, of which 158,409 bales went to England, and 24,643 to Canada, being an increase over the previous year of 9,552 bales to the latter country.

The stock on hand, August 31, 1888, was 3905 bales. Prices remained steady during the year; middling

cotton ranged from 8 3-4 and 9 5-8 in September, 1887, to
10 and 10 1-8 in August, 1888. The rates during the
year were 9, 9 1-2 and 9 3-4 cents.

ST. LOUIS WOOL AND FUR ASSOCIATION.

OFFICERS:

Moses Summerfield, *President.*

Albert Schott, *Vice-President.*

Benjamin Harris, *Secretary.*

The Association, although maintaining a separate organization, holds its 'Change for the transaction of business
at the Hall of the Cotton Exchange, South-West corner
Main and Walnut Streets, daily.

LIVE STOCK EXCHANGE.

The third Annual Convention and Election of the
Exchange, met October 27, 1888, and the following officers were elected for the ensuing year, as follows:

E. J. Senseney, *President.*

R. H. Mann, *Vice-President.*

DIRECTORS:

C. C. Daily,	W. L. Cassidy,
Samuel Scaling,	C. M. Keys,
J. G. Cash,	W. D. Little,
H. F. Parry,	James Moody,

T. J. Daniels.

The St. Louis Live Stock Exchange was organized
October 20, 1885, and is conducted at the National Stock
Yards. It aims to develop the general interests of the
business in live stock, to secure uniform rules and just
principles in all transactions in buying and selling. And, to
protect the common interest of the shipper or producer,
and the purchaser and utilizer of the production, as well.

The Exchange has accomplished valuable reforms in the model of stock cars and in the handling of live stock. It has been influential in the improvement of grades, and the introduction of valuable new breeds. The membership is made up of fair-dealing and liberal-minded men, whose influence extends to all shipping points and is exercised daily at the Exchange itself.

The Live Stock trade is of very special interest and value to this city, and it receives the careful, active and intelligent attention of the officers and members of the Exchange.

THE STOCK YARDS.

FOR CATTLE, HOGS, SHEEP, HORSES AND MULES.

There are two well appointed and extensive stock yards— the Union and the National — situated on opposite sides of the Mississippi river, but connected by transfer steam boats.

THE NATIONAL YARDS

Are situated at East St. Louis, and cover one hundred acres of ground, of which between seventy-five and eighty acres are under roof. The land and improvements cost one million, seven hundred thousand dollars. Their daily capacity is equal to 8,000 cattle, 25,000 hogs, 7,500 sheep, and 750 horses and mules. Cars are loaded and unloaded with dispatch. The pens are floored with timber and plank, and the avenues paved with stone. A perfect system of sewerage prevents mud. Each pen is provided with facilities for easy feeding and watering. There is a fine hotel on the grounds, a stock exchange, bank, telegraph and telephone offices. The offices of stock merchants and agents are convenient to the yards. These yards are so situated as to receive and ship by all the railroads connecting with St. Louis.

THE UNION YARDS

Are situated near the Mississippi river in the northern part of the city, and are reached by the Broadway street railroad. Twenty-five acres of ground are occupied by these yards, which have a daily capacity for 7,000 hogs, 2,500 cattle, 2,500 sheep, and 300 horses and mules.

A hotel and exchange, besides telegraph and telephone offices, and other conveniences for the dispatch of business, are near at hand. The facilities for handling stock are ample and include all the late improvements. The pens are roofed and floored. Stock buyers and commission merchants have offices at the yards.

The St. Louis, Kansas City and Northern (Wabash Western Division) railroad passes through the yards. Stock is taken from steam boats and ferry boats directly into the yards.

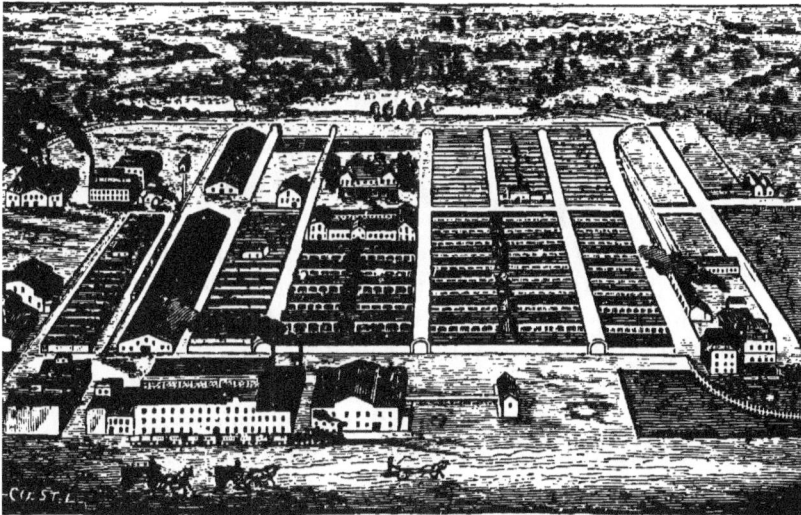

BIRD'S-EYE VIEW OF THE NATIONAL STOCK YARDS.

CHAPTER III.

MECHANICS' EXCHANGE, ST. LOUIS.

NO. 9 NORTH SEVENTH STREET.

OFFICERS FOR THE YEAR 1889:

WILLIAM A. RUTTER, *President.*

A. S. ITTNER, *First Vice President.*

F. P. HUNKINS, *Second Vice President.*

WILLIAM S. STAMPS, *Treasurer.*

RICHARD WALSH, *Secretary.*

DIRECTORS:

JAMES H. KEEFE,	JOS. L. GUEDRY,
JEREMIAH SHEEHAN,	SAM. MARSDEN,
BRYAN BRADY,	C. C. WEAVER,
THOS. P. McKELLEGET,	THOS. H. RICH,
THOS. MOCKLER,	MARK HUDSON,
STEPHEN O'CONNOR.	DANIEL EVANS.

The Exchange membership is composed of the master mechanics, builders and other master workmen of St. Louis. It is a body of substantial, reliable and intelligent men — formed into a business association for mutual benefit and protection, and for the advancement of "Mechanical and industrial interests in the city of St. Louis, and to inculcate just and equitable principles of trade."

The membership is composed of master builders, master plumbers and gas fitters, master painters, contractors in bricklaying, quarrying, building stone, stone cutting, stone masonry, stair building, roofing, plastering, lathing, sidewalks, fire proof work, sand, lime and cement, galvanized iron, hardware, lumber, brick, mill planing, iron railings, foundry, architectural iron and zinc work, electric bells, glass, fresco painting, steam and hot water heating, mantles, grates and tiles, tuck pointing, blacksmithing, civil engineering, printing and publishing, sewer building, etc.

The Exchange hall is a large and handsome chamber. It includes a reading room. Upon its files may be found the leading industrial newspapers, journals and magazines of the United States. These are free, but to members only and friends whom they introduce. The Exchange is open daily from 8 A. M. till 5 P. M.

THE MEXICAN AND SPANISH-AMERICAN EXCHANGE.

JOHN F. CAHILL, CONSUL FOR THE REPUBLIC OF MEXICO, 216 NORTH EIGHTH STREET.

The Mexican and Spanish-American Exchange is not an organized body, but it is presided over by the Mexican Consul, who, whilst actively and efficiently engaged in promoting intimate and fraternal intercourse between the Mexican Republic and the United States, is likewise deeply concerned to secure similar relations between this country and *all* of "Latin America."

The consulate is employing its talent and influence to develope and secure mutual trade and commerce between the city of St. Louis and the republics of South and Central America, as well as with the Republic of Mexico.

THE ASSOCIATED WHOLESALE GROCERS OF ST. LOUIS.

OFFICERS:

J. W. GODDARD, *President.*

JAMES H. BROOKMIRE, *Vice-President.*

WILLIAM E. SCHWEPPE, *Secretary* and *Treasurer.*

This Association is one of special value and importance to the Wholesale Grocery trade. The number of firms represented is about thirty, and one hundred individual members. It was formed five years since. It is one of the wealthiest commercial organizations of this city.

The wholesale Grocery Trade of St. Louis amounted to about forty million dollars for the year 1888.

THE MERCHANTS AND MANUFACTURERS ASSOCIATION,

Is an organization of special importance and value for the protection of the trades, especially in all matters relating to rates of freight, and has been of great utility in securing fair and just rates of railway freight and passenger fares.

THE BREWERS ASSOCIATION

Is composed of all the principal brewers of the city, amongst whom are the largest brewers in the United States. Headquarters office, 404 Market Street.

IMPLEMENT AND VEHICLE MANUFACTURERS ASSOCIATION.

This association is devoted to such specialties of manufactured products as belong—implements and vehicles—to those lines, and is designed to guide, govern and protect the interests of its members.

THE COAL EXCHANGE

Was established for the promotion of the coal business, and the regulation of prices.

BUILDING AND LOAN ASSOCIATIONS.

St. Louis has numerous Building and Loan Associations, which are conducted with special advantage to a large class of small and thrifty investors and shareholders. The number of these associations exceeds seventy.

ST. LOUIS FURNITURE BOARD OF TRADE.

OFFICE, LACLEDE BUILDING.

J. G. SMITH, *President.*

J. H. CONRADES, *First Vice President.*

I. F. MUELLER, *Second Vice President.*

GUSTAVE WOLF, *Treasurer.*

JAMES A. REARDON, *Secretary.*

H. S. TUTTLE, *Manager.*

ST. LOUIS MERCHANTS BRIDGE COMPANY.

OFFICE, CHAMBER OF COMMERCE.

SETH W. COBB, *President.*

C. C. RAINWATER, *Vice-President.*

JOHN D. PERRY, *Secretary and Treasurer.*

TERMINAL RAILWAY BRIDGE COMPANY.

OFFICE, LACLEDE BUILDING.

C. C. RAINWATER, *President.*

JOHN R. HOLMES, *Vice President.*

JOHN D. PERRY, *Treasurer.*

JOHN H. OVERALL, *Secretary.*

WESTERN COMMERCIAL TRAVELERS ASSOCIATION.

OFFICE, LACLEDE BUILDING.

OFFICERS FOR THE YEAR 1889:

M. C. WETMORE, President, St. Louis, Mo.; JOHN W. ELWELL, First Vice President, St. Louis, Mo.; J. C. MILLER, Second Vice President, Chicago, Ill.; H. C. McNAIR, Third Vice President, St. Paul, Minn.; H. M. HIDDEN,

Fourth Vice President, Kansas City, Mo.; CHARLES W. WELLS, Fifth Vice President, Indianapolis, Ind.; JONAS P. JOHNSON, Sixth Vice President, Omaha, Neb.; and THOS. RYAN, Secretary and Treasurer, St. Louis, Mo.

The board of Directors, Committees, Medical Director and Attorney are all citizens of St. Louis.

SOUTHERN HISTORICAL AND BENEVOLENT AID ASSOCIATION.

J. BOYCE, *President.*

ANTHONY BOYCE, *Treasurer.*

W. P. BARLOW, *Secretary.*

ST. LOUIS CHAPTER OF THE AMERICAN INSTITUTE OF ARCHITECTS.

H. G. ISAACS, *President.*

H. W. KIRCHNER, *Secretary.*

ST. LOUIS INSTITUTE OF ARCHITECTS.

T. W. BRADY, *President.*

J. F. MITCHELL, *Secretary.*

HOTEL RICHELIEU.

CHAPTER IV.

THE BANKING INSTITUTIONS.

The Banks of the City of St. Louis are twenty-one in number, *four* of which are operated under the National banking laws, and *seventeen* under the laws of the State of Missouri. The capital employed was, together with surplus, on the 31st December 1888. fifteen and a half million dollars. The statement of the manager of the Clearing House is given below.

These institutions are conducted in conformity with a policy, which while liberal. is conservative. The capital of private bankers—legitimately used in discounts of business paper—should be added to that of the banking institutions.

The limit of the legal rate of interest in Missouri is ten per cent per annum. The bank rate is nominally eight. but six per cent is the common one charged by banks. Loans on real estate in the city are made at five and six per cent, but chiefly at the latter rate of interest. More banking capital could be employed and is required to meet the healthy growth of the manufacturing and mercantile lines of trade.

BANK STATEMENT TO DECEMBER 31.

YEAR.	Capital and Surplus.	Deposits and due Banks.	Loans, Bonds and Exchange Maturing.	Percentage of cash to Deposit.
1887	$14,824,115	$45,878,586	$ 44,507,836	34
1888	15,460,866	52,289,979	46,852,313	37

BANK STATEMENT—CONTINUED.

YEAR.	Cash and Deposits to other banks.	Clearings.	Balances.
1887	$ 14,913,121	$ 894,527,731	$ 138,59,8622 00
1888	19,432,361	900,474,878	141,883,529 00

17

BANK DIVIDENDS DECLARED PAYABLE JANUARY 1, 1889:

Commercial Bank, 10 per cent, annual dividend.
Mullanphy   "   5   "   "   "
And the dividends of the following banks were each for
semi-annual periods, namely:
American, Exchange, Bremen and Continental, each 4
per cent; German-American, Mechanics, and Merchants'
National, each 3 per cent.

STATEMENT OF THE CLEARING HOUSE.

(FROM E. CHASE, MANAGER.)

AGGREGATE STATEMENT OF THE ST. LOUIS CITY BANKS;

FOUR NATIONAL, AND SEVENTEEN STATE BANKS, ON THE 31st DECEMBER, 1888, COMPARED WITH STATEMENT OF SAME ON 31st DECEMBER, 1887.

	Dec. 1888.	Dec. 1887.	DIFFERENCES.	
Capital and Surplus	$15,460,866	$14,824,115	Increase, $	636,751
Deposits payable on time	9,035,451	8,463,560	"	571,891
" " on demand to Banks	10,459,072	10,546,306	Decrease,	87,234
Deposits payable on demand to others	32,495,456	26,868,720	Increase,	5,926,736
National Bank Circulation	189,000	591,060	Decrease,	402,060
Liabilities	$67,939,845	$61,293,761	Increase, $	6,646,084
U. S. Bonds to secure Circulation	210,000	660,000	Decrease,	450,000
Good Loans and Bonds	46,852,313	44,507,836	Increase,	2,344,477
Cash, Checks and Exchange	9,501,935	6,519,075	Increase,	2,982,860
Cash, Coin,	2,467,259	2,267,953	"	199,306
" Currency	7,463,167	6,126,093	"	1,337,074
Real Estate, Furniture and Fixtures	1,445,171	1,212,804	"	232,367
Assets	$67,939,845	$61,293,761	"	$ 6,646,084

ST. LOUIS POST OFFICE — LARGE GROWTH OF ITS BUSINESS.

The remarkable growth in the mailable matter in letters, postal cards, papers, circulars, etc., delivered and collected at the post office of this city, is a very forcible proof of the enlargement of its trade and population.

MAILABLE MATTER FOR THREE PERIODS, ILLUSTRATIVE OF THE GROWTH OF ST. LOUIS:

DELIVERED.	1888.	1886.	1880.
Registered letters	199,251	183,994	125,389
Mail letters	36,768,477	26,027,857	12,533,151
Mail postal cards	7,546,159	4,445,983	2,600,275
Drop letters	13,200,197	6,004,009	2,082,535
Drop postal cards	6,998,502	3,819,638	1,648,222
Papers, circulars, etc	17,672,890	10,092,909	5,303,778
COLLLECTED.			
Letters	31,956,495	17,558,137	8,484,267
Postal cards	10,623,286	5,677,836	2,791,483
Papers, circulars, etc	7,856,983	3,648,244	2,752,419

FIRE INSURANCE AND LOSSES FOR THE YEAR 1888 CITY OF ST. LOUIS:

Amount of Insurance Premiums Paid.	Loss to Insurance Companies.	Percentage of Loss.
$4,134,079.12	$752,887.12	18.21

THE INSURANCE LAWS OF MISSOURI.

In no state are the laws relative to the reliability and competency of insurance companies more complete or more strictly enforced, than in Missouri. They require more than mere solvency, and enforce a fixed and very ample capital, which shall remain intact against contingent risks and losses. But, whenever such capital shall become impaired, notice is given by the state commissioner (whose office is at St. Louis) to "wind-up" or re-organize with ample resources—without delay.

"Bogus" insurance is suppressed as soon as found. It is always attempted in some obscure neighborhood, and has a short life.

CHAPTER V.

GRAIN AND FLOUR.

GRAIN.

The year 1888, was marked by fruitfulness in several of the cereal crops—notably of corn and oats—in the State of Missouri, and the adjoining states which ship to St. Louis, as their best market. In the quantity of wheat received, there was a moderate decline, whilst the receipts of the other cereals were largely increased over the preceding year.

The table of receipts of grain now given—for five years —shows a special deficiency in the receipts of wheat for several seasons, in consequence of poor harvests. But, the establishment of large flouring mills at points near this city—in the surrounding country—operated by St. Louis millers, take wheat for manufacturing, some of which would otherwise be marketed here and swell the volume of receipts.

RECEIPTS FOR FIVE YEARS WERE AS FOLLOWS:

BUSHELS.	1888.	1887.	1886.	1885.	1884.
Wheat.......	13,010,105	14,510,315	12,309,364	10,690,677	16,368,809
Corn	20,269,499	16,576,386	16,357,071	26,114,782	19,607,325
Oats.........	10,456,760	9,768,545	7,426,915	7,383,529	7,036,951
Rye	421,514	236,726	447,842	726,799	585,218
Barley.......	3,044,961	2,932,192	2,529,731	3,017,362	2,625,841
Total	47,202,842	44,024,164	39,100,923	47,933,148	46,224,144

INCLUDING FLOUR REDUCED TO WHEAT THE RECEIPTS WOULD BE AS FOLLOWS:

BUSHELS.	1888.	1887.	1886.	1885.	1884.
Wheat and Flour....	51,195,121	48,748,562	42,918,800	52,579,425	52,776,832

PLANT OF THE EXCELSIOR MANUFACTURING COMPANY.

SHIPMENTS FOR THE PAST FIVE YEARS:

BUSHELS.	1888.	1887.	1886.	1885.	1884.
Wheat......	4,412,506	6,238,268	2,429,462	2,332,609	7,177,982
Corn	15,904,750	13,841,172	11,848,995	20,491,416	16,533,259
Oats.........	5,414,764	3,780,729	2,764,922	3,680,829	3,082,360
Rye	275,233	175,352	337,018	636,640	700,526
Barley	324,832	291,337	215,377	210,340	169,781
Total......	26,332,085	24,326,858	17,595,774	27,351,834	27,663,908

DIRECT SHIPMENTS OF BULK GRAIN FROM ST. LOUIS TO FOREIGN COUNTRIES IN TONS:

TONS.	1888.	1887.	1886.	1885.	1884.	1883.	1882.
By Rail Eastward..........	121,657	128,522	30,853	52,186	147,202	141,904	107,528
By River to New Orleans...	201,072	325,442	232, 52	231,552	175,126	301,629	176,583
Total....	322,729	453,964	263,205	284,738	322,328	443,533	284,111

SHIPMENTS OF BULK GRAIN FROM ST. LOUIS BY RIVER TO NEW ORLEANS.

YEAR.	Wheat Bushels	Corn. Bushels.	Rye. Bushels.	Oats. Bushels.	Total.
1887 ..	3,973,737	7,365,340	....	217,722	11,556,799
1888 ..	1,247,952	5,844,042	....	160,584	7,252,578

The falling off in the shipments of wheat in 1888, was caused by the decreased crop of that year, and the advanced price. Wheat could not be shipped to Europe except at a loss! The rise in price occurred suddenly, and, wheat sent to New Orleans for export was *returned to St. Louis* and resold at a profit!

The falling off of shipments of corn for export, was occasioned by the short crop of 1887.

CORN.

The corn crop of the United States for 1887, as reported by the department of agriculture, was 1,456,161,-000 bushels. This was the *smallest* crop harvested since 1881. The yield per acre was 20.1 bushels against 22

284   ST. LOUIS OF TO-DAY.

bushels for the crop of 1886. The crop of 1888 is in
marked contrast with preceding year, and is the largest
ever grown, amounting to 1,987,790,000, and exceeds the
crop of 1887 upwards of five hundred million bushels.

CROPS OF THE GREAT CORN GROWING STATES FOR FIVE YEARS:

STATES.	Bushels. 1888.	Bushels. 1887.	Bushels. 1886.	Bushels. 1885.	Bushels. 1884.
Indiana..	125,478,000	71,400,000	118,795,000	131,994,000	104,757,000
Illinois ..	278,000,000	141,080,000	209,818,000	268,998,000	244,544,000
Iowa.....	278,232,000	183,502,000	198,847,000	242,496,000	252,600,000
Missouri.	202,583,000	140,949,000	143,709,000	196,861,000	197,850,000
Kansas ..	158,186,000	76,547,000	126,712,000	158,390,000	168,500,000
Nebraska	144,217,000	98,150,000	106,129,000	129,426,000	122,100,000
Total..		706,628,000	904,010,000	1,128,165,000	1,090,351,000

ST. LOUIS' ELEVATORS.

DESIGNATION BY NAME.	Capacity for Bulk Grain. Bushels.	Additional Capacity for Packages. Sacks.
St. Louis....................	2,000,000	200,000
Central A.......................	700,000	....
" B.......................	900,000	....
" C.......................	800,000	....
East St. Louis..................	1,000,000	165,000
Advance........................	600,000	....
Valley.........................	1,250,000	....
Union	1,500,000	.... ..
Venice.........................	600,000	....
Merchants......................	1,100,000	....
Union Depot....................	750,000	....
St. Louis (Salt) Warehouse......	750,000	....
St. Louis Warehouse............	200,000	....
Total Stored, Jan. 1888.....	12,150,000	365,000
" " 1887.....	12,150,000	365,600
" " 1886.....	11,800,000	365,000
" " 1885.....	10,950,000	365,000
" " 1884.....	11,700,000	415,000
" " 1883.....	10,700,000	415,000
" " 1882.....	9,650,000	415,000
" " 1881.....	5,650,000	415,000
" " 1880.....	4,950,000	415,000

SHIPMENTS TO NEW ORLEANS DURING 1888, OF FLOUR AND GRAIN:

Wheat. Bushels.	Corn. Bushels.	Oats. Bushels.	Flour. Barrels
1,250,752	6,418,233	1,981,794	313,327

GRAIN ELEVATOR, ST. LOUIS.

ST. LOUIS AND MISSISSIPPI VALLEY TRANSPORTATION COMPANY, ("BARGE LINE.")

HENRY C. HAARSTICK, *President.*

AUSTIN B. MOORE, *Vice-President.*

This Company does a very large carrying trade between this city and New Orleans and Port Eads—at the Jetty passage of the Mississippi—and is of very special value to the commerce of St. Louis, as a great carrier of grain destined for Europe.

The report of the National Bureau of Statistics, for the year ending June 30, 1888, states the quantity of maize—Indian corn—carried by this Company at 21 per cent of the exports to foreign countries.

This Company was incorporated in August 1881, with a paid up capital of two million dollars, and is popularly known as the "Barge Line."

THE CARRYING CAPACITY OF THE BARGE LINE

Is to *float*, at any time, of grain in bulk, four million bushels, and to *move* to the European vessels—waiting its reception at tide water—two and one-half million bushels, monthly. The line employs eleven towing steamboats and eighty barges.

ST. LOUIS FLOUR MILLS: THE OUTPUT OF 1887 AND 1888 COMPARED.

The number of barrels of flour manufactured during the last two years was as follows:

Flour manufactured in St. Louis for the year ending, Dec. 31, 1887, was 1,985,717 barrels: and in the same time of 1888, 2,016,619, being an increase of 30,902 barrels.

Flour manufactured by mills located outside, but owned and operated by citizens of St. Louis, for the year ending

December 31, 1887, was 842,373 barrels, and for the same time in 1888, was 1,029,446, being an increase of 187,073 barrels. Grand total output of 1887, 2,828,090 against 3,046.065 barrels in 1888, an increase over the preceding year of 217,975 barrels.

The flour output of St. Louis is second only to all others in the United States—Minneapolis having the first place for quantity, but all from *spring* wheat. The flour of this city, made from winter wheat, has always held the very highest reputation at the East and South, and in Europe, for its superior quality. It has always been in large demand for shipment to tropical countries.

THE TOTAL AMOUNT OF FLOUR HANDLED BY MILLERS AND DEALERS FOR THREE YEARS:

	1888.	1887.	1886.	1885.
Received	887,173	1,049,864	848,417	1,032,506
Manufactured.	2,016,619	1,985,817	1,807,956	1,841,529
Sold and Shipped Direct from Country Mills..	1,069,363	597,610	542,010	536,083
Total Barrels.......	3,973,155	3,633,191	3,198,383	3,410,118

AMOUNT OF FLOUR MANUFACTURED IN VARIOUS CITIES.

CITIES.	1888.	1887.	1886.	1885.
	Bbls.	Bbls.	Bbls.	Bbls.
Minneapolis................	7,056,680	6,379,264	6,168,000	5,221,243
St. Louis................	2,016,619	1,985,717	1,807,956	1,841,529
Baltimore	506,870	496,244	540,567	526,992
St. Paul................	250,000	316,000	194,500	225,000
Philadelphia................	240,000		240,000	
Milwaukee................	1,421,258	1,214,648	960,000	961,152
Buffalo................	1,500,000	637,885	706,384	752,862
Richmond			264,712	412,000
Toledo	250,000	305,000	310,000	
Detroit................	235,000	253,000	296,500	255,500
Chicago	435,000	514,870	494,789	
Duluth................			40,000	10,000
Kansas City................	26,987	165,000		
Peoria	90,000	105,600		

THE GEOGRAPHICAL POSITION OF ST. LOUIS RELATIVELY TO
THE GREATEST FOOD PRODUCING FIELDS
OF THE UNITED STATES.

St. Louis' position, relatively to the greatest food producing field of the nation — surpassing that of any country of the globe—is almost a central one. But, by reason
of its great water facilities, and numerous extensive railway systems — penetrating all those fertile fields — it
possesses superior advantages over some other western
sites. This city occupies the center of the great winter
wheat and Indian corn belt of the United States. A
table is here given of the crops for the year 1888 of
part of the states, but not including several in lesser
commercial relations with this city:

STATES.	Wheat. Bushels.	Corn. Bushels.	Oats. Bushels.
Missouri	18,496,000	202,583,000	34,909,000
Illinois	33,556,000	278,060,000	137,400,000
Iowa	24,196,000	278,232,000	67,090,000
Kansas	15,960,000	158,186,000	42,654,000
Nebraska	14,508,000	144,217,000	26,177,000
Total	106,716,000	1,061,278,000	308,230,000

A total of one billion, four hundred and tweny-six million, two hundred and
twenty-four thousand bushels wheat, corn and oats.

The wheat crop of the United States for the year 1888
was 414,868,000 bushels. And the five states named produced 26 per cent of the whole quantity.

The corn crop for the same year was 1,987,790,000
bushels. And, the five states yielded 53 1-2 per cent of
that quantity. The oats crop was 701,735,000 bushels.
And, the same states yielded 44 per cent of the whole
quantity produced in the United States, and are those
which are closely allied in business relations with this city.
And, if these five states—whose resources are very far

from being fully developed—have yielded so much of the whole production, then, when their entire area shall be brought under cultivation, the proportion will be yet greater, especially since most of the other states have reached their maximum in the yield of cereal crops.

THE AVERAGE VALUE OF EXPORTED WHEAT FROM THE UNITED STATES DURING 68 YEARS TO THE END OF THE FISCAL YEAR, JUNE 30, 1888.*

The subjoined table gives the foreign exports of wheat, and average value per bushel since 1820. It will be seen, that the lowest average value touched in 68 years was for the twelve months ending June 30, 1888. The average price of all wheat exported during that year was only 81 cents a bushel, against 86 cents in 1885, the next lowest year. Prior to 1866, the average had never been as low as $1.10, with two exceptions—1879 and 1884, when the price was $1.06. For the five years, ending June 30, 1870, the average was $1.43, a bushel, the highest for any similar length of time since the United States first commenced exporting wheat. In 1876, the average was $1.24, dropping in 1877 to $1.16, and again rising in 1878 to $1.33. Since then, there have been some considerable fluctuations from year to year, with the tendency gradually downwards, until, as already said, the lowest point of 81 cents per bushel was reached last year.

---

*NOTE.—These statistics of the wheat and flour exports; and, the acreage, production and exports of grain, were obtained from a reliable seaboard authority.—*Author.*

WHEAT AND FLOUR EXPORTED SINCE 1820.

EXPORTS OF WHEAT AND FLOUR FROM THE UNITED STATES.

(Flour Reduced to Bushels in the Total.)

EACH OF THE FIVE FISCAL YEARS ENDED AS GIVEN BELOW.	Wheat. Bushels.	Flour. Barrels.	Total Bushels.	Per ct. of Flour in Total.
1825.............	72,874	4,451,384	18,878,410	99.61
1830.............	125,547	4,651,940	23,385,247	99.46
1835.............	614,145	5,241,964	26,823,965	97.2
1840.............	1,842,841	4,092,932	22,307,501	91.7
1845.............	2,946,861	6,274,697	34,320,346	91.1
1850.............	10,184,645	12,284,828	71,608,785	85.77
1855.............	16,446,955	13,149,518	82,194,545	79.9
1860.............	38,808,573	15,778,268	117,699,913	67.
1865.............	138,306,907	19,757,733	237,095,572	42.09
1870.............	81,808,364	11,454,785	139,082,289	41.2
1875.............	224,019,376	16,797,684	308,007,796	27.2
Total for 55 years.	515,177,088	113,935,733	1,081,404,369	52.6

FISCAL YEAR.				
1876.............	55,073,122	3,935,512	74,750,682	26.32
1877.............	40,325,611	3,343,665	57,043,936	29.30
1878.............	72,404,961	3,946,855	92,139,236	21.42
1879.............	122,353,936	5,629,714	147,687,649	17.1
1880.............	153,252,795	6,011,419	180,754,180	15.2
1881.............	150,565,477	7,945,786	186,321,464	18.9
1882.............	92,857,276	5,733,194	118,656,649	21.7
1883.............	106,385,828	9,205,664	147,811,316	28.02
1884.............	70,349,012	9,152,260	111,534,182	36.9
1885.............	82,449,014	10,347,629	128,993,344	36.
1886.............	57,750,609	8,179,231	94,557,149	37.1
1887.............	100,809,212	11,328,872	151,789,136	33.5
1888.............	63,846,204	11,746,028	116,703,330	45.2
Total for 13 years.	1,078,423,857	96,605,829	1,608,742,253	27.0
Grand total since 1820..........	1,593,600,945	210,541,562	2,690,146,622	....

These figures show that the exports of flour for the last fiscal year were the largest on record, reaching 11,746,028 barrels—a gain of 400.000 barrels compared with the preceding year, and of 2.500.000 barrels compared with the year ending June 30, 1886. Of wheat, however, the shipments were the smallest since 1878 with one exception. Since 1880 there has been a gradual upward movement in the percentage of flour to the total exports of wheat and flour combined, and while in that year the percentage was only 15.2, in the year just closed it was 45.2.   This is an exceedingly gratifying condition of affairs.   Instead of exporting so small a proportion of flour the increase is now steady, thus giving American millers the benefit of this expanding trade.   Nearly one-half of all the wheat exports of the country goes now in the shape of flour.   The gain has been remarkably rapid.

In thirteen years, or since 1876, we have exported from this country over 1,000,000,000 bushels of wheat, and 96,600,000 barrels of flour; the aggregate value of the two being $1,797,267,367, while for the preceding 55 years we exported 515,177,088 bushels wheat and 113,935,000 barrels of flour, the aggregate value being $1,412,000,000.

THE VALUE OF EXPORTS OF FLOUR AND WHEAT SINCE 1820 TO JUNE 30, 1888, HAS BEEN AS FOLLOWS:

EACH OF FIVE FISCAL YEARS ENDED JUNE 30.	WHEAT.		FLOUR.		WHEAT AND FLOUR.	
	Value.	Average value per Bushel.	Value.	Average value per Barrel.	Aggregate value.	Average value per Bushel.
1825	$ 68,978	$0.94	$ 24,334,999	$5.46	$ 24,403,977	$1.29
1830	112,754	.89	34,708,090	5.31	24,820,844	1.06
1835	737,365	1.20	29,347,649	5.59	30,085,014	1.13
1840	1,817,067	.98	27,231,952	6.05	29,049,019	1.30
1845	2,900,785	.98	31,056,156	4.94	33,956,941	.98
1850	12,801,093	1.25	69,375,741	5.64	82,176,834	1.18
1855	21,864,762	1.39	75,775,220	5.76	97,639,982	1.18
1860	53,343,918	1.37	104,368,446	6.61	157,712,365	1.34
1865	178,470,444	1.29	133,356,875	6.74	311,827,319	1.31
1870	117,527,424	1.43	92,071,717	8.03	209,599,141	1.50
1875	296,540,060	1.32	114,401,066	6.86	410,941,126	1.33
Total for 55 years	$ 686,184,650	$1.33	$ 726,027,911	$6.37	$1,412,212,561	$1.30
FISCAL YEARS ENDED JUNE 30.						
1876	$ 68,382,899	$1.24	$ 24,433,470	$6.20	$ 92,816,369	$1.24
1877	47,135,562	1.16	21,663,947	6.47	68,799,509	1.20
1878	96,872,016	1.33	25,092,826	6.35	121,964,842	1.32
1879	130,701,079	1.06	29,567,713	5.25	160,268,792	1.08
1880	190,546,305	1.24	35,333,197	5.88	225,879,502	1.24
1881	167,698,485	1.11	45,047,257	5.66	212,745,742	1.14
1882	110,430,920	1.18	35,396,599	6.14	145,827,519	1.23
1883	119,879,341	1.12	54,824,459	5.95	174,703,800	1.18
1884	75,026,678	1.06	51,139,696	5.58	126,166,374	1.13
1885	71,088,456	.86	50,619,158	4.89	121,707,614	.94
1886	50,262,715	.87	38,442,900	4.70	88,705,615	.93
1887	89,8 3,761	.89	51,174,598	4.51	140,978,359	.92
1888	54,817,803	.81	53,860,303	4.58	116,703,330	.81
Total for 13 years	$1,272,646,020		$ 516,596,123		$1,797,267,367	
Grand total for 68 years	$1,958,830,670	....	$1,242,624,034		$3,201,454,704	....

ACREAGE, PRODUCTION AND EXPORTS OF GRAIN.

ACREAGE DEVOTED TO CEREAL CROPS IN THE UNITED STATES FOR THE PAST SEVENTEEN YEARS.

YEARS.	Wheat. Acres.	Corn. Acres.	Oats. Acres.	Rye. Acres.	Barley. Acres.	Buckwheat. Acres.	Totals. Acres.
1872	20,858,359	35,526,836	9,000,788	1,018,654	1,287,082	118,195	68,389,195
1873	22,171,676	39,197,148	9,751,760	1,150,355	1,587,106	134,152	74,112,137
1874	31,967,027	41,036,918	10,897,412	1,116,716	1,589,606	152,580	80,651,260
1875	26,381,512	44,841,371	11,915,075	1,359,788	1,789,302	575,580	86,863,178
1876	27,625,021	49,033,364	13,358,908	1,408,371	1,786,511	686,441	93,920,619
1877	27,277,546	50,369,138	12,826,148	1,413,852	1,611,654	649,923	93,150,256
1878	32,108,560	51,585,000	13,126,500	1,622,700	1,790,400	673,100	100,946,260
1879	35,430,052	62,368,863	16,144,593	1,842,303	1,397,717	848,389	118,631,923
1880	37,986,717	62,317,842	16,187,977	1,767,611	1,843,329	822,802	120,926,281
1881	37,709,020	64,262,025	16,831,000	1,789,100	1,965,510	828,815	123,887,150
1882	37,067,194	65,659,546	18,494,691	2,227,889	2,272,103	847,112	126,368,535
1883	36,455,593	68,301,889	20,324,962	2,314,734	2,379,009	857,349	130,683,536
1884	39,475,885	69,683,780	21,300,917	2,343,963	2,698,848	879,403	136,392,766
1885	34,189,246	73,130,150	22,782,620	2,129,301	2,729,359	914,384	135,875,060
1886	36,806,184	75,694,208	23,658,474	2,129,918	2,652,957	917,915	141,888,656
1887	37,641,783	72,392,720	25,920,906				
1888	37,378,148	75,672,763	26,997,376				

GENERAL PRODUCTION OF THE UNITED STATES FOR THE PAST SEVENTEEN YEARS.

YEARS.	Wheat. Bush.	Corn. Bush.	Oats. Bush.	Rye. Bush.	Barley. Bush.	Buckwheat. Bush.	Totals. Bush.
1872	249,997,100	1,092,719,000	271,747,000	14,888,600	26,846,400	8,432,500	1,664,331,600
1873	281,254,700	932,271,000	270,340,000	15,142,000	27,044,191	7,887,700	1,538,892,881
1874	308,102,700	850,148,500	240,369,000	14,990,800	32,552,500	8,016,600	1,455,180,290
1875	292,136,000	1,321,069,000	354,317,500	17,722,100	36,908,600	10,082,100	2,032,353,300
1876	289,356,500	1,283,827,000	320,884,000	20,374,800	38,710,500	9,668,900	2,002,822,100
1877	364,194,117	1,342,558,000	406,394,000	21,169,500	34,441,460	10,177,000	2,278,934,046
1878	420,122,400	1,388,218,750	413,578,580	23,812,780	42,245,630	12,246,820	2,302,254,850
1879	459,301,093	1,772,989,846	407,970,712	19,863,652	44,149,479	11,851,758	2,716,336,300
1880	380,280,000	1,194,916,000	416,481,000	24,540,829	45,165,346	14,617,535	2,718,193,501
1881	501,185,170	1,617,025,100	488,250,610	20,704,950	41,161,330	9,486,200	2,963,029,570
1882	421,086,160	1,551,066,895	571,302,402	29,058,585	48,953,926	11,019,353	2,629,319,089
1883	512,765,000	1,735,628,182	343,628,000	28,457,584	50,137,097	7,668,454	2,689,384,466
1884	357,112,000	1,936,176,000	629,409,000	21,756,000	61,206,652	11,116,022	2,989,881,500
1885	357,218,000	1,665,411,000	624,134,000	21,756,000	58,360,000	12,626,000	3,015,423,000
1886	456,329,000	1,456,161,000	659,618,000	24,489,000	59,428,000	11,869,000	2,842,579,000
1887	114,868,000	1,987,730,000	701,735,000	20,693,000	56,812,000	10,844,000	3,192,740,000

COMPARATIVE STATEMENT.

RECEIPTS, SHIPMENTS, STOCK, AND CONSUMPTION OF COTTON FOR FIVE YEARS.

	1887-'88.	1886-'87.	1885-'86.	1884-'85.	1883-'84.
Receipts	527,900	411,832	472,682	291,056	297,122
Stock on hand Sept. 1st.....	3,910	9,924	1,609	1,518	4,588
Total bales.........	531,810	421,756	474,756	292,574	301,710
Shipments.................	522,806	416,344	458,268	286,402	295,068
City Consumption.........	1,419	1,302	4,000	......	5,124
In Compress Aug. 31.......	3,910	4,140	9,924	1,609	1,518
Unaccounted for..........	......	......	2,099	4,563	......
Total bales.........	528,135	421,756	474,291	292,574	301,710

TABLE SHOWING THE GROSS AND NET RECEIPTS OF COTTON AT ST. LOUIS.

SEASON.	Gross Receipts. Bales.	Through Shipments. Bales.	Net Receipts. Bales.
1887-'88..........	527,900	271,028	256,872
1886-'87..........	411,832	167,698	244,134
1885-'86..........	472,682	246,017	226,665
1884-'85..........	291,056	103,312	187,744
1883-'84..........	297,122	80,599	216,523
1882-'83..........	456,858	160,098	296,760
1881-'82...........	369,579	129,060	240,519
1880-'81..........	398,939	97,586	301,353
1879-'80..........	496,570	172,286	324,284
1878-'79..........	335,799	117,083	218,716
1877-'78..........	248,856	61,561	187,295
1876-'77..........	217,734	69,258	148,476
1875-'76..........	244,598	84,788	159,810
1874-'75..........	133,969	39,679	94,290
1873-'74..........	103,741	24,323	79,418
1872-'73..........	59,709	......	......
1871-'72..........	36,421	......	......
1870-'71...........	20,270	......	......
1869-'70..........	18,518	......	......
1868-'69..........	16,696	......	......

The receipts of cotton to March 13th, 1889, are thirteen thousand bales in excess of those of the preceding year.

18

REPORT OF COTTON COMPRESSED AT ST. LOUIS.

Year ending Aug. 31.	Receipts.	Shipments.	Stock.
1888	256,809 bales.	257,044 bales.	3,910 bales.
1887	258,234 "	264,110 "	4,140 "
1886	240,183 "	231,868 "	9,924 "
1885	203,584 "	203,493 "	1,609 "
1884	228,414 "	231,484 "	1,518 "
1883	304,300 "	301,451 "	4,588 "
1882	259,151 "	265,637 "	1,739 "
1881	317,195 "	316,537 "	8,225 "
1880	358,124 "	351,818 "	7,467 "
1879	237,437 "	237,101 "	1,161 "
1878	205,861 "	206,537 "	825 "

OFFICERS OF THE ST. LOUIS COTTON COMPRESS COMPANY.

WILLIAM M. SENTER, *President.*

JEROME HILL, *Vice-President.*

J. H. REIFSNYDER, *Sec'y and Treas.*

OFFICERS OF THE PEPER COTTON COMPRESS COMPANY.

CHRISTIAN PEPER, *President.*

R. B. WHITTEMORE, *Sec'y and Treas.*

NATIONAL BOARD OF TRADE.

COMMITTEE ON REPRESENTATION AND EXTENSION.

J. A. PRICE, - - - - - - - Scranton.

J. S. T. STRANAHAN, - - - - - Brooklyn.

S. S. GUTHRIE, - - - - - - - Buffalo.

J. A. GANO, - - - - - - - Cincinnati.

WM. H. PARSON, - - - - - - New York.

A. F. HIGGINS, - - - - - - New York.

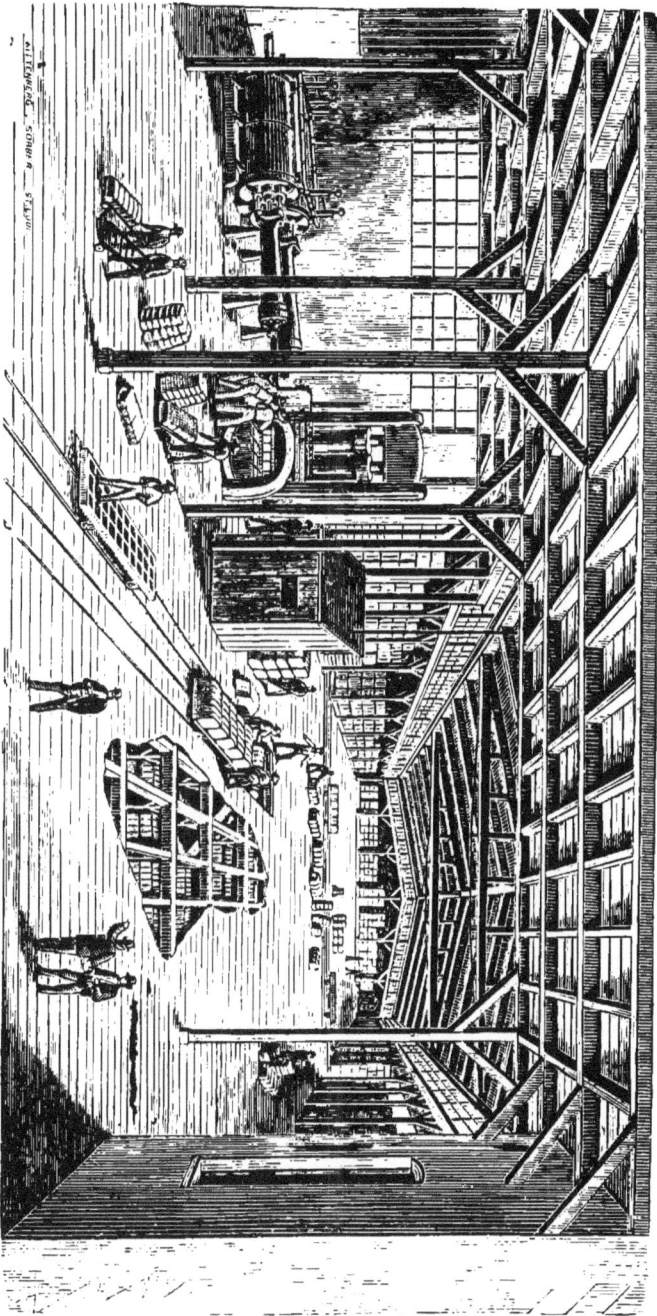

INTERIOR VIEW OF THE WORKS OF THE ST. LOUIS COTTON COMPRESS COMPANY.

CHAPTER VI.

THE ST. LOUIS WOOL MARKET.*

The improvement of the market for wools, during 1888, over that of 1887, was very marked, especially towards the close, both in the volume of receipts and prices. Although the receipts of wool, in 1887, were about 7 per cent less than for 1886, it did not indicate that St. Louis was losing so valuable a trade—gained by special and protracted effort. The receipts at other large primary markets showed a much greater falling off—varying from 8 to 25 per cent of the quantity of the preceding year.

The general deficiency was to be attributed, in part, to wool being held at interior points for a higher price, but more to an actual deficiency in the clip of the United States, at large, in 1887 — estimated by the government statisticians at twenty million pounds.

It is well known, that dealers in wools—throughout the entire country—did not find the business of 1887 profitable. But, the experience of the dealers of this city, for the year 1888, is just the reverse. Whilst the middle men were the sufferers in 1887, the wool growers who sold with the market did exceedingly well, and manufacturers generally enjoyed a prosperous year.

Early in the year 1888, improvement set in. A very marked and encouraging change was realized, yet the slow

---

*NOTE.—These details of the wool market were obtained from the firm of S. Bienenstok & Co., and from Frank & Hellendall, wool merchants, South Main street.—*Author.*

and uncertain action of the Congress of the United States upon the question before it—of reduction of the duty on foreign wools—led to hesitancy on the part of manufacturers. And, by July, the price of wools dropped to the lowest point of the year and were as low as in 1887. But, shortly after that date, wools began to advance, and confidence in the stability of values was largely restored—after many months of hesitation and doubt—and sales were made on a hopeful market. Early in September, buyers conceded the opinion, that wools were *too low* in view of the favorable prospects. That opinion was confirmed by the current business down to the close of the year. During the intervening period wools sold freely at advanced prices—acceptable to both seller and buyer.

The political contest having ended—stability of prices was soon established; and the business in wools wore a most cheerful and encouraging aspect. The dealers and wool growers were well satisfied with the year's business. The latter are encouraged to increase and not diminish their flocks. The factors and dealers are likewise most cheerful—having made up their losses of last year by the large business of 1888. The prices obtained in excess of those of '87 averaged from 15 to 25 per cent. The receipts of this market have exceeded those of '87 by upwards of two million pounds, and the total to December 31, 1888, is 19,626,629 pounds, exclusive of receipts by wagon.

From reliable data, the wool clip of the United States for 1888, is largely less than the previous year, when the deficiency — as stated above — was twenty million pounds. Hence the last year's business is the more gratifying, and illustrates — by comparison — the large growth in the wool trade of St. Louis. Besides, the receipts at other primary wool markets show, that this city is the only one whose receipts have increased.

RECEIPTS AND SHIPMENTS OF WOOL TO AND FROM ST. LOUIS
FOR FIVE YEARS:

| YEAR. | WOOL. | |
| | Receipts. | Shipments. |
	Pounds.	Pounds.
1888	19,626,629	21,463,998
1887	17,347,186	17,392,858
1886	18,563,614	17,825,630
1885	21,193,031	25,145,815
1884	12,391,806	17,665,858

THE FUR MARKET OF ST. LOUIS.

The market in peltries (of wild animals) and furs in 1888-'89, is noted for a large increase in the quantity. There has been no diminution in the proportionate volume of beaver, mink, coon and fox, but an increase in muskrat. Oppossum and skunk are specially in request, and prices of all descriptions continue well maintained.

No public record is kept by the sixteen dealers of the receipts and shipments; but, whilst it is well understood, that larger receipts than heretofore has been the rule, the number of bales, packs or pounds cannot be stated with any accuracy; and, therefore, the value in dollars is unknown. It must not be supposed, however, that the trade in furs and peltries—which, at a very early period of the business history of the village and town of St. Louis, constituted almost its sole trade—has diminished. But, it will surprise some persons of intelligence and general information to be informed, that with the exception of buffalo and wolf pelts (very few of the latter and none of the former), the receipts of furs and peltries—in number and pounds—are greater to-day than in the palmiest days of the "fur trade of St. Louis." Besides, although the market prices are less, the money value is greater than formerly. St. Louis is the largest original receiving and shipping market in furs in the United States. Europe, as formerly, takes the bulk — three-fourths of all—of the furs and peltries marketed in this city. They are purchased by agents for the account of the foreign dealers, and are in ready demand.

The buffalo—the wild cattle of the North American " pampas" — have disappeared! The ruthless hunter or reckless sportsman may no more gratify his greed or pursuit of "glory" in the chase and slaughter of the noble bison! Now, the roseate hues of the setting sun fall not upon him, but upon Texas "long horns," and " short horns" of European strain, which graze upon the grounds trodden by the former monarch of the plains!

HIDE MARKET OF ST. LOUIS FOR YEAR ENDING DECEMBER 31, 1888.*

The hide market of St. Louis has gained such increased proportions as to claim a position of great prominence in the trade of the city. Tanners of Illinois, Indiana, Ohio, Michigan and Wisconsin, find it to their interest to purchase their stocks at St. Louis. Pennsylvania and other Atlantic States, make large purchases from dealers here. Tanners from numerous points buy through hide brokers of this city. They have found by experience, that in general, the quality of the hides received at St. Louis is specially good and desirable; and, that the dealers bestow the most careful attention to the delivery of the exact grades of hides as sold.

The hide business of the year 1887, was an unprofitable one to St. Louis dealers. It was owing to a current decline in prices, which dropped fully twenty-five per cent

---

* NOTE.—These details of the hide market were derived from Frank & Hellendall, Dealers, South Main Street.—*Author.*

during the season. Dealers were compelled either to sell at a loss, or hold for an improved market. But, on the contrary, the business of the year, closing December 31, 1888, was a very satisfactory one—both to the shippers and dealers and was scarcely less so to tanners—who purchased their stocks at this market. Up to May 1st, the ruling prices were low and unsteady. They were lower than for a number of years prior to the decline, which came with the previous year, (1887), and had still continued. After that date, however, a steady demand set in and prices advanced on all descriptions of hides—fully ten per cent.

There was no feeling of speculation, and sales were freely made at current quotations. All hides offered on the market—coming from interior points of shipment—were readily taken by dealers, who promptly resold to tanners. Accordingly, there was no accumulation of stock. This occasioned a very easy and pleasant market during the remainder of the year. Shippers were satisfied; and, both dealers and tanners were gratified. The tanners enjoyed a profitable business through the current rise in the prices of leather.

The receipts of hides at this market for the year ending December 31, 1888, were nearly twenty-five per cent greater, and the shipments were thirty per cent in access of the preceding year, (1887). Reference is made to the accompanying tables—showing the actual receipts and shipments for several years past.

Saint Louis is a popular market with shippers from both sides of the Mississippi river—commencing at St. Paul, and following the river to, and hundreds of miles below this city. And, by rail from Texas, Arkansas, Indian Territory, New Mexico, Colorado, Wyoming, Montana, Nebraska, Kansas, Iowa, Illinois and Missouri.

Our hide dealers find such satisfaction expressed by shippers with the fair treatment they have received, and from the general outlook for constant enlargement of the receipts, that they confidently expect St. Louis will become the largest interior hide market of the United States.

HIDES RECEIVED AT, AND SHIPPED FROM ST. LOUIS FOR FIVE YEARS.

YEAR.	RECEIPTS. POUNDS.	SHIPMENTS. POUNDS.
1888	31,814,049	40,296,581
1887	26,175,992	31,476,328
1886	19,978,698	23,407,160
1885	20,864,833	25,386,095
1884	16,305,415	21,797,724

PROVISIONS: HOGS PACKED AT ST. LOUIS.

In provisions, during the past year (1888), the market St. Louis made very considerabe advances as a distributing market. The receipts and shipments of hog products—in smoked and salted meats, barreled pork and lard—for the last two years were as follows:

YEAR.	Received. Pounds.	Shipped. Pounds.
1887	114,568,211	149,998,707
1888	220,613,987	246,238,457

PACKING FOR THE LAST TWO YEARS.

WINTER AND SUMMER RESULTS.

	Hogs.		Hogs.
1888—Winter	369,790	1887—Winter	370,866
" —Summer	280,000	" —Summer	313,591
Totals	649,790		684,457

The partial failure of the corn crop of 1887, reduced the number of hogs packed for the seasons between November 1887, and same date in 1888 about five per cent.

302 ST. LOUIS OF TO-DAY.

Most of the packing points had a similar experience. Nevertheless, as a centre for receiving and distributing the products of the hog, St. Louis has maintained its position as a great distributing market. The receipts were *ninety-one per cent* more in 1888 than for the previous year. And, the shipments were *sixty per cent* more during the same period, as is shown in the first of the preceding tables. Of the shipments—a moderate amount went direct to Europe, more to Eastern points, but the greater portion to the Southern States.

NATIONAL STOCK YARDS.

RECEIPTS OF CATTLE, HOGS, SHEEP, HORSES AND MULES, FROM JANUARY 1, TO DECEMBER 31, FOR FIFTEEN YEARS:

YEARS.	Cars.	Cattle.	Hogs.	Sheep.	Horses.
1874	17,264	234,002	498,840	41,407	2,235
1875	13,938	232,183	181,708	46,316	2,385
1876	18,052	234,671	333,560	84,034	2,616
1877	24,344	322,571	426,109	119,174	2,364
1878	31,003	317,830	833,446	82,549	2,534
1879	35,641	333,155	1,163,748	99,951	4,338
1880	38,294	346,533	1,262,234	129,611	5,963
1881	42,232	406,804	1,308,514	226,124	8,377
1882	29,178	356,434	642,871	303,753	14,284
1883	33,393	332,625	843,672	272,852	17,054
1884	37,866	390,569	1,079,827	277,697	14,703
1885	33,864	311,702	1,145,546	245,793	12,176
1886	28,542	397,244	984,995	212,101	16,398
1887	29,838	387,709	772,171	315,546	29,286
1888	30,150	453,918	652,127	368,848	27,713

THE SHIPMENTS FOR THE YEAR ENDING DECEMBER 31, 1888, FROM THE NATIONAL STOCK YARDS:

Cars.	Cattle.	Hogs.	Sheep.	Horses and Mules.
18,406	329,182	253,988	313,536	25,995

HORSES AND MULES.

St. Louis is the most important market for horses and mules in the United States. It leads all other markets in the number of marketable saddle, carriage, and heavy draught horses and serviceable mules. The war department of the United States obtains all its horses for cavalry service at this market.

RECEIPTS AND SHIPMENTS OF HORSES AND MULES AT THE ENTIRE MARKET, INCLUDING THE NATIONAL AND UNION STOCK YARDS, FOR SIX YEARS:

YEARS.	Receipts.	Shipments.
1888	58,458	61,192
1887	57,948	59,222
1886	42,032	39,798
1885	39,385	35,610
1884	41,870	39,544
1883	44,913	44,543

To these figures should be added a large number of horses and mules—*driven* to the different stables of the commission dealers—from the country, and are not recorded at the Stock Yards.

The demand for horses and mules has grown with the increased supply, and all desirable stock found a ready sale.

RECEIPTS AND SHIPMENTS OF CATTLE, SHEEP AND HOGS TO, AND FROM ST. LOUIS—AT THE ENTIRE MARKET, INCLUDING THE UNION AND NATIONAL STOCK YARDS, FOR SIX YEARS:

YEARS.	RECEIPTS.			SHIPMENTS.		
	Cattle.	Sheep.	Hogs.	Cattle.	Sheep.	Hogs.
1888	546,875	456,469	924,239	336,216	316,676	294,869
1887	464,828	417,425	1,052,240	277,406	287,018	324,735
1886	377,554	328,985	1,264,471	212,958	202,728	520,362
1885	386,320	362,858	1,455,535	233,249	233,301	789,487
1884	450,717	380,822	1,474,475	315,433	248,545	678,874
1883	405,090	398,612	1,351,785	249,523	217,370	609,388

LEAD IN PIGS. WHITE LEADS, LINSEED OIL.

PIG LEAD.

St. Louis remains, as for many years past, the largest market for lead and white lead paints in the United States.

The receipts of lead for year 1887, was 1,380,758 pigs, of eighty pounds each. And, for 1888, 1,815,687 pigs, or one hundred and forty-five million, two hundred and fifty-four thousand, nine hundred and sixty pounds! The shipments out, during same years, were for 1887, 759,892 pigs, and for 1888, 1,285,354 pigs, one hundred and two million, eight hundred and twenty-eight thousand, three hundred and twenty pounds, for the year 1888. The increase of receipts of lead were

ST. LOUIS SHOT TOWER.

434,929 pigs, and of shipments in 1888, over the previous year, was 525,462 pigs, or forty-two million, thirty-six thousand, nine hundred and sixty pounds.

WHITE LEADS, ETC.

Saint Louis' pre-eminence as a market for lead is to be attributed almost wholly to its extensive manufacture of the products of that metal—in lead pipe, sheet lead, paints, etc.

This city is the greatest manufacturer of white lead paints, and shot, of any other place. Three white lead corroding plants of this city have a capital of two million dollars invested in their business.

LINSEED OIL.

Two of the plants engaged in the manufacture of linseed oil, produced 1,050,000 gallons in 1888, as against 550,000 gallons for the previous year. They employ a capital of about a half million dollars in their business.

BALING CLOTH FOR THE COTTON STAPLE.

QUANTITY MANUFACTURED AND ON HAND AT, AND SHIPPED FROM ST. LOUIS, FOR FIVE YEARS.

YEARS.	Manufactured.	On Hand December 31st.	Shipped Out.
1888	12,000,000 Yards.	8,000,000 Yards.	181,104 Pieces.
1887	15,000,000 "	1,500,000 "	360,609 "
1886	16,000,000 "	1,500,000 "	325,609 "
1885	7,500,000 "	350,000 "	280,996 "
1884	6,000,000 "	850,00 i "	190,965 "

RECEIPTS OF BAGGING IN FIVE YEARS.

YEARS.		YARDS.
1888. 50,806 Pieces.............		2,520,300
1887. 78,473 "		3,933,650
1886. 49,904 "		2,495,200
1885.		2,948,050
1884.		657,450

RECEIPTS OF LUMBER AND LOGS, BY RIVER AND RAIL, AT ST. LOUIS, IN 1888.

	FEET.
Lumber by River............. 108,478,966
" " Rail............... 485,748,000
	594,226,966
Logs by River—about.......... 33,000,000
	627,226,966

HARDWOODS, ETC.

The receipts of oak, ash, yellow pine and poplar in this market have continued very large.

In hardwoods, St. Louis holds the supremacy over all other markets, and will continue to do so. After the white pine of the North is exhausted, the Southern States now supplying this market, will furnish an unlimited quantity of yellow pine, poplar and cypress; the latter two for doors, sash and blinds.

Poplar is making rapid strides in public favor, and has now reached a stage of progress that promises it a more prominent recognition than ever before.

E. JACCARD JEWELRY CO., S. E. COR. OLIVE AND SIXTH STS.

CHAPTER VII.

THE BUSINESS TONNAGE IN LEADING ARTICLES, RECEIPTS AND SHIPMENTS TO AND FROM ST. LOUIS, FOR THE YEARS 1887 AND 1888.

RECEIPTS:

ARTICLES.	1888.	1887.
Flour, barrels manufactured	2,016,619	1,983,717
" " handled	3,973,155	3,633,194
Wheat, bushels	11,670,440	14,510,313
Corn, "	19,916,299	16,576,386
Oats, "	9,819,800	9,763,545
Rye, "	410,550	236,726
Barley, "	3,194,146	2,932,192
All grain received, (including flour reduced to wheat)	62,890,439	48,748,562
Hay, tons	107,884	85,394
Tobacco, hogsheads	27,140	37,592
" (packages leaf)	6,962	......
Wool, pounds	19,626,629	17,347,186
Cotton, bales	527,900	520,063
Hides, pounds	31,814,049	26,175,977
Butter and Cheese, pounds	11,248,777	9,234,043
Potatoes and Onions, barrels	695,137	301,636
Cattle, head	546,875	464,828
Sheep, "	456,669	417,425
Hogs, "	929,230	1,052,240
Meats—hog products—pounds	220,613,987	114,568,211
Horses and Mules, head	58,458	57,048
Rice, packages	74,181	79,604
Lumber and Logs, feet	627,226,966	675,144,047
Coal, tons	3,449,000	2,649,000
Coke, "	168,939	191,687
Cement, barrels	393,989	366,106
Railroad Iron, tons	39,789	138,312
Iron and Steel, "	99,890	153,479
Pig Iron, "	149,370	178,760
Iron Ore, "	91,375	180,878
Zinc "	43,269	45,904
Lead, in 80-pound pigs	1,853,781	1,432,054
Nails, kegs	596,579	706,472
Coffee,* bags	192,940	184,312
Salt, barrels	330,110	394,676
" sacks	24,649	32,060
" bushels in bulk	254,700	320,490
Boots and Shoes, cases	488,514	362,446
Bagging, yards manufactured	12,000,000	15,000,000

* NOTE.—The receipts for the past four years averaged 241,834 bags; the decrease in 1887 and 1888 is owing to reduced consumption on account of increase in cost.

THE GREAT STEEL BRIDGE, SPANNING THE MISSISSIPPI RIVER AT ST. LOUIS.

THE FREIGHT TRAFFIC ACROSS THE MISSISSIPPI RIVER AT ST. LOUIS.

THE BUSINESS OF THE BRIDGE, FERRIES AND TRANSFER COMPANY.

In 1887, total freight going East, 1,729,481 tons. Going West, 4,474,531 tons. "
In 1888, " " " 2,104,140 " " " 4,426,761 " "

THE BUSINESS TONNAGE IN LEADING ARTICLES, RECEIPTS· AND SHIPMENTS TO AND FROM ST. LOUIS, FOR THE YEARS 1887 AND 1888.

SHIPMENTS.

ARTICLES.	1888.	1887.
Wool, pounds	21,463,998	17,392,858
Cotton, bales	528,135	501,867
Hides, pounds	40,296,581	31,476,338
Wheat and Flour, in bushels Wheat	16,483,723	17,865,755
Flour, (alone) barrels	2,652,405	2,594,881
Meats—hog product—pounds	246,238,457	149,998,707
Manufactured Tobacco, pounds	....	1,298,250
Ale and Beer, packages	2,310,268	2,340,650
Nails, kegs	561,818	541,4c8
Lumber, feet	....	344,434,000
Pig Iron, tons	51,760	50,489
Iron Ore, "	123,537	219,877
Zinc " "	20,995	19,038
Lead, 80-pound pigs, each	1,293,919	766,807
Zinc and Spelter, slabs	*24,360	708,326
Barbed Wire, pounds	....	27,000,843
White Lead, "	39,135,340	34,267,439
Dried Fruit, sacks and barrels	98,569	137,694
Bagging, rolls	181,104	360,609

CONCLUSION.

A RESUME OF THE PROGRESS AND PROSPECTS OF THE CITY OF ST. LOUIS OF TO-DAY.

PROGRESS.

The growth of the city of St. Louis in all its staple manufactures, and established industries continues steady and rapid. It supplies machinery and an infinite variety of its productions, as well as merchandise of every de-

19

scription, to a wide district of surrounding territory, including some in which its merchants and manufacturers
compete successfully with other cities in their own fields.

The receipts of this market for the last year, ending
December 31, 1888, in all the great staples of grain,
cotton, wool, furs, hides, meats, butter, tobacco, lead,
zinc, coal, cattle, sheep, hogs, horses, mules, etc.—were
greater than its predecessor.

The shipments during the same period of all the
products of farm and forest, of mines and factories, including sales of merchandise and commodities, were in
volume and value in excess of the preceding year.

At the present date, March 15, 1889, the construction
of dwelling houses and business blocks in active progress
is larger than usual, outdoor work being facilitated by the
present mild season. But, the opinion is justified—from
what is now known — that the private, corporate and
municipal buildings and improvements which will be constructed within the city limits the present year will surpass
in magnitude and value those of any previous year in
its history.

At no time hitherto, was the outlook so full of promise of extensive and large results—in economic values—in
all that relates to PRODUCTION, CONVERSION AND EXCHANGE
in its trade and industries.

And, foremost of all in material wealth and values
of the city—ITS REAL ESTATE—there is not in it at the
present time any inflation of prices, but a *bouyancy* which
strikingly reflects its grand future! And, whilst the
realty of this city is largely dependent for its practical
value upon the general prosperity, it possesses an *intrinsic*
value—through its rare advantages of site and surroundings—which is potent in strength to help every other
interest and give them lasting vitality.

PROSPECTS.v

PRIVATE, CORPORATE AND MUNICIPAL BUILDING AND WORKS
OF IMPROVEMENT PLANNED AND UNDERTAKEN.

PRIVATE AND CORPORATE.

Briefly given, the following may be named as a few of
the larger works planned the present year, some of which
are under construction. The Merchants' Railway Bridge
Company, composed exclusively of St. Louis capitalists,
have begun the erection of another steel railway bridge—
a counterpart of the present magnificent structure spanning the Mississippi. It is expected that the new bridge
will be completed by 1891. The needs of an enlarged
and growing commerce loudly calls for its early construction. And, as necessary adjuncts of the bridge, another
company of St. Louis' wealthy and enterprising men, will
build surface and elevated railway tracks and depots at the
East End—river front of the city.

Also, the score of great railroad corporate lines which
enter this city—pouring their daily tides of human beings
into the Union Passenger Depot, which for a long time
past has been inadequate in its accommodations to the
demands for space, and the convenience and comfort
of the millions of railway travelers who each year come to
St. Louis—have at length resolved to build a new depot.
They will soon begin the work of erecting a new passenger
union depot whose plan, dimensions and appointments
will be in accordance with the best modern improvements
in such structures and ample for the requirements of
another decade.

The buildings and realty improvements commenced
and contemplated by private citizens and syndicates of
capitalists, are the construction of both private and public
boulevards and parks; of business blocks for stores and

offices; new manufacturing plants and the enlargement of existing ones. Also, of dwellings—residences suited to the means and wants of every class of citizens—built by capitalists, for sale and rent. They will be provided—and some replete—with modern conveniences, and built with suitable regard to taste and health. Some of the residences—intended by their builders for their own family homes—will vie in cost, elegance and beauty wlth, if they do not surpass, any of the splendid dwellings heretofore erected in this city.

MUNICIPAL.

The municipality through its legislative body and with the approval of the mayor has recently decided to build a new CITY HALL — upon the eligible site of Washington square, of six acres of ground. A large sum of money is now lying in the city treasury, being a special appropriation for the purpose. The cost will be not less than one million dollars. The site belongs to the city—by purchase many years since.

The board of Public Works has under construction additions to the present grand system of sewerage, equaled in effective utility by only two other cities of the United States (Cincinnati and Nashville). Also, the opening, construction and paving of new streets, including further re-construction with granite blocks. The building of new water works of greater strength and capacity, is energetically pressed. The plans include the construction of a *conduit* of seven miles length and a diameter of nine feet, and other radical improvements. These great works are to be completed within five years. They will furnish daily fifty million gallons of wholesome water. The plant is adapted to supply *double* that quantity at a moderate additional outlay. The full cost has been provided for in cash appropriations and will be met, together with the full sum of the Water Bonds annually maturing, out of the current water revenues by the year 1893.

FINALLY, the facilities for rapid transit within the city limits and extending into the suburbs, which now comprise upwards of 160 miles in length, of street railways, nearly all of which are double tracked, will—during the present year — be much increased. The motive power to be utilized will continue to be that of the cable system or electric motors on all the principal street passenger railway lines.

A system of *elevated street railways* of considerable magnitude and importance, is now under consideration in the city legislature. Fewer property owners now than formerly object to the elevated railway system, while many of the most cautious citizens earnestly approve it.

LASTLY, it can be said — cannot be controverted—that rarely has a city of this or any other country made, within the term of a short decade — such substantial progress in every element of solid growth as the city of St. Louis. No city to-day possesses a foundation more substantial. Not a single drawback is in view, or can be adduced upon good judgment, that can prevent its steady development or mar its splendid prospects. But, the contrary is the case, in numerous tangible evidences of greatness possessed by the present city, which presage a future of surpassing wealth and power!

BUILDING OF THE INDEPENDENT ORDER OF ODD FELLOWS.

APPENDIX.

The figures of the assessments reported to the Mayor are made to the end of the fiscal year, the 9th of April, but are handed to him the preceding month, and prior to the assembling of the City Board of Equalization. The table presented on page 90 is made from the record in the Comptroller's office, and shows the assessment *after its revision* by that Board.

THE WESTERN COMMERCIAL TRAVELERS' ASSOCIATION OF ST. LOUIS.

MODERN METHOD OF EFFECTING SALES TO DISTANT DEALERS THE "DRUMMER."

The system—adopted at the period of the civil war and continued ever since—of taking orders from distant dealers at their places of business, through an agent of a city merchant, has become an established custom.

The agent, known as a "commercial traveler" more recently, but "a drummer" formerly, is, almost invariably, a *gentleman*— in manners, character and life. He has—must have—tact, push and principle. Upon him depends—in a large measure—the reputation of his house or employer. If he speaks truthfully, and represents his goods fairly, his employer is benefitted by the increased respect and confidence of the customer. And, the salesman stands surely *in the esteem* not only of his employer, but in the hearty regards of all with whom he deals. But, if by any ill conduct, he should acquire the displeasure of his customer, then, the principal or employer is damaged, and the agent loses the friendship of both!

The traveler—who is chosen by his employer for character and qualifications—is expected to possess good judgment, a keen appreciation of motives, and clear discrimination of facts, diligently learned, when making up his opinion of the fitness of a *new* customer. And, he should exercise his wits at all times in dealing with an *old* customer, so as to value him according to his true worth. The credit of an honorable customer is sometimes temporarily effected by business mutations which he cannot control, and to cut him off entirely might result in serious consequences to the creditor—the principal of the agent. In other cases, he will be called upon to communicate cautiously with his house in respect to circumstances and appearances affecting the credit standing of a customer, which perhaps could not be known *in time* through any wide-awake " commercial agency."

The extraordinary success of the St. Louis Western Commercial Travelers' Association in acquiring, not only its large membership of twenty-five hundred, but in its efficiency as a " live " organization, are matters of surprise to the thoughtful observer. In fact, the association is a successful life indemnity company—of fraternal members. The legal representatives, upon the demise of a member, receive an early payment of the " assurance " in the sum of five thousand dollars! This sum is readily raised by an assessment of two dollars—made upon each member. What a grand gift that large sum is to bereaved wife and children!

The St. Louis Western Commercial Travelers' Association is the largest of any similar association west of the Alleghany mountains. It is ably officered and managed—by men of high character and intelligence, in active sympathy with its commendable objects, and with the men who form its worthy membership.

ST. LOUIS AS A SEAPORT.

A NEW YORK BUSINESS PAPER'S VIEW OF IT, JANUARY, 1889.

A recent issue of the New York *Globe*, a weekly business review, contains an article on "St. Louis as a Seaport," which is of interest to the people of this city and the West. The paper says:

The unknown author of a song which we have not heard since we were on blue water in an old wooden ship, years ago, may

have had in his prophetic eye the future ''old salt '' of St. Louis
when he wrote :

> He called for his sextant and took the moon,
> And a big, bright star took he
> On the deck of his schooner, and worked a Lunar,
> As he sailed down the Mississippee—ippee,
> As he sailed down the Mississipp—ee!

But the subject of our heading is one about which St. Louis
is in dead earnest, and has good reason to be, if the Lucas
steamship proves itself able to tussle with old Neptune on salt
water. The Mississippi River and Ocean Navigation Company
propose to build steel vessels, carrying 1,000 tons of freight on
seven feet draught, with a long and very deep movable keel,
to be lowered when needed at sea. The space for this keel,
which would be the *well* in a center-board vessel, is so long that,
practically, the ship is composed of two hulls bound together at
the stem and stern for a sufficient distance to insure solidity, and
each having a permanent keel sufficient to give steadiness and
steerage qualities when in smooth water. Those who have
battled with the sea in North Atlantic gales, or off Cape Horn,
will need to have faith in the strength of material and mode of
construction and in the judgment of experts in order to feel quite
easy regarding the ability of the movable keel to stand the strain
that will be put upon it : but, the prospectus reminds scientific
croakers of Dr. Lardner's prediction, that no steamship could be
built that would cross the Atlantic! We see but three things
needed for complete success : Capital, and surely an ample amount
can be secured to build one trial ship. Proof of its mechanical success will insure all the capital required. But, there should
be such reform of our tariff as will permit the importation of
Spanish-American products in exchange for our flour, provisions
and manufactures. St. Louis is admirably situated for trade
with all the ports on the Gulf and Carribbean Sea, many of
which, like St. Louis, are on rivers which are not navigable by
ordinary sea-going vessels, and to which it would be a great
boon to be able to receive American cargoes without trans-
shipment.

Such a commerce would richly compensate St. Louis for trade
which might be diverted from her by the changes wrought in the

multiplication of railways. The statistics furnished in the company's prospectus of commerce with Europe and with the country of our South American neighbors—"so near. and yet so far." under our present conditions—are instructive, and so astounding as to make an American, who believes himself to be sane, to disbelieve in the sanity of the nation.

DIRECT LINE OF STEAMERS BETWEEN ST. LOUIS AND BUENOS AYRES.

FROM THE ST. LOUIS REPUBLIC, OCTOBER, 1888.

It having come to the notice of a *Republic* reporter, that important news had been received by the promoters of the Mississippi River and Ocean Navigation Company, more generally known as the Lucas ship enterprise. he went to the office of Mr. John F. Cahill yesterday to ascertain the truth of the rumor. This gentleman, to whom is due in great part the success which has so far attended the enterprise. stated that within the past few days he had received from representatives of the Argentine Republic the most positive assurances, that the government of that progressive South American Republic would ratify the provisions of the concession to the River and Ocean Navigation Co. of St. Louis. which has already been sent direct from here. It was carried in duplicate by an influential gentleman specially commissioned for this purpose, to the city of Buenos Ayres. For several months past. the attention of the Argentine and other governments of Spanish America has been attracted to the importance of the Lucas ship, as it is known that in those countries there are very few railroads, and all transportation of import and export has to be carried on by rivers. This is particularly true as to the great commercial city of Buenos Ayres. whose population of nearly 450,000, and commerce of many hundreds of millions annually, are dependent on the costly transfers of freight and passengers from and to the numerous lines of ocean steamships. which are prevented from going within many miles of the city of Buenos Ayres—because of the bars and shallow water in the River La Plata. The Argentine government was on the point of making an appropriation of $9,000,000.00 for removing two bars and deepening the river to 25 feet—which would take many years to accomplish—when their representatives in this country called their attention to the Lucas ship. Investigation was made, opinions of competent engineers were sought, and the plans of the Lucas ship pronounced practicable, and its application desirable from an economic and commercial standpoint. This resulted in the submission of a very liberal offer to the River and Ocean Navigation Company, in the form of a concession from the Argentine Republic—from the original of which are translated the following provisions—for the establishment of a line of steamships between the ports of St. Louis and New Orleans in the United States, that of Buenos Ayres and one other port which the Argentine government may designate.

PROVISIONS OF THE FRANCHISE.

1. The steamers of the River and Ocean Navigation Co., of the Lucas patent, will make one or more trips monthly between the ports of St. Louis, New Orleans and Buenos Ayres and another port to be hereafter designated.

2. The average speed of these steamers is to be 20 miles per hour on the ocean.

3. The Argentine Republic will guarantee to the company for ten (10) years twenty-five (25) per cent of the net products of its capital, which is to be five millions of dollars($5,000,000.00) in gold or its equivalent.

4. When the capital invested shall produce more than 12 per cent of interest annually, the company shall deliver into the treasury the excess until all the sums obtained by it as a guarantee shall have been re-imbursed.

5. For the immediate construction of two ships the Argentine government will guarantee the amount of stock the company may deem necessary to issue, and, if deemed requisite, a company may be organized for this purpose.

6. The Argentine government will guarantee 5 per cent annually on the sum of $1,000,000.00 to be employed in the construction of two ships destined for navigation between Buenos Ayres and New Orleans and ports of the Mississippi Valley, and two that are to be used in the river service of the interior.

WATER COMMUNICATION A NECESSITY.

NOVEMBER, 1888.

Hon. John Drayton. consul at Tuxpan. Mexico, in a letter to Mr. Mitchel. Secretary of the New Orleans Chamber of Commerce. states that the exports from Tuxpan, amount to nearly $2,000,000 yearly, and consist principally of vanillia. chicle. hides. deerskins, dyewood. ce lar, mahogany, honey. sarsaparilla, rubber. coffee and fruit, nearly all of which go to New York.

Further on in his letter the consul says :

" Now. there is no reason why New Orleans, with the whole Mississippi Valley to back her with all of its produce and manufactures. cannot place merchandise of all classes here as reasonable as New York. if not more so. for she is but two days and a half from any of these ports. So. if she cannot put in more steamers and offer the same inducements and accomodations as New York for this trade then it must continue in the old course. The trade natually belongs to her. Draw a line from New Orleans to the City of Mexico and you will see that Tuxpan is the nearest port on it. At any rate it would be worth the while to send out commissioners to examine the prospects and put a line of steamers to run the coast. for there are many merchants who would go to New Orleans to purchase their supplies if there were convenient transportation facilities to transact their business.

The lands are very fertile. producing two crops of corn on the same acre every year. also all vegetables and fruits. Sugar lands are excellent and need very little cultivation after the first year. and last six. eight or ten. without re-planting. producing two and three hogsheads to the acre. For enterprises a sugar refinery. paper mill. powder mill. would do well if properly managed. Petroleum abounds in many localities."

VIEWS OF ALEXANDER VON HUMBOLDT, UPON AN ISTHMUS ROUTE.

The Baron. Alexander Von Humboldt. the distinguished traveler and author of " Cosmos." explored Central America about the year 1800. He spent considerable time in extensive researches. His opinions as a scientist are entitled to the greatest weight upon the practicability of a marine route to India, via the narrow neck of land which unites the two continents. He may be quoted as reliable authority favorable to the feasibility of the construction of a passage through from ocean to ocean. Humboldt voiced the desire of every nation for the opening of the speediest and cheapest route from Western Europe to Eastern Asia, including all the countries lying between, which, since his time had come to be among the chief producing and commercial nations of the globe. Now, after the lapse of more than sixty years, the short and direct passage is demanded a hundred times more cogently by the emergencies of commerce. It is is reasonably assumed, that the people of the United States cannot afford to leave the great work of opening the Isthmus to be done after the beginning of the twentieth century—now only a decade distant—but should begin it at once.

EXTRACTED FROM THE NEW YORK FINANCIAL AND MINING RECORD'
JANUARY 5, 1889.

As long since as February 21, 1827, Gœthe, in a conversation with Eckerman—who noted the great German's word that same night—about what Humboldt had written upon the subject of a passage-way through the Isthmus of Panama, remarked as quoted by Eckerman:

" Humboldt, who has, with a great knowledge of his subject, given other points where by making *use* of *some* streams which flow into the Gulf of Mexico, the end may be better attained than at Panama. All this is reserved for the future and for an enterprising spirit. So much, however, is certain, that if they succeed in cutting such a channel that ships of any burden and size can navigate through it from the Mexican Gulf to the Pacific Ocean, *innumerable benefits would result to the whole human race* civilized and uncivilized. BUT I SHOULD WONDER IF THE UNITED STATES SHOULD LET AN OPPORTUNITY ESCAPE OF GETTING SUCH WORK INTO THEIR OWN HANDS. It may be foreseen that this young State, with decided *predilection for the West will, in thirty or forty years, have occupied and peopled the large tract of land west of the Rocky Mountains.* It may, furthermore, be seen

that along the whole coast of the Pacific ocean where Nature has
formed the most capacious and secure harbors, important commercial towns will gradually arise for the furtherance of a great
intercourse between China and the East Indies and the United
States.   In such a case, it would be *not only desirable but almost
necessary*, that a more rapid communication should be maintained
between the Eastern and Western shores of North America,
both by merchant ships and men of war, than has hitherto been
possible with the tedious, disagreeable and expensive voyage
around Cape Horn.   I therefore repeat that it is *absolutely indispensable for the United States to effect a passage from the Mexican
Gulf to the Pacific Ocean;* and I am certain they will do it."

In that same notable conversation Goethe said that he should
like to see " England in the possession of a canal through the
Isthmus of Suez."   ,

NEW NATIONAL BANK.

CITY OF ST. LOUIS, MARCH 15, 1889.

THE CONTINENTAL APPLIES FOR A CHARTER, AND WILL
INCREASE ITS CAPITAL TO $2,000,000.00.

The first practical result of the Act of Congress *making
St. Louis a central reserve city* under the national banking law,
came to light yesterday, when it became known that the Continental Bank had resolved to nationalize and increase its stock
from two hundred thousand to two million dollars.   Application
was forwarded by the bank last night to the Comptroller at
Washington for a charter, and subscription books will be
opened at the bank to-morrow, the 16th.   The stock will be
awarded in the order that subscriptions are offered.   *The Continental National Bank* will be an entirely new institution, but
*will be under the same management which has been in charge for
the past eight years* and which has been conspicuously successful.
*During that time the deposits have increased from about $400,000
to over $3,000,000.*   The new bank will liquidate the Conti-
nental Bank, take such of its assets as the directors may approve.

and assume to pay its depositors. Since St. Louis was made a central reserve city the inducements for operating under the national bank law are very much increased, the removal of the 10-per cent restriction on interior national banks naturally bringing to this point largely increased lines of deposit. *It is conceded by well-informed citizens* that St. Louis is not over-banked, but, on the contrary, *is a fine field for more bank capital.* It has been a matter of comment that St. Louis has fewer national banks than any other city on the continent of similar size and wealth. Chicago, for instance, has twenty-two national banks, employing $16,000,000 capital; Baltimore seventeen national banks, with $10,000,000 capital; Cincinnati thirteen banks and $9,000,000 capital, while St. Louis has only four national banks, with $3,000,000 capital.

The officers of the new concern will be George A. Baker, President; J. M. Thompson, Vice President; Chas. W. Bullen, Cashier. Directors—J. M. Thompson, C. S. Freeborn, H. A. Crawford, I. G. Baker, Geo. W. Parker, Joseph Hill, R. C. Kerens, Chas. F. Gauss, H. L. Morrill, L. B. Tebbetts and George A. Baker.

A HUMANITARIAN PROJECT.

AN EMERGENCY HOSPITAL.

ESTABLISHMENT OF A NEW INSTITUTION FOR THE STRICKEN AND INJURED.

The design of the projectors in the establishment of an *emergency hospital* in this city is in the line of true humanity. The duty of the early care of the unfortunate —stricken upon the daily battle field of human life in a great city—necessarily falls upon the able. The new institution will supply almost the only want — *emergency* — in the numerous and admirably appointed infirmaries and hospitals of this city.

The new hospital is to be established at No. 410 North Eleventh street, a very eligible spot in view of its centrality. It will be under the auspices of the St. Louis Mullanphy Hospital,

with its corps of surgeons and physicians. Also, of the Sisters of
Charity, who are well known for their intelligent care of the sick.
A prospectus says of the proposed establishment: " The need of
an 'Emergency Hospital' in St. Louis has long been felt by the
manufacturers, builders, steam and street railroad, telegraph
and telephone companies, and by others whose employes are
especially endangered by accident. When the saving in suffer-
ing and life, which is insured by the prompt action and efficient
means at the command of an institution of this character is considered, it must commend the 'Emergency Hospital' to the
favorable consideration and liberal support of the benevolent
citizen, as it does to the business community. It may not be
out of place to say to those who have not given the subject
attention, that emergency hospitals are not by any means new
or their efficiency a matter of experiment. On the contrary,
there are many in operation in a number of cities in this country,
as well as in the cities and large manufacturing districts in
Europe, where they have been successful and have demonstrated
by actual trial not only their efficiency but their necessity.

Physicians will be in constant attendance and will always accompany the ambulance to the scene of accident, fully prepared
to render all possible assistance and relief, afterward conveying
the injured to their houses or to the hospital, as may be desired.
Ambulances, fully equipped for any emergency, will be kept in
readiness to respond at a moment's notice to any call for accident cases, thus lessening to a great degree the danger from
loss of blood which is increased by delays. *The ministrations of
the 'Emergency Hospital' in all its departments will be absolutely
free.* No charges whatever will be made for the services of physicians or nurses, use of ambulance, nor for that of the hospital while
the injured remain there. The feature of the hospital ren-
ders it necessary that it shall depend for the means of its
establishment and support on voluntary contributions from the
benevolent people of this city, and it is confidently hoped that
the generous liberality which has ever characterized the citizens
of St. Louis will not be wanting in this particular instance.
Especially is it hoped that those whose employes are liable to
accident will assist liberally towards the establishment and
future success of an 'Emergency Hospital' in our city. Telephone calls for the ambulance will be promptly responded to at
any hour of the day or night.''